Praise for

LINCOLN'S GAMBLE

"Brewster has pulled off his task with aplomb. He navigates a clear path through conflicting accounts, giving us the context necessary to understand why the Proclamation was just so difficult for Lincoln to write. . . . Brewster's greatest achievement in this book is to bring nuance back to a story that is often paved over with heroism . . . transforming Lincoln from an American saint back into a man."

—*Pittsburgh Post-Gazette*

"A readable and heavily researched account."

—*Civil War Times*

"Brewster gets inside Abraham Lincoln's mind, revealing his struggles with the limited powers of his office. Here is Lincoln, the man, surprisingly ambivalent about the decision for which he is most remembered. A masterful psychological portrait."

—George Stephanopoulos

"Journalist Brewster presents an interesting exploration into what was going on in Lincoln's mind and life during the time before the signing. . . . Of value to anyone interested in this great event in US history."

—*Choice* magazine

"Brewster helps us understand, with an engaging narrative style, that [the Emancipation Proclamation] was not designed as a noble gesture to boldly free 4 million slaves from bondage but as a strategic weapon to decisively turn the tide of the struggle to bring rebellious states back into the Union."

—*Arrive* magazine

"Brewster brings elegant clarity to the tangle of conflicting ideologies, loyalties, and practicalities that pushed the proclamation forward, ultimately ensuring Lincoln's legacy as the Great Emancipator."

—*Publishers Weekly*

"A highly readable, vigorously researched account of the fraught six-month period in which the Emancipation Proclamation came into being . . . Brewster is particularly good as a close reader of Lincoln's drafts of the document and their evolving intent. . . . A sturdy, instructive, well-written book."

—*Kirkus*

"Readers of this expertly told tale may note parallels to other times in American history when the lack of a clear mission hampered war efforts. Yet this, finally, is a story of courage and leadership, a stirring account of how Lincoln, perhaps our greatest warrior-president, took firm control of the war, gave clear direction to his generals, and, with his historic proclamation, established a purpose worthy of the sacrifices so many made in that epic American ordeal."

—H. R. McMaster, author of *Dereliction of Duty: Lyndon Johnson, Robert McNamara, the Joint Chiefs of Staff, and the Lies that Led to Vietnam*

"A very readable account of the process whereby Lincoln, his cabinet, and key congressional figures sorted priorities and prepared the public for the promise of a 'new birth of freedom' that would save the Union and remake the republic. . . . Always engaging and informed."

—*Library Journal*

"In this historical essay about the Emancipation Proclamation, Brewster explores the six months between Lincoln's July 1862 decision to issue it and actually doing so in January 1863. Inspired by a 1922 article on Lincoln by W. E. B. Du Bois, the purpose of which was to portray Lincoln as great but imperfect, Brewster sets as his goal a quest for the 'real' Lincoln. . . . Featuring vignettes of figures who met Lincoln during his formulation of the proclamation, Brewster's work illuminates Lincoln's lines of thought during this turning point in American history."

—*Booklist*

"This story has been told before, but never as well, with such a firm grasp of the revolutionary implications of Lincoln's decision, or the multilayered levels of Lincoln's quite tortured thought process. Although Lincoln is the most written about figure in American history, Brewster's book is a major entry in the Lincoln sweepstakes."

—Joseph J. Ellis, author of *Founding Brothers*

"It's hard to act from strength and a higher moral conviction when the war you're waging is not going well. But in this wonderful study, Todd Brewster authoritatively evokes the strategy of our best president to change the terms of the Civil War and thereby the destiny of his nation."

—Ken Burns

"With its original approach and tight pacing, this is one of the best Lincoln-related works in recent years. Its scholarly credentials are all in place, but more casual audiences will be drawn to this work because of its intensity and drama. Give this one a read, but be prepared to not want to put it down until it's finished."

—*Books in the Park* blog

"[Brewster's] detailed account is an important addition to understanding the Proclamation and the circumstances of its genesis."

—*What Would the Founders Think?* blog

ALSO BY TODD BREWSTER

The Century

The Century for Young People

In Search of America

I, Abraham Lincoln, President of ...
States of America, and Command...
of the Army and Navy thereof, d...
claim and declare that hereafte...
fore, the war will be prosecute...
ject of practically restoring the con...
lation between the United States
of the states, and the people ther...
states, that relation is, or ~~may be~~ sus...
disturbed.

That it is my purpose, upon the ...
of Congress to again recommend the ...
a practical measure tendering pecu...
the free acceptance or rejection ...

LINCOLN'S GAMBLE

*The Tumultuous Six Months That Gave
America the Emancipation Proclamation and
Changed the Course of the Civil War*

TODD BREWSTER

SCRIBNER

New York London Toronto Sydney New Delhi

SCRIBNER

An Imprint of Simon & Schuster, Inc.
1230 Avenue of the Americas
New York, NY 10020

First Scribner trade paperback edition August 2015

SCRIBNER and design are registered trademarks of The Gale Group, Inc.,
used under license by Simon & Schuster, Inc., the publisher of this work.

For information about special discounts for bulk purchases,
please contact Simon & Schuster Special Sales at 1-866-506-1949 or
business@simonandschuster.com.

The Simon & Schuster Speakers Bureau can bring authors to your
live event. For more information or to book an event contact the
Simon & Schuster Speakers Bureau at 1-866-248-3049 or
visit our website at www.simonspeakers.com.

Book design by Ellen R. Sasahara

Manufactured in the United States of America

3   5   7   9   10   8   6   4   2

ISBN 978-1-4516-9386-7
ISBN 978-1-4516-9389-8 (pbk)
ISBN 978-1-4516-9390-4 (ebook)

The handwritten manuscripts of the first and final drafts of the Emancipation Proclamation (pages 255–56 and 267–70) and Lincoln's Letter to Hodges (pages 275–77)
are from the Abraham Lincoln Papers, Manuscript Division, Library of Congress.

The first printed edition of the Emancipation Proclamation (pages 263–65) is
provided courtesy of the Alfred Whital Stern Collection of Lincolniana, Rare Book
and Special Collections Division, Library of Congress.

The handwritten manuscript of the preliminary Emancipation Proclamation
(pages 259–62) is provided courtesy of the New York State Library.

The photo of Abraham Lincoln is provided courtesy of the Library of Congress.

for Sylvia

CONTENTS

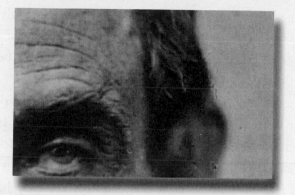

INTRODUCTION

A MAN, IMPERFECT

T HE INSPIRATION FOR this book comes from a short passage in the writings of W. E. B. Du Bois, the African-American intellectual who cofounded the National Association for the Advancement of Colored People in 1909 and whose work on behalf of racial equality set in motion the civil rights crusades of the twentieth century. What Du Bois wrote about the sixteenth president is worth reexamination.

"Abraham Lincoln was a Southern poor white, of illegitimate birth, poorly educated ... unusually ugly, awkward, [and] ill-dressed," Du Bois claimed in a 1922 issue of the NAACP magazine, *Crisis*. "He liked smutty stories and was a politician down to his toes." The judgment at first blush seems unduly harsh (even Du Bois's own faithful readers apparently greeted it with considerable outrage), and as a summary of a life of such commanding importance, it also appears a little beside the point.

On a couple of his observations, Du Bois's description of Lincoln is also simply incorrect. The first president born in a state outside of the thirteen original colonies (Kentucky), Lincoln grew up in Indiana and settled in Illinois, which at the time formed the western edge of the country. He may have been Southern in sensibility, carrying many of the same racial prejudices as those against whom he would later wage war, but he was Western in spirit, in his willingness to broach the new and the untried, to question old traditions and to start over.

The reference to "illegitimacy" is suspect as well. It comes from an almost certainly erroneous and yet often repeated story that Lincoln's father was not the struggling farmer Tom Lincoln, as maintained by most all biographers, but Abraham Enloe (or "Enlow," as the spelling is in doubt), a wealthy North Carolina landowner who, in a story that began to be whispered as early as 1865, entered into an extramarital affair with the family servant girl, Nancy Hanks. When she became pregnant by him and gave birth to a son, whom she named Abraham, presumably after his father, Enloe schemed to shield himself from the shame by sending Hanks off to Kentucky, where she eventually married Tom Lincoln, providing young Abraham with a last name. Though a photograph of a young Wesley Enloe, Abraham Enloe's acknowledged son, did carry an uncanny resemblance to the young Abraham Lincoln, no concrete evidence supported the story. Still, the tale persisted and does to the present day (as a Google search amply demonstrates). It was helped along by William Herndon, Lincoln's law partner, who, in his 1889 three-volume biography, repeated the story in part to reinforce his belief that Lincoln rose from the lowest depths of any of our great men, climbing "from a stagnant, putrid pool, like the gas which, set on fire by its own energy and self-combustible nature, rises in jets, blazing, clear, and bright." The story of Enloe, and others, questioning Lincoln's paternity, even inspired a 1920 book, *The Paternity of Abraham Lincoln*, with the unfortunate subtitle *An Essay on the Chastity of Nancy Hanks*. There, the author refutes claims that Lincoln was fathered by the legendary South Carolina senator John C. Calhoun, by the adopted son of Chief Justice John Marshall, by Enloe, or anyone else other than Thomas Lincoln.

Still, Du Bois was right on most everything else: Abe Lincoln was indeed fond of the bawdy tale. He was also ungainly, homely, self-educated, the product of a dirt-poor upbringing, almost always disheveled in his appearance, and possessed of a gift for politics, though if it reached "down to his toes," as Du Bois claimed—a reference that seemed to deny Lincoln any instinct *but* the political—it was still not enough to prevent the country from collapsing into its bloodiest war, a civil war, almost from the moment when Lincoln was elected president on November 6, 1860.

No matter. For Du Bois, all of this was mere preamble anyway. "The world is full of illegitimate children," he continued. "The world is full of folk whose taste was educated in the gutter. The world is full of people born hating and despising their fellows. To these I love to say: see this man. He was one of you and yet he became Abraham Lincoln."

He *became* Abraham Lincoln. It is an appealing, though, even for Du Bois's time, unoriginal thought. Through the decades, many have adopted the idea that Lincoln's most important gift was that he was educable, that he, like other underestimated political figures, grew to his greatness while in office, that events and Lincoln's response to those events conspired to make Lincoln *Lincoln*, that he listened and watched and studied his way to greatness, often with the help of those around him. In 1864, he spoke, with humility, of no claim to have controlled events, but rather "that events have controlled me," and the abolitionist Wendell Phillips once proclaimed that if Lincoln could be said to have grown in office, "it is because we have watered him."

Still, the old rail-splitter is often credited (perhaps erroneously) with saying that "by age forty, a man is responsible for his own face," a milestone he realized in 1849, twelve years before he reached the presidency, and one could also claim that Lincoln grew to greatness through a steady climb *to* the office, beginning in 1838 with his speech before the Young Men's Lyceum of Springfield, Illinois, when, a mere twenty-eight years old, he warned, with prescience, that the greatest threat to the American nation was not some powerful invading country—no Bonaparte, Alexander, or Caesar—but the threat from within. "If destruction be our lot we must ourselves be its author and finisher," he told his audience, responding in part to mob violence that had led to a lynching in St. Louis, Missouri, and another murder in nearby Alton, Illinois. "As a nation of freemen we must live through all time or die by suicide."

Of Lincoln one could certainly say that he grew *after* the office—after his death, as we came to appreciate a new contour to the American idea, one birthed by him, and as a kind of shimmering mysticism began to attend his memory, a vision of Lincoln as the American Christ figure, killed on Easter weekend (he was assassinated on Good Friday) for the "sin" of granting freedom to the oppressed, a god-man, not a man-man, flawless, porcelain, divinely touched, someone to be worshipped more than understood. Among those who had suffered through the Civil War, much of the latter half of the nineteenth century was spent in an effort to wring meaning from their suffering. They had witnessed so much loss, so much destruction; they now *needed* to make meaning of it, lest the six-hundred-some thousand dead soldiers (and an uncounted number of civilians) be seen as having perished in vain. As early as July 1862, Lincoln, recognizing that this was no ordinary American war—most importantly because it involved Americans killing Americans—pushed Congress to pass legislation creating the first national resting places for those who died in service to their country. In the years following the end of the war, tens of thousands of bodies, most of them lacking any identification, were removed from their primitive battlefield graves to be brought to these new national cemeteries, where their deaths could be given recognition. (Union soldiers' bodies, that is; the corpses of Confederate soldiers were left to the work of small groups of Southern women who banded together to recover what they could.) It wasn't so much the war that created the Union. It was the death from that war and the need to come to terms with it.

But Lincoln's death was the big one. If his violent end could be rendered meaningful, if it could be said that he died for some transcendent purpose, then those who'd perished in the struggle over which he presided would follow his heavenly path. So the lesson was passed on to the next generation, the after-war generation: Lincoln was not simply to be saluted for his service, he was to be "sanctified." By his blood, he had reconciled us; through his pain, we had been healed. By 1909, on the centenary of Lincoln's birth, the apotheosis was complete. More than twenty-two counties and thirty-five cities had been named for Lincoln. There had also been (failed) proposals to christen new states—what became Wyoming and the Dakotas—with his name. It almost didn't matter that so much of what had happened since the end of the war had undone the promise of equality (such as it was, a promise distinct, as we will see in this book, from the promise to end slavery), that the Jim Crow era had put a stain on Lincoln's legacy, that much of what had been gained had been given back; Lincoln had injected the question of equality into the American consciousness as something central to our national identity, as a core element of the American conversation.

In the same year, 1922, that Du Bois wrote the passage above, the Lincoln Memorial was dedicated, a Hellenic temple containing a statue of the seated president that measured nineteen feet from bottom to top and all of it on an eleven-foot pedestal. If this Lincoln were standing, he would rise to twenty-eight feet tall. At the dedication, the poet Edwin Markham reprised his 1900 verse, including the now oft-quoted line "The grip that swung the ax in Illinois / Was on the pen that set a people free."

This hagiographic episode continued, with Lincoln books on every conceivable aspect of his life and career, many of them setting out, Parson Weems style, to create the Lincoln legend: "Honest Abe," "Abe, the Redeemer," "Lincoln: Man of the People," "Master of Men," and, of course, "The Great Emancipator." Thankfully, the trend long ago abated. A tempering of the Lincoln myth occurred in the post–World War II era, with some authors going too far in the other direction, laying him out to be racist, incompetent, devious, and certainly no subject for national reverence. Still, the cascade of Lincoln volumes has continued unabated, and a glance through the entire list shows just how inventive the researching mind can be. In addition to traditional biographies and histories there is *The Life of Abraham Lincoln for Young People: Told in Words of One Syllable*; *The Personal Finances of Abraham Lincoln*; *Abraham Lincoln on the Coming of the Caterpillar Tractor*; and, first published only a decade ago, *The Physical Lincoln*, including the following chapters: "Lips," "Gut," "Skull," "Muscles," "Skin," "Eyes," "Height," and "Joints." According to WorldCat, the global online library catalog, 23,274 books and updated and new editions of books have been written on Lincoln. (So how original am I? As you read this, you are holding the 23,275th.)

But neither growth nor myth nor the overzealous debunking of myth is enough to understand Lincoln, and Du Bois alone, it seems, recognized this nearly a hundred years ago. For his short passage continues with his arguing that Lincoln became Lincoln not by denying or even transcending the impurities of his past but by holding on to them, embracing them, his virtues coexisting with his failings, his achievements coming both because of what he believed and in spite of what he believed. We all would like to think that a man's education and experience forms a progressive line; the more he learns, the better he is. This is only natural, said Du Bois, a desire to whitewash our heroes, to remember only the fine and the brave and the good about those we revere and to whom we look for guidance. "We yearn in our imperfection towards perfection—sinful, we envisage Righteousness." But life is rarely so cleanly lived (okay, it is *never* so cleanly lived), and in our lifting up of those we admire, we forget, Du Bois wrote, "all that was small and mean and unpleasant," rendering the image of our forebears "remote, immense, perfect, cold and dead." Drawing on his own words, he might also have said that we remove the notion that we could become them, that the great are no greater than us.

This book chooses one slice of Lincoln's life, one six-month period from July 1862 to January 1863, as the target for discovering the real Lincoln that Du Bois preferred to recognize. In this noteworthy slice of time, a hinge moment, the focus of the Civil War shifts from being about the restoration of the Union to the abolition of slavery; loyalty to the principles of the nation begins to supersede loyalty to the states; war itself—the conduct of armies—turns to a new brutality, prefiguring the twentieth century's global conflicts; and the American ideal of liberty is joined by the ideal of equality.

It is also an in-between moment for Lincoln. He is not yet the revered god he would become, yet the awful responsibility that has been thrust upon him means that he is already history's object to mold. He is both racist and not. He invites black leaders to the White House and tells them that the Negro has brought on this war, that whites and blacks can never coexist, and that it would be best for all if they would all move somewhere else—all while the Emancipation Proclamation lies in his desk drawer, a work in progress. He issues that Emancipation Proclamation and then withdraws it, resubmits it and then offers to take it away. An agnostic, he prays for God's mercy. A constitutionalist, he suspends one of the most treasured civil liberties. A man of principle, he displays a coarse willingness to compromise.

In the task of freeing men and women, he becomes a tyrant. A civilian, he masters the art of war, yet hundreds of thousands die cruel deaths under his leadership. He is Lincoln and he was human. "I love Lincoln," concluded Du Bois. "Not because he was perfect, but because he was not and yet triumphed."

I.

A FUNERAL: JULY 13, 1862

H IS MELANCHOLY DRIPT from him as he walked," wrote William Herndon of his law partner, Abraham Lincoln, in what is still the most important book ever written about the sixteenth president. Of course, Herndon knew Lincoln best in the years before he became the nation's most embattled chief executive, back in the 1840s and 1850s, when he was a young Springfield, Illinois, attorney, newly married to a difficult woman and with a once-promising career now going in reverse. Lincoln may have had reasons to feel depressed—*melancholy*, Herndon's word, was the word for that day, *depression* not yet a term of diagnosis—

but he didn't need reasons. Depression was not an episode to him; it was his persistent, lifelong companion. He wept easily, felt sorrow deeply, and viewed existence as a grim series of injustices. Lincoln, it was said, didn't merely observe the pain of others, he absorbed it, crawled into the frame of those whom he cared for and suffered their misery as if it were his own.

Imagine the scene, then, on July 13, 1862, as the president, Navy Secretary Gideon Welles, Secretary of State William Henry Seward, and Seward's daughter-in-law Anna Seward traveled together in a horse-drawn carriage to Oak Hill Cemetery in Georgetown for the burial of the infant son of Lincoln's secretary of war, Edwin Stanton. Only months before, Lincoln had taken this same journey, through the same crowded dirt-and-gravel streets, the carriage pulled awkwardly through mud and rain, after his own eleven-year-old son, Willie, succumbed to the dreaded typhoid fever. "My poor boy, he was too good for this earth," the president lamented then to the former slave Elizabeth Keckley, who washed and dressed Willie's dead body. "God has called him home."

The Civil War, the war precipitated by Lincoln's election, killed both boys, albeit indirectly. The hostilities delivered thousands of wounded soldiers to Washington, where warehouses, churches—virtually all available spaces—were quickly converted into makeshift clinics to care for the suffering. Little was known then of the role germs play in disease, and water was scarce, making unsanitary conditions the norm and infection rampant. The overcrowding led to pressure on the sewerage mains and, ultimately, fecal contamination of the water supply.

Widespread typhoid, dysentery, and smallpox were the result. Among the soldiers fighting the war, infection was at least as stubborn a threat as the enemy (and, in the end, twice as deadly), but disease also passed to the civilian population. The stationing of Union troops along the Potomac River, which the soldiers used as a latrine, made the residents of the White House (or Executive Mansion, as it was then called) particularly vulnerable to infection since they received their drinking water from the heavily polluted river.

Early in February 1862, typhoid struck both Willie and his younger brother, Tad. For a while, Lincoln and his wife, the eccentric and much-maligned Mary Todd Lincoln, shuttled between the two, until it became clear that Willie was the one in graver danger. In her memoir, written after the war, Keckley recalled a presidential reception held on a day when Willie took a dramatic turn for the worse, with Mary in a long satin and black lace dress traipsing up and down the stairs, attending to the boy on one end and feigning interest in her guests on the other, the sounds of the Marine Band arriving to the sickbed as "soft, subdued murmurs, like the wild, faint sobbing of far off spirits."

Willie was the favorite child of both parents, and he was popular among the executive staff as well. He was known for his playful imagination—he and his friends built a "fort" on the White House roof, a child playing war while a devastating real war ensued throughout the nation—and his charm reminded many of the president's own. When he finally passed, Mary was inconsolable and took to bed. She would never recover from the loss, wearing mourning clothes the rest of her life (a year of black, followed by lavender with a touch of white, but, being Mary, always only the "very finest" and most "genteel" black, lavender, and white), certain that Willie was taken from her as divine punishment for the lavish lifestyle she sought, and sought to distraction. While churchgoing, she was hardly devout and could not attach to the Christian notion, repeated to her by minister and friend alike, that the dead are in a better place, far happier than they had ever been on earth. Instead, she pursued the relief of spiritualists, holding séances—not uncommon in a day when there was so much young death—where she believed she was communicating with the boy's spirit. "Willie lives," she told her half sister. "He comes to me every night and stands at the foot of the bed with the same sweet adorable smile he always has had." But even this little comfort was, for her, fleeting, a cruel hallucination erased by the disinfectant shine of the next morning's sun. For Mary, there appeared to be no escape from her private hell.

As for Lincoln, he scarcely had time to indulge his grief. Even as Willie's body lay in the Green Room and plans were being formed for the boy's funeral, the president had to tend to eight-year-old Tad's own battle with the same illness, moving his work into his son's room to be closer to the boy, listening for his voice calling for him in the night, and then emerging, his tall frame wrapped in a gown, his bony feet gripped by slippers, to manage the boy's needs. Tad would eventually recover, but the entire episode—two children stricken (one dead, one deathly ill) and the war going on—was, he said, his life's "greatest trial."

A torrential rain arrived the day of Willie's funeral, winds ripping through the capital, destroying trees and pelting the mourners as their caravan moved through Washington to a vault at the top of a hill. Here Willie's body was placed—temporarily, it was presumed, until it could accompany his parents back to Illinois, and eventually it did, though only when the body of the murdered Abe Lincoln made the journey to Springfield in 1865.

So, now, in July 1862, moving to the rhythm of another funeral dirge, this one to observe the burial of yet another innocent victim of the war's pestilence, even as the federal army retreated from defeat after defeat, the casualty toll approaching 150,000 on each side, 300,000 overall, how could Lincoln not feel a deep and painful association with his own recent loss?

The president's two professional companions on this passage formed a stark contrast. Gideon Welles was a Connecticut Yankee, a big, tall, white-whiskered figure sporting a comically ill-fitting brown wig that shook out of place when he spoke. Lincoln affectionately called him Father Neptune. A onetime Jacksonian Democrat who read for the law but pursued a career as a journalist, Welles had broken with the Democrats in the 1850s over slavery, joining the emerging Republican Party and starting a new newspaper, the *Hartford Evening Press*, which promoted Republican ideas. A member of the Connecticut legislature, he was the Republican candidate for governor in 1856, though he received only 10 percent of the vote.

Four years later, when Welles met Lincoln, the future president was fresh from the commanding success of his Cooper Union speech in New York City, where he had introduced himself to the Eastern political establishment and carefully laid out the argument for the federal government's regulation of slavery in the Western territories. While visiting Hartford, Lincoln sought out Welles with the hope of securing his support at the upcoming Republican nominating convention in Chicago. The two sat outside Brown and Gross's Bookstore at the corner of Main and Asylum Streets, drawing attention from bystanders who had recently become aware of Lincoln's growing reputation, pushed forward first by the Lincoln-Douglas debates of

1858 and then by the Cooper Union speech. Lincoln's lanky form, two-thirds legs, shrank when he sat so that he faced his host more or less eye to eye. Yet even with Lincoln in this pose, Welles found him "every way large, brain included." The following day in his paper, Welles gave readers a nuanced picture of the man whose rapid fame had invited both curiosity and caricature. "He is not Apollo," Welles offered, "but he is not Caliban." Lincoln "was made where the material for strong men is plenty" with a "huge, tall frame . . . loosely thrown together." Still, "his countenance shows intellect, generosity, good nature."

Going into his meeting with Lincoln, Welles had favored Salmon P. Chase, the Ohio governor, for the Republican nomination. Like Welles, Chase was a strong and outspoken opponent of slavery and was conservative on government spending and the protection of states' rights, two subjects that the Connecticut reformer, as a former Democrat, found attractive. But on this visit to Hartford, Lincoln deeply impressed Welles. To Welles, Lincoln was an accomplished speaker, "earnest, strong, honest, simple in style, and clear as crystal in his logic."

Welles switched his support to Lincoln at the Chicago convention, and Lincoln, as president-elect, rewarded him with the post of navy secretary. This political appointment was aimed at getting a New Englander into the cabinet, and Welles had little familiarity with naval affairs. Lincoln once joked that he himself at least knew the difference between a stern and a bow, more, he ventured, than Welles knew. Still, Welles performed capably at his post, earning Lincoln's respect, and he kept him in wise counsel.

Welles's disdain for slavery led him to a pronounced dislike for the South in general. An inveterate diarist—certainly the most valuable among the Lincoln administration insiders—he was dismissive of what he came to see as the "diseased imagination" of the Southern landowners, little Ivanhoes inspired by reading too many Walter Scott novels, thinking themselves "cavaliers, imbued with chivalry, a superior class, not born to labor but to command," who held the North in contempt as weak, religious, moral, dull. Years later, at the close of the war, he acknowledged its inevitability. "[Southerners] came ultimately to believe themselves a better race," he penned in an 1865 entry. ". . . Only a war could wipe out this arrogance and folly."

Seward was Welles's superior in every measurement but size. A short, thin reed of a man sporting a painful-looking beak for a nose (Henry Adams found him reminiscent of a "wise macaw"), he was dashing and brilliant, known for throwing off restraint in favor of the bold statement of principle or at least appearing to do so, his political face blending so well with his private face that it was hard, Adams wondered, to tell "how much was nature and how much was mask."

As a senator from New York, and former governor of the Empire State, Seward had been the favorite over either Chase or Lincoln for the 1860 Republican presidential nomination. Seward had planned for it. In his mind, and in the mind of many others, it would serve as the much-anticipated cap to a career that had been animated by his forthright and eloquent opposition to slavery. In a justly famous speech delivered on the Senate floor in 1850, Seward had argued that a "Higher Law" was superior to the slavery-tolerating Constitution, a "law of nature and of nations" that had been "bestowed upon them by the Creator of the universe," and he implored his Senate colleagues to be most faithful to this law, even when it conflicted with the nation's founding document. "We cannot . . . be either true Christians or real freemen," he concluded, "if we impose on another a chain that we defy all human power to fasten on ourselves."

Such claims naturally put Seward at odds with Southern leaders, who rightly felt the New Yorker's finger wagging at them, and they traded verbal jabs with him throughout the decade, the worst exchange, perhaps, coming after the Supreme Court's *Dred Scott* decision of 1857, when Seward charged that President James Buchanan and Chief Justice Roger Taney had conspired in that infamous ruling, which declared that Congress had no power to legislate a ban on slavery in US territories (invalidating the Missouri Compromise of 1820) and African-Americans (slave or free) had no rights under the Constitution of the United States. Seward's charge of collusion, which compared Buchanan and the justices to England's Charles I and his courtiers, "[subverting] the statutes of English liberty," prompted Buchanan to declare that Seward was not welcome at the White House, and years later Chief Justice Taney acknowledged that if Seward had been elected president in 1860, Taney would have refused to administer him the oath of office.

Undaunted, Seward continued to let his mouth outpace his discretion. A few months after the *Scott* decision, he declared that the growing sectional conflict over slavery put the country on the path of "an irrepressible conflict" where the choice would be "either entirely a slaveholding nation, or entirely a free-labor nation." It almost seemed as though Seward were saying to the South, "Bring it on," an explicit rejection of the accommodationist approach of those who argued that the clash of wills between North and South was but "accidental, unnecessary," the work of fanatic fringes on each side that would surely prove "ephemeral." In fact, Seward's tone misrepresented his views.

Like Lincoln, he favored a gradual, legislative end to slavery, but he was a confrontational speaker, and rare for a Northern politician in this time, he dared to challenge the South, mistakenly thinking that disunion was not a serious possibility, that the threat of secession was nothing more than a bluff.

As the 1860 convention neared, Seward had tried to broaden his appeal by sounding more moderate, assuring delegates that he felt the South was "sovereign on the subject of slavery" within its own borders. But the past continued to haunt him. Adopting his colorful phrase as their own, members of the New York delegation supporting him branded themselves "the Irrepressibles," making it even harder for the New York senator to escape his lively rhetoric, and this while the rest of the gathered delegates in Chicago—an amalgamation of Free-Soilers, Know-Nothings, Nativists, and former Democrats who made up the nascent Republican Party—saw a clash with the South as something they wanted very much to avoid, not encourage by nominating the man Southerners most resented.

Despite their common views on ending slavery, Welles and Seward were antagonists, and their animosity predated their service in the Lincoln administration. For his part, Welles found Seward unattractively ambitious, an opportunist whose employment of Thurlow Weed, a cigar-chomping political boss, to manage his political career struck the New Englander as crass. Seward, in turn, resented Welles for his support of Lincoln at the nominating convention, where the future navy secretary helped lead not only Connecticut but all New England away from supporting Seward. Once Lincoln was elected, Seward opposed the appointment of Welles to the cabinet, preferring that Lincoln select only former Whigs, not ex-Democrats such as Welles.

The tension between Welles and Seward had a more recent history, too. In 1861, in what became the opening scene of the Civil War, federal troops stranded at Fort Sumter in hostile South Carolina had been in desperate need of provisions. Welles ordered the USS *Powhatan* to be readied from its pier in Brooklyn for service in supplying the South Carolina fort. At the same time, however, Seward was scheming for the same ship to help protect Fort Pickens at Santa Rosa Island, Florida. While Welles was navy secretary, Seward assured the president that "Uncle Gideon" would not mind Seward's meddling. Yet Welles did of course mind, and when he heard of it, the whole plan had to be scuttled. The episode only confirmed Welles's feelings toward Seward, whom he thereafter referred to as "the trickster." Even after Seward died in 1872, Welles could not contain his wrath over this experience and others, publishing a small book in which he vented his rage. In *Lincoln and Seward*, Welles accused the onetime Lincoln rival of entering "upon his duties [as secretary of state] with the impression . . . that he was to be the *de facto* president."

Welles's opinion of Seward was shared by others in the Lincoln cabinet, particularly Chase. Seward was pictured as an arrogant, self-aggrandizing figure who could be charming, yes, but whose flair for the dramatic often offended more people than it pleased. Seward even dared to show his haughtiness to Lincoln, criticizing the president to his face with the air of one convinced that he could have done a better job. Yet Seward's brilliance was undeniable and his input critical. After Lincoln's nomination, he became a loyal supporter of the Republican candidate and declared himself a Unionist first—joining in Lincoln's view that preservation of the Union was the first and only important goal.

Working side by side with Lincoln on the writing of the president's first inaugural address, Seward, in a reversal of roles, softened Lincoln's text, making it less combative toward the South, removing the president's threat to reclaim federal property seized by the secessionists, and moderating the tone Lincoln had assumed toward the Supreme Court over the *Dred Scott* decision.

Seward even contributed to one of the most powerful statements Lincoln ever made: the closing paragraph of his first inaugural address, which the president had initially penned as a challenge to the rebels: "With *you*," he wrote, in the tone of a bark, "and not with *me*, is the solemn question of 'Shall it be peace, or a sword?'" Seward suggested replacing it with an outstretched hand: "We must not be aliens or enemies but fellow countrymen and brethren." He also proposed a commanding image of optimism and reconciliation: "mystic chords . . . proceeding from so many battle fields and patriot graves," which Seward, writing for Lincoln, imagined "will yet again harmonize in their ancient music when breathed upon by the guardian angel of the nation." Lincoln, the better poet, improved on this image to make it into one of history's most commanding lines of political oratory—looking forward to the moment when "the mystic chords of memory, stretching from every battle-field and patriot grave, to every living heart and hearthstone, all over this broad land, will yet swell the chorus of the Union, when again touched, as surely they will be, by the better angels of our nature." But it was Seward who pushed Lincoln toward it.

So the carriage ride to James Stanton's funeral on that thirteenth day of July 1862 was not exactly a meeting of friends, more accurately the convening of three men of character thrown together by both ambition and circumstance, each of them deeply connected to, and responsible for, the nation's great test: Welles in charge of the naval campaign, Seward as chief diplomat, and Lincoln at the center of it all. The war, to put it mildly, was not going well.

The Union Army had met with considerable success in the winter and spring of 1862, securing control of Missouri and western Tennessee, capturing New Orleans, and defeating the Confederates at the massive battle of Shiloh. But the Confederates had since regrouped and humiliated the North in the Virginia peninsula, rendering General George B. McClellan's strategy there a failure. The former engineering instructor at West Point, himself a West Pointer, had risen to fame off an early battle success in the western region of Virginia. Out of this the Pennsylvania native had earned the nickname Young Napoléon, but the moniker fit him more favorably as a comparison of inflated egos than as a comparison of tactical brilliance. As an officer, McClellan was good at one thing: organizing and training troops. But there it all stopped. Like a skilled stage actor who freezes in the opening-night lights, McClellan could rehearse but not perform. Worse, he blamed his failures on others, repeatedly overestimating the strength of his enemy and stalling for more time, then pleading for more troops, receiving them, and pleading for even more time. He elicited an impressive loyalty from his soldiers, who revered him as a "soldier's general," probably because his passivity helped keep them out of danger, which may be a virtue for an officer but only if not taken to the extreme. Frustrated by his general, in March Lincoln relieved McClellan from his position as general in chief of the Union Army, still leaving him to lead the Army of the Potomac, the primary Union fighting unit in the Eastern Theater of the war. Now the failure of that army's Peninsula Campaign, aimed at capturing the Confederate capital, Richmond, had cast a dark shadow over the North's prospects. Bungled by McClellan, it was probably the last chance for the Union to make it a short war.

McClellan's failures were failures of courage. He could not abide risk. But they were also, to some degree, failures of intention, and with him, the two fit comfortably. Like many of the West Point officers serving the Union, McClellan was a Democrat. He did not share the Republican Party's antipathy toward the South, nor did he see the eradication of slavery as a worthy war goal. Slavery should end, he believed, but only gradually, not forcibly, and with respect rendered to both master and slave. After the war, he pronounced "a prejudice for my own race," adding that he couldn't imagine learning "to like the odor of either Billy goats or niggers," but such racist pronouncements were not in his mind inconsistent with a repugnance for slavery.

McClellan was particularly uncomfortable with bringing a war against his own people. Throughout his life, he had found himself inclined toward Southern culture and Southern thinking, preferring it to Northern ways, even as he held firm in his belief that the South's decision to secede was wrong. He believed in the integrity of the American nation. Thus, while he fought for the Union Army, he fought primarily for the cause of *union*, wanting to see the country restored to its prewar geography and seeing the clash between North and South as essentially a pique brought on by "ultras," with both sides equally to blame. Naturally such a confusion of sympathies led him to a stuttering war plan. He wanted to successfully prosecute the battle against the South, but he wanted to limit the risk, too, both for his own soldiers and, ironically, for the "enemy" as well. It was a rebellion, and he intended that it remain a rebellion, not a full-scale war.

To radicals and abolitionists, even to some in Lincoln's cabinet, such as Stanton, the McClellan stutter was something just short of treason.

In early July, only days before the funeral of Stanton's baby, a peeved Lincoln had boarded the steamship *Ariel* out of Fort Monroe and journeyed to visit McClellan at his Harrison's Landing, Virginia, headquarters along the James River. The purpose of the visit was to spur the morale of the troops involved in the disappointing Peninsula effort. On that, the trip was a success, the soldiers cheering the presidential visit in competition with the sounds of cannons fired in a show of enthusiasm. But Lincoln was also there to confront McClellan on his lack of success. The president had been pained by the army's failures, and it was taking a toll on him. He was losing sleep and had lost interest in eating. "I cannot take my vittles regular," Lincoln had said, when pressed on his increasingly gaunt appearance. "I kind of just browse around."

The setting had its own presidential significance, having been the ancestral home of William Henry Harrison, the ninth president of the United States and one of ten prewar presidents who had owned slaves. (Harrison, it was later rumored, also fathered several children with one of his.) The property had since passed on to others, who abandoned it when the war broke out, leaving the elegant Georgian mansion that was the centerpiece of the estate to be crowded now with wounded and dying soldiers. Two rooms, *Harper's Weekly* reported, were reserved for amputations.

Lincoln toured the ranks of soldiers, doffing his hat in respect to them. As grave as the scene must have felt, the pairing of the two men was also somewhat comic. Little Mac, as his soldiers affectionately called him, was striking in his crisply ironed uniform, his mustache carefully trimmed, his chest puffed out in a display of patrician arrogance. Next to him was the shabby but towering Lincoln, six feet four inches before you added his trademark stovepipe hat, riding in on horseback ("like a pair of tongs on a chair back" in one soldier's description), unusually self-conscious, especially around men of arms. The two of them engaged in a stare-down (a "stare-up" for the diminutive general) over policy. McClellan thought Lincoln his distinct inferior, which he was if you looked only at birth status and formal education; while Lincoln thought McClellan some stunted genius, whom Lincoln had been too quick to favorably judge when he appointed him to lead, and he was suffering for it now.

McClellan, whose self-esteem was once described by a writer in *Harper's* as swelling to "elephantiasis" proportions, decided here, at Harrison's Landing, to educate Lincoln with what the general proudly described to his own wife as "a strong frank letter." McClellan felt forced, by conscience, he said, to counsel the president, even if such advice did go beyond the scope of his duties as an army officer. Lincoln was used to McClellan's imperious pronouncements; nonetheless, this statement had to have startled him. In the letter, McClellan laid out a defense of the kind of warfare he preferred and had been practicing: cautious, limited, between armies alone, not citizens, and conducted with decorum. A gentleman's war. Fearing that doubts over his progress were leading many in Washington to push for a more aggressive approach to the South, the general asserted that victory should only be pursued according to the "highest principles known to Christian Civilization," which, to McClellan, included a prohibition on the "confiscation of property, [on] political executions of persons," and on "forcible abolition of slavery." None of these "should be contemplated for even a moment," he wrote. "Military power should not be allowed to interfere with the relations of servitude, either by supporting or impairing the authority of the master." It was not only advice, but an attempt by McClellan to demonstrate his preeminence among the Union's senior officers and reclaim his "rightful" position as general in chief. McClellan was always an officer who kept one eye on his troops and the other on destiny.

Lincoln read the letter as the two sat on the deck of the president's boat. Then, in what must have been the most pregnant of pauses, Lincoln placed it in his pocket and said nothing more other than to coolly thank his general for providing it to him. The two men emerged from this private scene to mount their steeds and slowly greet each division of weary soldiers. Lincoln's awkward handling of his horse's reins brought great amusement to the troops. They had suffered mightily, with 1,734 dead and 8,066 wounded, their regimental colors, the *New York Times* reported, "torn almost to shreds by the balls of the enemy," but having their president there to thank them was a "tonic."

On the way home, Lincoln's ship stalled, going aground at Kettle Shoals in the Chesapeake, and the president took the opportunity for a bracing dip in the river. The water may have cleared his mind, but if so the respite was temporary. For only days after his return to Washington, Lincoln rode with Welles and Seward to James Stanton's funeral, and both the relative privacy of the situation—a simple, small carriage; three men with a lot on their minds—and the nature of their mission, attendance at a baby's funeral, encouraged Lincoln's resolve. As he bounced along in the rain, the president's reactions to McClellan's demanding message no doubt competed with memories of Willie, and with thoughts of the morbid scenery formed by Washington's dead and dying, of the general downturn in the prospects for the Union, of his wife's slide toward insanity, of the bitter rivalries among the members of his cabinet, and, increasingly, of his own rising insecurities, to push him toward a monumental decision. Rejecting McClellan's advice in its totality, Lincoln abruptly informed his companions that he had determined he would utilize the power of the executive order to do what his enemies had long claimed he would do, but which he, torn between highly regarded principles that competed inside him for preeminence, had mightily resisted. His mind was now made up on all aspects except timing. He was ready, he said, to free the slaves.

II.

"IN REGARD TO YOUR SLAVES . . ."

BETWEEN THE TIME when Abraham Lincoln was elected president and the time when he assumed office, seven Southern states, acting in anticipation of what they regarded as the new president's plans to end their long-standing practice of chattel slavery (where both slaves and their progeny are deemed to be the property of the slaveholder), seceded from the Union. Once the Confederate attack on Fort Sumter plunged the nation into civil war, four more states followed these first seven. Long-standing abolitionists and members of his own Republican Party urged Lincoln to make the battle lines distinct and declare this war's mission as the destruction of the South's "peculiar institution." Upon hearing the news from Sumter, Senator Charles Sumner of Massachusetts made his way hurriedly to the Executive Mansion, where he informed Lincoln "that under the war power the right had come to him to emancipate the slaves." Lincoln demurred. While he held firm to his belief that slavery should not be extended to the new territories acquired in the war with Mexico, the president said he had no intentions to disrupt the practice where it already existed. Lincoln's mission, then, was nothing more than to restore the Union, to bring the South back and bring it back with slavery intact. Indeed, throughout 1861, Union commanders ordered their troops to be faithful to the Fugitive Slave Act of 1850. As hundreds and then thousands of slaves threw themselves in front of advancing Union forces, convinced that the war was for them, for their freedom, and their future in America, they were captured and returned to their owners. Some Union commanders even allowed slave owners to conduct searches of their Union campgrounds and reclaim their runaways. One can only imagine the brutal fate that awaited them upon capture.

This was no war to end slavery. It wasn't even a war, insisted Lincoln. It was an insurrection of states that, as far as he was concerned, were still part of the Union and still guaranteed the rights of the slavery-protecting Constitution. The administration's military efforts were exclusively for the "suppression of rebellion," the "preservation of the Union," and the "chastisement of treason," and when, after Sumter, Lincoln called up seventy-five thousand militiamen to counteract the Southern uprising, they were told to use care not to interfere with the property of those in the seceded states. The order was clear: *leave the slaves in slavery.*

Why? Why was it so difficult for Lincoln to decide to free the slaves? It's a simple question that has dogged his reputation for 150 years. Why? Why did the man who would become revered for generations as the Great Emancipator hesitate to do his "emancipating," and if it did take him so long, what is so "great" about that? Surely an issue of such moral gravity demanded action absent of even the slightest uncertainty, yet Lincoln hesitated and hesitated repeatedly, dodging the subject as if he simply did not want to confront its consequences, of which there would be many—some known, some unknown. Why?

The answer is as unreachable as the search is tantalizing. But whoever pursues it must first confront the fact that the Lincoln who rode with Seward and Welles to James Stanton's funeral in July 1862 was not, and had never been, an abolitionist. No matter how powerful his statements about the evils of slavery, and he made many, he had never, ever prescribed the complete and immediate end to the institution, which, say, Frederick Douglass, William Lloyd Garrison, and Wendell Phillips—all famous antislavery activists of Lincoln's day—did.

Sure, he was a politician and therefore worked in the realm of the possible, not the ideal or the pure. Lincoln would never have been nominated for president in 1860 if he had shown himself to be a true friend to the abolitionists' cause. We know this by the lesson of Seward, who, while also advocating a slow, negotiated end to slavery, was looked upon as more radical than Lincoln, if only for his persistent and eloquent moral pronouncements on the subject, which *precisely because they were so persistent and eloquent* effectively denied him the nomination he had long expected would be handed to him by acclamation. We know, too, from Lincoln himself, who turned to Charles Edwards Lester, a clergyman and author, and said, "I think Sumner and the rest of you would upset our applecart altogether if you had your way. We'll fetch 'em; just give us a little time. We didn't go into the war to put down slavery, but to put the flag back, and to act differently at this moment would, I have no doubt, not only weaken our cause but smack of bad faith; for I never should have had votes enough to send me here if the people had supposed I should try to use my power to upset slavery."

Over the years, many of Lincoln's champions have taken this "Lincoln was just being a politician" point of view, arguing that he put on a public face, a political face, one that obscured his real feelings, his abolitionist feelings, as an explanation for his ambiguity on the subject. By this perspective, Lincoln understood that he could not end slavery *at all* if he exposed his true belief that slavery needed to be ended *immediately*. Ironically, many in the South shared this "closet abolitionist" view of Lincoln, or more precisely, they did not see much of a distinction between those, like Lincoln, who publicly advocated a gradual and negotiated end to slavery and those who cried out for its immediate extinction, the former being, to them, just a mask for the latter, a more polite way of delivering the same death blow, maybe even worse, as it appeared to hide the speaker's real intentions behind a softer message that was perhaps nothing more than a foil. But from either perspective, is the picture accurate? Did Lincoln secretly want slavery to end *immediately*? The answer, again, is almost certainly no.

It is hard for modern minds to comprehend the importance of slavery to the economic growth of the United States. It is harder still to connect with the way that slavery, in the New World more than anywhere else, came to be equated with the subjugation of the African race. There was slavery, of course, long before there was an America, but most of the history of slavery is of whites enslaving whites. The word takes its origins from the Latin *sclavus*, for "Slav," and grew out of the practice of importing peoples from Eastern Europe to work in Mediterranean societies from roughly the 1200s to the 1400s.

The discovery and development of the New World, with its abundant natural resources, presented an opportunity ripe for commercial exploitation, but one that required a pool of labor large enough to meet the demand. At first this was fulfilled by the flow of white, indentured servants from Europe. But that source slowed in the eighteenth century and was replaced by the forced migration of African peoples at a rate of more than five African slaves for every new European settler. The greatest concentration of African slave labor during this time was in the Caribbean, but once it became apparent that the larger slave population afforded the sugar plantations there a dramatic advantage over their competitors, ever-larger numbers of African slaves were brought to the American mainland. By the mid-eighteenth century slavery was being practiced in all thirteen original colonies.

It remains a historical mystery why the slavery of African peoples began to be preferred over the slavery of whites, but speculation centers on the conjunction of several convenient factors. Many in Europe considered slavery to be cruel and unjust only when it targeted Christians, and by the mid-1700s most of that continent had been converted, while the non-Christian Africans remained "heathens." Slavery was also common in Africa itself—that is, with Africans enslaving other Africans—and that meant that half of the slave trader's work had already been done for him: he didn't need to "enslave" anyone, just bargain for the right to sell these slaves abroad. And finally, many Europeans saw the color black as marking the African as different from the rest of the world's people. This "color-coded" racism, as one historian describes it, may even have assuaged some of the guilt associated with the practice of slavery by confirming an "otherness" that "made it psychologically easier to treat [slaves] with the brutality that the slave trade often necessitated." Indeed, the stories of innocent Africans orphaned from their families, prodded through holding pens and onto the fetid slave ships, where they faced an Atlantic passage rife with violence and degradation, are legendary.

Still, as slavery grew in the colonies, moral objections abounded, and how could they not? This was after all the beginning of the Enlightenment. Liberty was on the lips of most forward-looking people, and if the American Revolution was about anything, it was about freedom, equality, and the supremacy of rational thinking. The Revolution did indeed lead to the end of slavery in most Northern states, with New England and Pennsylvania leading the way, but it remained strong in the South. The Southern economy had become too dependent upon slavery to forgo its advantages.

Two critical historical developments hardened the Southern states' position: The first was the invention in 1793 of the cotton gin, which provided a method for processing large amounts of short-staple cotton, the kind that could be grown inland (long-stem cotton, which is easier to remove from its seeds, could only successfully be cultivated along the coastline, where the growing season was longer). The second was the acquisition of new territories that became the Southern states of

Alabama, Mississippi, and Louisiana, along with the forced removal of the Native American populations living there. With a new method for harvesting cotton and new land upon which to harvest it, a robust Cotton Kingdom arose, dominating the Southern economy of the early nineteenth century and dependent on an ever-increasing number of slaves. The most that antislavery activists could achieve in these days was an end to the merciless slave trade (and even that ban was repeatedly violated), but slavery itself continued to flourish. Despite the assertion of human rights that lay at the core of the American Revolution, slavery was far stronger in the early 1800s than it had been before the Revolution. There were seven hundred thousand slaves in 1790, 4 million by 1850.

Lincoln did not pay much attention to slavery early in his career. He abhorred it and said so, but he was a traditional Whig, interested more in economic development than in advancing the cause of social progress, and anyway, he believed slavery would ultimately follow an unaided path to extinction just as the Founders, he argued, had intended it to. Writing to his slaveholding friend Joshua Speed, Lincoln acknowledged "your rights" and "my obligations under the Constitution, in regard to your slaves," before admonishing him to "appreciate how much the great body of the Northern people do crucify their feelings, in order to maintain their loyalty to the Constitution and the Union." But Lincoln's attitude was more pitying than indignant. "I confess I hate to see the poor creatures hunted down, and caught, and carried back to their stripes, and unrewarded toils," he wrote, "but I bite my lip and keep quiet." Lincoln still had something of the old Kentucky boy in him, the historian Richard Hofstadter wrote in a seminal 1948 essay, his "regard for the slaves" being "more akin to his feeling for tortured animals than it was to his feeling, say, for the common white man of the North."

Only with the passage of the 1854 Kansas-Nebraska Act, guided through Congress by Lincoln's Illinois rival Senator Stephen A. Douglas, did slavery became the single most urgent subject of the day, one demanding the attention of every politician. Lincoln publicly denounced slavery for the first time in October of that year, even as he found himself stymied by how to abolish it. The 1854 act repealed the 1820 Missouri Compromise, which had banned slavery in the Nebraska Territory, and it divided that territory into two parts, Kansas and Nebraska, ordering that the question of slavery be addressed in each through popular sovereignty. In other words, if the people of Kansas wanted slavery, they could have it; if they didn't, they wouldn't.

To Douglas, who assumed that the new territories would reject slavery, the Kansas-Nebraska Act was a convenient way to settle the issue away from the stage of national politics and thus make it easier for him to run for president by his not having to choose a side on this divisive issue. To Lincoln, the new law was an abdication of national responsibility. Congress had rejected the letter and spirit of legislative compromise and replaced it with an invitation to violence. He suspected that the issue would now bring partisans from both sides to Kansas, armed with "bowie knives and six shooters," pro-slavery activists from the South "flushed with triumph and tempted to excesses," while those of the North would counter them, feeling betrayed and "burning for revenge." Speaking in Peoria in October 1854, Lincoln countered Douglas with his warning, declaring, "One side will provoke; the other resent. The one will taunt, the other defy." The spiral would have no end. "And if this fight should begin," he told his audience, "is it likely to take a very peaceful, Union-saving turn? Will not the first drop of blood so shed, be the real knell of the Union?"

Lincoln's vision was sadly prescient. Far from reducing tensions, the Kansas-Nebraska Act raised the argument over slavery to a new, and highly dangerous, pitch, one exemplified by "Bleeding Kansas" (journalist Horace Greeley's compelling phrase), the period of four years or so from 1855 to 1859 when violence erupted between pro-slavery and antislavery advocates who flooded the state to battle over the issue. Within a couple of years, Douglas became so hated in the North, he observed that he could have journeyed from Chicago to Boston over a path illuminated by nothing more than the lights from his burning effigies.

The nation's freshly energized clash over slavery was perhaps most dramatically exhibited on the floor of the US Senate when, in 1856, the abolitionist senator Charles Sumner of Massachusetts, using sexually charged language that struck at the South's conception of chivalric honor, accused Senator Andrew Butler of South Carolina—who had cosponsored the Kansas-Nebraska Act with Douglas—of having taken on a mistress ("the harlot, slavery") and of further exhibiting a "lust for power" that would now lead to the "rape" of the "virgin territory" of Kansas. Two days later, while Sumner was working at his desk on the Senate floor, Preston Brooks, a South Carolina congressman who was Butler's cousin, entered the chamber and, after waiting for the scene to be free of women (whom he wished to protect from his deed), took a gold-headed cane from his side and brutally beat Sumner to unconsciousness. "I did not intend to kill him," said

Brooks calmly afterward, "but I did intend to whip him." While bloodied, Sumner survived, and Brooks resigned from Congress for his assault, not so much in disgrace as to offer his constituents the opportunity to judge him for his unorthodox behavior, which they did by mounting rallies in his honor and reelecting him to his seat.

By the time Lincoln and Douglas faced off in seven celebrated debates as part of the 1858 Illinois US Senate campaign, the issue of slavery had pushed aside all others, and the threat it had brought to the territorial integrity of the nation had become real. In a justly famous speech opening his Senate campaign, Lincoln asserted that the nation could not endure "half slave and half free," setting the stage for his debates with Douglas. To Lincoln, the Kansas-Nebraska Act and the *Dred Scott* decision now combined to form the threat that slavery would not, as he had long expected, expire of its own accord; indeed, it appeared poised to spread and flourish throughout an expanded nation. But to Douglas, the problem was not the spread of slavery. That argument, he claimed, was a red herring, since slavery was intimately wrapped up with the climate of the South and the South alone. It would not spread to the territories because slavery had no reason to exist in regions where cotton could not be grown. No, said Douglas, the real threat was the persistent efforts of Lincoln and others to "abolitionize" American politics, to force the rules and regulations of one region upon another. Could the nation really not endure "half slave" and "half free"? Why not? It had been that way for eighty years.

Those who watched Lincoln in these historic debates were in awe of his talents and struck by his unusual bearing. "In repose,

I must confess," wrote a reporter for the *New York Evening Post,*
" 'Long Abe's' appearance is *not* comely. But stir him up and the
fire of genius plays on every feature. His eye glows and sparkles,
every lineament, now so ill formed, grows brilliant and expres-
sive, and you have before you a man of rare power and of strong
magnetic influence."

The debates, which have since been held up as a model of
political discourse, were almost exclusively about slavery, but
the arguments the men put forward drew the outlines of two
opposing concepts of a free society. Lincoln spoke for a kind of
rights-oriented nationalism that predated the Constitution and
embraced the Declaration of Independence's assertion that "all
men are created equal." Douglas was the proponent of popular sovereignty, of a procedural model of American democracy
where the government does not assert a preferred way of life for
its people, rather it lets people choose their own values and prac-
tices, subject to the consequences of their decisions. In Douglas's model, the morality is in the process, not the decisions that
come from it. In Lincoln's, fundamental truths are inviolable no
matter the virtue of the "process."

Given that distinction, one might think that Lincoln *would* be
an abolitionist, a "right" being by definition fundamental, not
subject to compromise *precisely because it is a right.* Yet that was not
the case. As he would through the first half of his presidency,
even this Lincoln, the Lincoln of the Lincoln-Douglas debates,
claimed no interest in disturbing the practice of slavery where it
existed, only to preventing its threatened spread to the new territories. Lincoln advocated a gradual, negotiated, and peaceful
end to slavery. That could well mean that "ultimate extinction,"

as he told Douglas, would take a hundred years or more (what a thought; a hundred-year phaseout would have maintained slavery in the United States until 1958), but if so, Lincoln could live with that schedule.

The key here, to Lincoln, was the law. On the one hand, he laid claim to a "higher law"—Seward's term—protecting humanity from involuntary servitude, a "natural law," if you will, as described by the Declaration of Independence, a creator-given law endowing "all men" with "inalienable rights." This fundamental principle, Lincoln argued, distinguished the American Revolution from other revolutions, for its central achievement was not simply to exchange one regime for another but to rescue the "common right of humanity" from the "divine right of kings." Slavery was incompatible with the American idea because slavery sprang from the same tyrannical spirit that monarchs claimed as their birthright: the power to live off the labor of others, to say, "You work and toil and earn bread, and I'll eat it." The slaves themselves understood this better than anyone else, Lincoln argued, once illustrating his point with a story: "The ant who has toiled and dragged a crumb to his nest will furiously defend the fruit of his labor, against whatever robber assails him. So plain, that the most dumb and stupid slave that ever toiled for a master, does constantly know that he has been wronged. So plain that no one, high or low, ever does mistake it, except in a plainly selfish way; for although volume upon volume is written to prove slavery a very good thing, we never hear of the man who wishes to take the good of it, by being a slave himself."

But this calculation was problematical. The Declaration was a *declaration*, a call to war authorized by assembled delegates in the interest of establishing a revolution. Having never been voted on by a duly elected body of representatives, it was not "law" in a political sense, and to the degree that one could assert a "higher law" on the subject of slavery—*real* law, as opposed to a statement such as the Declaration—it was in the form of the US Constitution, which actually protected slavery. Lincoln may have been a moralist, but he was also, perhaps even primarily, a lawyer, resigned to working with the law *as it was*, not *as he wished it to be.*

In the debates, Lincoln cited a historical argument to claim that the Founders, while tolerating the practice, intended for slavery to end. For one, he said, the Constitution set a date allowing for an end to the slave trade, 1808 (Article I, section 9). Why, he asked, would they have set this date if they intended for slavery to continue? For another, the authors of the Constitution avoided using the term *slavery*—the word appears nowhere in the document—so offended were they by its practice. Even when asserting that fugitive slaves needed to be returned to captivity with their masters (Article IV, section 2), he argued, the Constitution reads that "no person held to service or labor in one State under the laws thereof escaping into another, shall . . . be discharged from such service or labor, but shall be delivered up, on claim of the party to whom such service or labor may be due." Wouldn't it have been much easier, Lincoln asked, to simply say that a slave escaping his master must be apprehended and returned? The Framers, he concluded, did not want to stain their document with reference to a shameful practice they hoped would be extinct before the nation had even grown from infancy.

Yet Lincoln's task remained difficult. However euphemistically it might be worded, the Constitution, in its fugitive-slave clause, undeniably protected slavery, and the document's ratification by the Southern states was well known to have depended upon its protection of slavery; to claim something otherwise was to argue against the historical record. Lincoln also faced the (very) inconvenient fact that the Founders, with one or two exceptions, were slaveholders themselves. Some of them may have been reluctant slaveholders, but they were slaveholders nonetheless. (Washington's will called for the freeing of his slaves upon his death; Madison, while a slaveholder his entire life, was an early advocate for freeing the slaves and sending them back to Africa; and Jefferson, well, what can we say about the author of "all men are created equal" who fathered children with the slave girl Sally Hemings and upon his death had his slaves sold off to pay his commanding debts?) Finally, an equally awkward detail was that Congress had reinforced its support for slavery when it passed the Fugitive Slave Act of 1850, which, responding to the North's unwillingness to comply with the practice of returning escaped slaves, now required Northern officials to return them under penalty of a fine. As part of the Compromise of 1850, the act had even earned the vote of Daniel Webster, the great orator and Massachusetts senator, who hoped that it would spare the country from the civil war that seemed to be the only alternative. It didn't, and Webster's son, Fletcher Webster, fighting for the Twelfth Massachusetts Infantry, would succumb to a bullet at the Second Battle of Bull Run.

In a sense, the debate between Douglas and Lincoln was one of priority. Did the "equality-claiming," God-centered, "natural law–avowing" Declaration take precedence over the "slavery-protecting," secular, law-focused Constitution, or the Constitution over the Declaration? Were the two documents mutually exclusive, or could they be seen in a dependent formation, the notion of "equality" becoming a fundamental precondition for the sort of representative democracy that the Constitution, well, "constituted"? Lincoln certainly thought this, having described equality as the "sheet anchor of American republicanism" and, in another brilliant image, this one borrowed from the book of Proverbs, the Declaration as the "apple of gold" framed by the Constitution's "picture of silver," with the picture (think *frame* here) made for the apple, "not the apple for the picture."

Yet if the Lincoln-Douglas argument was one of priority, it was also one of interpretation, and here Douglas appeared to have the clear upper hand. To the Illinois senator, as well as many Southerners, the issue was not that the "all men are created equal" phrase of the Declaration did not carry the power of law. Because even as a declaration, the Founders, in Douglas's convincing analysis, had never intended their notion of equality to apply to anyone other than the white race, the only race that, in its superior bearing, was capable of self-government. After all, Douglas pointedly reiterated, the author of the Declaration, Thomas Jefferson, was himself a slaveholder. "Did he intend to say in that Declaration that his negro slaves, which he held and treated as property, were created his equals by divine law, and that he was violating the law of God every day of his life by holding them as slaves?" No, it was clear. "This government was made on the white basis, by white men for the benefit of white men and their posterity forever." It cared not for "the negro, the savage Indians, the Fee-Jee [Fiji Islanders], the Malay, or any other inferior or degraded race."

Assuming the posture of moral rectitude, Douglas reassured his audience that he, Douglas, believed slavery was wrong, and he was certain, too, that the people of Illinois assembled before him would join with him in its condemnation, but nothing in the Constitution or the Declaration of Independence demanded that the people of all states believe this. "Why should Illinois be at war with Missouri, or Kentucky with Ohio, or Virginia with New York," he argued, "merely because their institutions differ?" To demonstrate the foolhardiness of imposing the North's morality upon the South, Douglas reminded his audience that at the time of the framing of the Constitution, twelve of the thirteen states in the Union permitted slavery. "Suppose this doctrine of uniformity preached by Mr. Lincoln, that the States should all be free or all be slave, had prevailed," Douglas said forthrightly, ". . . what would have been the result? Of course, the twelve slave-holding States would have overruled the one free State, and slavery would have been fastened by a constitutional provision on every inch of the American republic, instead of being left, as our fathers wisely left it, to each State to decide for itself." Douglas might have added that the author of the Declaration was also a fierce advocate for the present, believing that the past is past and that the earth belongs "in usufruct"— that is, to the enjoyment of—the living, that self-government presupposes a cycle of "decay and renewal" or it isn't "self-government," and when you recognize that principle of Jefferson's, well, who looked like the truer descendant, Lincoln, who sought to bind society to a nonlegal document written nearly a hundred years before, or Douglas, who championed the right of each state to decide the slavery question for itself, in the here and now?

In the debates, Douglas described Lincoln, disparagingly, as a lover of the Negro race. But this was all a feint, one to which Lincoln responded with unfortunate vigor. "I am not, nor have I ever been, in favor of bringing about in any way the social and political equality of the white and black races," he told a crowd in Charleston, Illinois. How could he, he went on, when there is "a physical difference between the white and black races which I believe will forever forbid the two races from living together on terms of social and political equality"? To Lincoln, slavery was wrong not because it treated one race of people as inferior to another race; that, he was clearly prepared to do himself. It was wrong because it violated the most fundamental principle of liberty: the freedom to do as one pleases and to reap the harvest of one's own labors. This was Lincoln's notion of "equality," not our own.

Douglas likened Lincoln to "the little Abolition orators who go around and lecture in the basements of schools and churches"—another belittling insult, at least for its time, one intended to make Lincoln look impatient, fanatical, religiously motivated, and self-righteous. Douglas accused Lincoln of being a disciple of "Parson" Lovejoy—that would be Owen Lovejoy, the abolitionist congressman from Illinois—and as "worthy of a medal" from "Father" Giddings and "Fred Douglass," a reference to Ohio congressman and abolitionist Joshua Giddings and to Frederick Douglass, the former slave whose powerful writings and speeches had made him a leading voice for the abolitionist cause. This was quite a charge since most people in that day saw abolitionists not as virtuous warriors, but as rabble-rousers, inciting the slaves to rebellion and the country to war, and it was true. Some abolitionists wanted the Union to be broken. William Lloyd Garrison, for instance, referred to the Constitution as "a covenant with death" and welcomed disunion as a way to part with the South, which he considered incapable of reform.

Once again, Lincoln declined the opprobrium. He had no

intention of "abolitionizing" the Republican Party, he asserted, and on this his argument was particularly strong. While Ohio Republicans, led by Salmon Chase, had refused to enforce the Fugitive Slave Act, Lincoln did not favor such a challenge in his own state. To him, the law was the law. Ample material in Lincoln's history suggested that he, like Douglas, fretted that a sudden, open path to freedom, the kind that the abolitionists sought, would wreak havoc on the nation. "Free them, and make them politically and socially, our equals?" he asked of a Peoria crowd in 1854. "My own feelings will not admit of this; and if mine would [not], we well know that those of the great mass of white people will not. Whether this feeling accords with justice and sound judgment, is not the sole question, if indeed, it is any part of it. A universal feeling, whether well or ill-founded, can not be safely disregarded." In other words, most people don't want an immediate end to slavery and the advance toward full equality, so who am I to say that there should be?

If this last sentiment sounds more like popular sovereignty than moralism, more Douglas than Lincoln, it only further demonstrates Lincoln's painful ambivalence about emancipation. His conscience could not abide the immorality of slavery, but his certainty that the two races could not live peacefully together in true equality (nor should they, in his judgment), and his fears, joined by so many, that an immediate and total end to slavery could result in a bloody rebellion, driven by the revenge of the slaves on their former masters and those who supported them, or, worse, an even bloodier clash between North and South, dividing the nation, made him uncomfortable with any plan that did not take gradualism as its philosophy and popular consensus as its partner. Yet was there a gradual path to be found on an issue divided by such absolutes? Four years after his celebrated verbal contest with Douglas, two years into the bloody national struggle he had so feared, caught up in this miserable 1862 summer of death, Lincoln, his confidence shaken by months of failure, set himself to sketch a document he hoped would wrest the nation from the grip of annihilation.

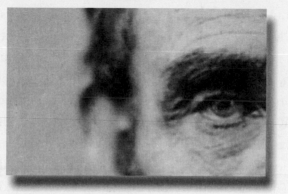

III.

NERVE CENTER

OTHER THAN HIS summer cottage at the Soldiers' Home (a three-hundred-acre sanctuary on the Maryland border) and the White House itself, the most familiar destination for Abraham Lincoln in the summer months of 1862 was the War Department telegraph office situated just a few hundred feet from the Executive Mansion. "His tall, homely form could be seen crossing the well-shaded lawn between the White House and the War Department day after day with unvaried regularity," wrote Homer Bates, one of the telegraph operators who worked there, in a memoir published decades later. On the cooler days, Lincoln would toss a gray plaid shawl over his shoulders "in care-less fashion." Sometimes he would stay all night, but when he did not and opted instead to return to the White House for the evening, he was most often accompanied by one of the telegraph operators or by a small guard of soldiers, the latter under Secre-tary of War Stanton's firm order to ensure the president's protec-tion, even though Lincoln had what one observer described as an "almost morbid dislike for an escort," preferring the ease of movement to protection from assassination. "If they kill me, the next man will be just as bad for them," he said.

For Lincoln, the telegraph office had the quality of a sanctu-ary. "I come here to escape my persecutors," he told one op-erator, by which he meant the office seekers who arrived at the White House looking for positions in his administration. They competed with the throngs of people who would arrive on pub-lic days at the White House asking for favors (days he described, albeit approvingly, as his "public baths"), making Lincoln's time at the White House rarely his own. But the telegraph room was more than a refuge. It was the nerve center of the war, a place where Lincoln, using the most advanced technology of his day, could keep up with the news from the battlefronts and issue or-ders delivered with the speed of electricity.

Less than two decades had passed since Samuel Morse and his partner, Alfred Vail, working on a grant from Congress, had strung the first telegraph wire between Washington and Balti-more, allowing Morse, sitting in the Supreme Court chamber in the US Capitol, to type out a dot-dash message in code and have it successfully received by Vail at Baltimore's B&O Railroad sta-tion forty or so miles away. The phrase he used—the biblical exclamation "What hath God wrought!" from the book of Numbers—was what the daughter of the US patent commissioner had suggested when Morse gave her the honor of choosing his historic communication, a shrewd move that no doubt curried favor with her father. But for Morse, the expression also seemed an appropriate retort to those who considered his work—electric sparks carrying words across great distances in an instant—to be dangerous, alien, ungodly, magical. (This was nearly thirty years before the telephone.) No, said Morse, the telegraph is God's work, for "only He could have carried me thus far through all my trials and enabled me to triumph over the obstacles, physical and moral, which opposed me." Less than a year later, when James K. Polk was inaugurated as the eleventh president, Morse was on the platform, tapping out details of the event for stories that landed on the streets with record speed.

By the time of Lincoln's presidency, the nation's many competing telegraph companies had been amalgamated into the legendary Western Union, and over fifty thousand miles of telegraph wire had been threaded across the nation. From the telegraph, Lincoln, at home in Springfield, had learned the results of both the Chicago convention that nominated him and the 1860 election that made him president.

Lincoln did not know Morse personally, but the inventor's story was in at least one respect an illustration of the progressive principles that the future president espoused. Morse had started his professional life as a portrait painter and completed two notable large canvases, one of the House of Representatives in action, with sixty-some members faithfully represented, each having sat individually for Morse's brush, and another of the Salon Carré gallery at the Louvre museum in Paris, containing meticulous renderings of the specific works displayed there.

Morse's early aspiration was to be an American Titian or Michelangelo, painting large scenes of history. He also had dreams of democratizing art for Americans, of popularizing painting by educating the American people on the great historical works that he felt they needed to learn. That was part of the idea behind his *Gallery of the Louvre*: to "collapse distance" by bringing great art to Americans who would likely never get to travel to a place such as Paris. Still, his own work, while impressive (many pieces are in prestigious museum collections to this day), received little public acclaim, and feeling rejected, he turned his attention to other professions, including politics (he twice ran unsuccessfully for mayor of New York City) and science, where, collapsing distance in another way, his patent to establish the first single-wire, electromagnetic telegraph became the basis for an industry that transformed human communication.

Like so many American politicians during this time, Morse thought of himself as carrying the torch for the revolutionary generation, but in his case this was no mere historical allusion; John Adams, James Monroe, and the Marquis de Lafayette had sat for his brush and, presumably, conversed with him as they did. Despite his pedigree, Morse offended both sides of the national divide of the late 1850s: Southerners because he objected vigorously to secession; Northerners because he supported slavery, which he regarded as benefiting both slave and slave master since it allowed for a "weak and degraded race" to toil under the guidance of noble Christian guardians.

Morse reserved a special wrath for the "implacable" and "headstrong" abolitionists, whom he described as "freedom-shriekers, Bible-spurners . . . Constitution and Union haters," and as "demons in human shape." He argued that "a more wretched, disgusting, hypocritical crew have not appeared on the face of the earth since the times of Robespierre." That last reference was effective, since the story of the excesses of the French Revolution still rang loudly as a warning against the call of the righteous mob.

Morse was no fan of Lincoln's (he once referred to him as an "imbecile," his administration as "bloodthirsty"), but Lincoln was a fan of Morse's telegraph and the spirit of invention that it represented. In 1858, while running for the US Senate against Stephen Douglas, Lincoln delivered a lecture to the Young Men's Association of Bloomington, Illinois, establishing his theory of progress. He had already earned his own badge as an inventor, having patented an apparatus for lifting boats stuck on sandbars. (The invention, highly impractical, was never produced.) In his lecture, Lincoln wove an elaborate analysis of human history, arguing that what distinguishes man from other animals is his ability to refine and improve the work of those who have come before him. The beaver, Lincoln said, builds its home the same way that beavers did five thousand years ago, but man is the only animal who actually improves on the workmanship of his forebears. Out of what he is given from his ancestors, man "dig[s] out his destiny."

By this logic, Morse's telegraph served as a riveting example of human achievement, American-born. It wasn't only invention; it was invention with purpose—a *democratic* purpose, a vision of a technology that was fast, cheap, and available to everyone. Seen this way, the telegraph also fit well with Lincoln's notion of the Founders' unfinished achievement in human liberty. What Washington, Jefferson, and Madison had done was epic; now those who succeeded them had to take that expression of freedom one stride deeper.

For Lincoln the telegraph became the means by which he could both track the progress of the war and direct his army in response. As a chief executive, his time in the telegraph office was unprecedented. No president in history (none before, none since) assumed the role of commander in chief the way that Lincoln did, actually planning the war instead of limiting himself to the political mission for which the war was being fought, and the telegraph office was where he did it.

In his early months as president, Lincoln made little use of this new technology. The White House had no telegraph system, and dispatches had to be sent by aides standing in line at the local Western Union station, no different from anyone else. As late as May 1862, Lincoln was sending barely a telegram a month. But shortly after that, he began to pick up the pace such that, by July, the telegram was his favorite mode of communication, and the War Department telegraph office was his daily haunt.

Upon his arrival, the president's routine, as recalled by Charles Tinker, another of the operators, was to head first to the drawer containing the most recent wires and read them over, beginning at the top and going through the pile until he came upon the last one he had seen on his previous stopover. Then Lincoln would cryptically pronounce, "Well, boys, I am down to the raisins." The comment, as with so many exchanges with the president, came with a story, this one of a little girl who celebrated her birthday by eating large portions of her favorite foods, including a serving of raisins for dessert. When she later took violently ill, the family sent for a doctor, who arrived just as she was "busy casting up her accounts." Noticing some "small black objects" at the bottom of the vessel, he pronounced the danger as having passed, for, having dispelled the early courses of her meal, she was, as he put it, "down to the raisins." (In fact, one would expect the raisins to depart first—last in, first out—but that was not how Lincoln told it.)

For someone whose speeches generally lasted hours—literally—the telegraph was a new and exciting way to communicate. Terse, unemotional, it was a medium of crisp communication: facts and the occasional aside. The telegram did not tolerate nuance nor "story" nor the kind of literary and political ambiguity that characterized so much of Lincoln's other writing. Inspired, perhaps, by a medium that demanded language of purpose over language of decoration, Lincoln one day in June (there is no record of what day) turned to Major Thomas Eckert, chief of the War Department telegraph office, and asked "for some paper, as he wanted to write something special." Special, indeed. While listening to the clatter of the telegraphers crowded into the room with him, Lincoln began to compose the language that would free 4 million people from bondage.

The story is almost too charming to be believed, and in fact it is disputed. It, too, comes from the telegraph operator Homer Bates's book and only Bates's book, published in 1907, forty-five years after the fact. Furthermore, it clashes with the version of the story told by the painter Francis Carpenter, for whom Lincoln, in 1864, sat for *The First Reading of the Emancipation Proclamation.* Carpenter asserted that Lincoln wrote the document on the steamer on the way back from his fateful July 8 meeting with McClellan at Harrison's Landing, yet the artist claims to have gotten this information not from his extensive conversations with Lincoln but from a reading of an 1865 biography authored by Lincoln's friend Joseph Hartwell Barrett. There, Barrett alluded to Lincoln beginning the proclamation "as early as July," which of course is hardly a definitive date marker and indicates nothing about the return trip from Harrison's Landing. Vice President Hannibal Hamlin, never known as a Lincoln confidant (they did not even meet until after the election put them in office together), claimed in 1879 that Lincoln first showed the proclamation to him on a carriage ride to the Soldiers' Home. Hamlin didn't provide a date for this meeting, but remarked that it was before the cabinet saw it. "He met me one day and said, 'Where will you be this evening?' 'I am going out of town,' I replied. 'No, you are not, sir.' 'Indeed, I am, sir, unless you command me.' 'Well, I do command you. I want you to spend the evening with me at the Soldiers' Home.' I met him at the Executive Mansion, and we started to drive to the Home. As soon as we had started he withdrew from his pocket the rough draft of the proclamation and read it to me. Naturally, I was delighted and told him so. He was much moved at the step he was taking."

Finally, there is Gideon Welles's version. In his much-cited diary, Welles asserts that Lincoln began writing the document in earnest only after opening up about it to Welles and Seward on the way to James Stanton's funeral. Yet, like so many quarrels over history, the ill fit of one shard against the next probably suggests that the truth lies somewhere between the splinters. Lincoln may have started the draft in the telegraph office in June and removed it to show to Hamlin on a day that same month. Or Lincoln may have been so negatively inspired by McClellan's self-righteous scolding at Harrison's Landing that he got a pen out the moment he left the dock for his return trip to Washington. Whenever he started it, he would have needed to refine it, maybe while sitting with the cipher operators, waiting for dispatches from the front. It was not, after all, the kind of document that flows uninterrupted from the pen. Finally, as Welles claimed, Lincoln may have begun a serious commitment to it only after speaking to Welles and Seward, motivated by their seeming approval, or maybe by the fact that the idea was no longer protected in his head, but was now out in front of him, not simply a thought, and a dangerous one at that, but an *expressed* thought, now, and appearing a bit less dangerous because it had been expressed.

Eckert's contribution to the scenery on this subject may be the most appealing, if only because his story carries a feeling of simplicity that belies the moment. Here we have the image of a man, a president, this president, this *mythic* president, sitting at a desk in a simple office, surrounded by technicians unimpressed by his being among them (because he was *always* among them) and busied by their own important work on the conduct of the war. Yet, while glancing at the spiders crawling on a web dangling from the ceiling above him (more on that in a moment), he inscribes words that will profoundly shift the nation's, if not the world's, history. With nothing more than pen and paper, he will free a race from servitude.

Eckert is himself interesting. As a young man growing up in Ohio, he became excited by Morse's telegraph and scratched together enough money to travel to New York to see it. Upon his return to Ohio, he pursued a future as a telegrapher, helping to initiate the first line on the Fort Wayne railroad in the 1850s. From there he went to North Carolina to join in a gold-mining operation and was in the South when the war broke out in 1861. While attempting to flee, he was challenged as a Union spy, but survived arrest when the Confederate vice president, Alexander Stephens, whom Eckert knew from Stephens's days as a congressman in Washington, interceded on his behalf. Once he was back in the North, Eckert's reputation as a telegraphy expert led him to a job in the War Department and eventually as an aide and telegraph operator for General McClellan. In February 1862, Secretary of War Stanton moved him from McClellan's staff to run the War Department telegraph office, a move that McClellan resented, and that is how he began working directly with Lincoln. (After the war, he had a substantial career in the telegraph business, culminating in his years as president and chairman of Western Union, which he was on his death in 1910.)

"I procured some foolscap and handed it to him," Eckert recalled, in Bates's account of the moment when Lincoln began writing the 1862 proclamation. "He sat down and began to write. . . . He would look out the window a while and then put his pen to paper, but he did not write much at once. He would study between times and when he had made up his mind he would put down a line or two, and then sit quiet for a few minutes. After a time, he would resume his writing, only to stop again at intervals to make some remark to me or one of the cipher-operators as a fresh despatch from the front was handed to him."

Whatever is the correct story of the Emancipation Proclamation's authorship, as Lincoln wrote it the same perplexing questions had to be going through his mind. He needed to craft an order that could withstand judicial scrutiny, but how? Could the slaves be freed without a constitutional amendment and, if so, under what power of Congress? They were, after all, "property," at least in a legal sense, and the Constitution protected private property from government taking. Yet if not as an act of Congress, how was emancipation to be realized? Certainly an executive order of emancipation would be beyond the powers of the president, but not, Lincoln concluded, if such an order were issued as furtherance of the executive's war powers. On the way to the funeral of Secretary Stanton's child, Lincoln told Seward and Welles that he was determined to emancipate the slaves *as an act of military necessity.*

For Lincoln, then, the Emancipation Proclamation had to be written with great care to emphasize this power and only this power. The ironies were rich: if he freed the slaves as an act of military necessity, its justification was not moral, but strategic. None of the usual Lincoln poetry about the evils inherent to one man's serving as a master to another—none of this—had any place in the document. Since military strategies are by definition provisional, to be lifted once the mission is complete, emancipation as Lincoln was writing it could only be temporary. Then, too, as an act of war, the freeing of the slaves for reasons of military necessity could only be done for the slaves in the Confederate states, in the states actually in rebellion. Since there was no military necessity to free slaves in states that were not in rebellion—Kentucky, for instance, and Maryland and Delaware, or even in those parts of the states in rebellion where the Confederacy had already surrendered—those slaves would be left in their shackles, untouched by the proclamation. This meant that as he sat working in the telegraph office, Lincoln, a man history admires for his profession of moral absolutes, was authoring a document of astonishing relativity—freedom for a time only and only for some, not all.

Another cruel twist Lincoln had to contemplate was that the states in rebellion—the very states that would be targeted by the proclamation—were no longer in the control of the federal government; they were in control of the Confederacy. So the proclamation would, essentially, be unenforceable in the only places where it had application. Of course, when the Union Army successfully invaded Confederate territory, the slaves there could be freed but, again, only as an act of war.

As it was already, thanks to the Confiscation Act of 1861, an invading Union force could free those slaves *whose labor was being used in the service of the Confederate Army*, but Lincoln had opposed this measure and only signed it under pressure. Once it was law, he was reluctant to enforce it. He felt that the act was constitutionally suspect, and as he expected, it immediately raised objections throughout the crucial Border States. It also prompted swift retaliation by the South. Indeed, within months the Confederate Congress passed its own law, the Sequestration Act of 1861, asserting the power to seize Union property. Then, just to show that they could, Confederate officials grabbed Thomas Jefferson's home at Monticello, which was at the time owned by a Union navy captain, Uriah P. Levy of Pennsylvania.

One final and crucial paradox was inherent to Lincoln's authoring the emancipation policy as an act of war. Lincoln's prime constitutional issue with the South was over secession. The war, he had repeatedly said, was to save the Union, first and foremost. This was the official argument between North and South: the South claiming that it had an inherent right to secede, a right established by the language of Jefferson in the Declaration of Independence, no less, when he asserted that legitimate governments "[derive] their just powers from the consent of the governed," and Lincoln claiming that the secessionist states did not have that right, that governments are established in perpetuity, and that ours was established as a contract—the Constitution, that is—between the states. For the contract to end, both sides needed to agree on its termination, not one.

To Lincoln, then, the rebel states were just that—states in rebellion—not a sovereign nation engaging in war with the United States. Yet if this was not war in the legal sense of the term, then how could the proclamation he was authoring be justified as a legal use of executive war power? Less than a year later, the Supreme Court, in what is known as the *Prize Cases*, would narrowly decide, 5–4 (three recent Lincoln appointees siding with the majority), that the powers of war could indeed be assumed by Lincoln, under the Constitution, even in a civil war, for civil wars "may be prosecuted on the same footing as if those opposing the Government were foreign" invaders. But Lincoln was writing the Emancipation Proclamation in 1862 before the *Prize* decision had been handed down, and he had no idea how the Court might regard this act. Opting for "military necessity" as the justification for freeing the slaves appeared to give him the best chance of staying within the law, but what if the Court overruled him?

Lincoln worked on these issues quietly, without consultation with his officemates or anyone else. Words came slowly to the president. On no day, recalled Eckert, did Lincoln fill a single sheet of paper. On each occasion, he would ask Eckert to "take charge of what he had written" and be certain that no one saw it. Eckert faithfully locked the pages in his desk. Lincoln told Eckert that he did not mind if Eckert himself should read it, only that Lincoln "should be glad that no one else will see it." This went on nearly every day for several weeks, with Lincoln sometimes writing no more than a line or two or editing his work by putting question marks in the margin next to certain phrases, "studying carefully each sentence."

As he worked, Lincoln became intrigued by a large spiderweb he noticed outside the office window. The web had already captured the fascination of the other men in the room, so much so that the spiders had affectionately been dubbed "Major Eckert's lieutenants" by Assistant Secretary of War Peter Watson. On the president's first mention of it, Eckert told Lincoln to keep an eye out, as the spiders would soon come out to pay their respects to him. "Not long after a big spider appeared at the cross-roads and tapped several times on the strands, whereupon five or six others came out from different directions. Then what seemed to be a great confab took place, after which they separated, each on a different strand of the web." Lincoln found the scene a welcome distraction from his work.

Each new phrase he wrote came accompanied by fear for its consequences. After all, what he was writing was revolutionary, and it was not hard for the imagination to conjure all manner of disastrous results for the country if the policy that Lincoln now considered was in fact declared. Upon hearing the news that the slaves were being emancipated, forever altering the mission of the war, McClellan and others in uniform who had been willing to fight for the Union but not for ending slavery might be inspired to a coup d'état, bringing down the Lincoln presidency. Even without such a challenge from the leadership of the armed forces, a change in mission as controversial as this one could render the Union Army a squabbling and ineffectual mess with soldiers and officers holding a multitude of conflicting loyalties, some wanting to rid the nation of slavery, others not, and many concerned that the seizing of property—even property in human life—was not a fair way to fight a war.

Abolitionists might crow in success and, crowing too much, turn the tide of public opinion against the president. That wouldn't be hard. While the tide was shifting, most white Americans, even Northern white Americans, were for preserving the Union but against emancipating the slaves. Disappointed by the extent of the emancipation, perhaps abolitionists would not crow at all but choose instead to disparage Lincoln for once again opting for a complicated and limited expression of freedom (for that is what he was composing, no simple opening of the gates of liberty), raising their voices even more loudly against him. Remember, many fierce abolitionists had thought that the Union was not worth saving, that the South should be cut free to stand or fall on the support of its own, immorally constructed foundation, and while that notion may not have had support among the broader population, in many ways the country had already been adapting itself to a future separation. The development of the railroads in the 1850s had seemed to signal the coming divide, with Southern lines more regional, Northern lines more national, and few lines connecting the two antagonistic regions with each other. A proclamation of emancipation could reverse that trend, making the North responsible for destroying the Southern economy and, by destroying it, ultimately responsible for rebuilding it as well.

Emancipation might also prove a failure even as a military tactic, either because the freed slaves would choose to stay with their masters and fight for the South, bolstering the Southern cause rather than eroding it, or because freeing the slaves would precipitate what so many, including Lincoln, had long dreaded:

an all-out race war, a bloody expression of long-suppressed rage that would spread uncontrollably, engulfing the nation. Congress's decision to end the slave trade in 1807 had been driven in part by this fear, for if the flow of slaves from Africa continued unimpeded, it could have led to what some worried would be a "dangerous" imbalance of the races, threatening white rule. Many in mid-nineteenth-century America knew of the Nat Turner slave revolt of 1831, and at least some had historical knowledge of the successful slave insurrection against white masters in the French colony of Saint-Domingue (modern-day Haiti) in the 1790s. There, whites, outnumbered by slaves ten to one, faced near genocide. Indeed, the rebellion in Saint-Domingue had so frightened Napoléon it was one of the main reasons he agreed to the Louisiana Purchase. A French empire in North America had no chance, he concluded, as long as the slave question remained unresolved.

Finally, there was more recent history in the form of the martyrdom of the abolitionist crusader John Brown. Brown's disastrous attack on Harpers Ferry in 1859, intended to spark a slave rebellion, was a ludicrous, perhaps even a mad, act—ill conceived, poorly executed (the first person killed was a free black man), and quickly put down by federal troops led by Lieutenant Colonel Robert E. Lee, the very same Confederate general who would later lead the Army of Northern Virginia, bedeviling Lincoln and McClellan.

In all, sixteen people died in the attack on Harpers Ferry, including two of Brown's sons. At first the raid solidified the image of the abolitionist movement as the work of raging moralists. Yet when the state of Virginia rushed Brown to trial on charges that included treason and then sentenced him to a hanging, which he faced with dignity, firm in his convictions, he became a peculiarly ambiguous symbol for the war. He was at once a violent criminal and a man of honor, a prophet warning of the conflagration that was to come. "How do you justify your acts?" Virginia senator James Murray Mason demanded of Brown as part of a Senate investigation of the Harpers Ferry raid. "I think, my friend, you are guilty of a great wrong against God and humanity," replied Brown. ". . . And it would be perfectly right for anyone to interfere with you so far as to free those you willfully and wickedly hold in bondage."

Even his detractors found Brown irresistibly interesting, but as a political association he was too hot to handle. The *New York Herald* blamed Seward for the crazed raid, saying that he, as the "arch agitator," was ultimately responsible for the insurrection. But Seward was quick to deny the charge and called for Brown's execution as "necessary and just." In his 1860 Cooper Union speech, Lincoln, too, rejected any sympathy for Brown. "John Brown was no Republican," he said; he was nothing more than "an enthusiast," who "broods over the oppression of a people till he fancies himself commissioned by Heaven to liberate them." Yet, two years later, Brown had indeed become a touchstone of the North-South competition—still seen as a fanatic, perhaps, but for Northerners he was now "our fanatic"—and the subject of the Union Army's most popular marching song, "John Brown's Body," immortalized as a "soldier of the Lord" whose "soul is marching on." Forced, punitive emancipation had been Brown's cause. What would happen if it became not the illusion of a violent extremist but a prime war goal backed by the arms and political power of the federal government?

While consumed with fantasies about what new dangers an

act of emancipation might unleash on the nation, Lincoln also had the very real threat posed by radical members of his own Republican Party who found his delaying both morally and militarily suspect. In their frustration they had taken it upon themselves to force his hand. Two acts were passed to challenge the president. The first, the Militia Act of 1862, authorized the use of "persons of African descent" for "the purpose of constructing intrenchments, or performing camp service or any other labor, or any military or naval service for which they may be found competent," and mandated that any escaped Southern slave who performed such services would, along with his family, "forever thereafter be free." In the second act, Congress made legal the seizure of the property of *all Confederate loyalists* (in contrast to the first Confiscation Act, which had been limited to those aiding the military prosecution of the rebellion) as well as the freeing of their slaves. By loyalists, Congress meant anyone who had taken an oath to the Confederacy or was a public officer to it as well as anyone who had simply aided and abetted the Confederate cause.

Taken together, the two acts were a direct affront to Lincoln and his generals, accompanied as they were by claims that there were "not brains enough at Washington to put down the insurrection" and that the federal government remained too respectful of constitutional rights. "The people," one abolitionist wrote, "are anxious that Congress should really feel that we are at war," that the president is ready to do some damage to the enemy, rather than remain "bound hand and foot by the Proslavery regard for the Constitution in which he was educated." Abolitionists argued that Lincoln needed to adjust his priorities, stop using the softer term *rebels* and call them *enemies*, and to show that he deemed "*their* property and *their* Negroes" to be "not half so precious as the lives of our brave and noble soldiers." They wanted a leader, not a "moderator between contending factions," as top Ohio Republican William M. Dickson claimed.

Moderates within the Republican Party urged Lincoln to veto the second Confiscation Act. Illinois senator Orville Browning told the president this was his chance to show that he could stand up to the radicals. A veto would create a "storm of enthusiasm within the Border States," he promised, a message that had considerable appeal to Lincoln in this moment. As the legislators were debating the two bills, the president had been hosting a group of Border State congressmen, arguing (unsuccessfully) that they accept his offer to begin gradual, compensated emancipation. A veto of this radical Confiscation Act might please the fence-sitters in Kentucky and Maryland, but doing so would risk the support of his own party. Lincoln asked for some changes in the act, including the removal of the parts he was certain would be reversed by the courts. Then, unwittingly proving Dickson's point about the president craftily playing both sides, he signed the bill even as he sent a veto message for Congress to read. He had authored "a veto that was not a veto" for an act he signed yet never intended to enforce.

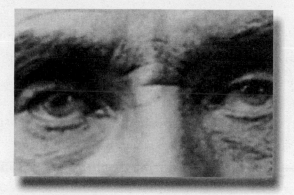

IV.

FIRST READING

HAVING AWKWARDLY BLUNTED the challenge from the Congress on the second Confiscation Act, Lincoln got set to tell the entire cabinet about his own tentative path to emancipation, the one he had already announced to Welles and Seward. On July 22, 1862, he did just that. What we know about the scene comes essentially from two sometimes-conflicting sources: Welles, who wrote about it both in his diary and in an article on the history of emancipation that he published a decade later, and Francis Bicknell Carpenter, the artist, who, inspired by his love for the president and the transcendent importance of the proclamation act, convinced Lincoln to allow him to spend six months at the White House composing a massive painting immortalizing the moment. The work, *First Reading of the Emancipation Proclamation*, now hangs near a staircase at the US Capitol, but just as important for the recall of this episode is the book that Carpenter published a few years later, *Six Months at the White House with Abraham Lincoln: The Story of a Picture.*

Carpenter's tale begins in 1864 with the artist standing on a receiving line at the White House, waiting to meet Lincoln for the first time. As Carpenter approached him, the president, dressed all in black except for a pair of white gloves, appeared haggard, worn, the war having distorted his face, but he lit up at their greeting. "Oh yes, I know; this is the painter," Lincoln said, grabbing his hand. (An intermediary had told him of Carpenter's interest.) Pulling up to his full bearing, the president then asked playfully, "Do you think, Mr. Carpenter, that you can make a handsome picture of *me*?"

Carpenter set up in the State Dining Room, working assiduously under the morning light streaming in from the portico and at night under the kerosene glow of the great chandelier. Lincoln passed regularly before him, remarking to guests, "Oh, you need not mind him; he is but a painter," and engaged the artist from time to time with stories. Despite having a deserved reputation for telling the vulgar tale, Lincoln, Carpenter reassures his readers, never related anything "which would have been out of place in a ladies' drawing-room."

While Carpenter considered the proclamation to be "unparalleled for moral grandeur in the history of mankind," his interest as an artist, he offered, was in merely documenting the meeting, not enlarging it. Eschewing the tradition of the history painter, he saw no need for allegory or decoration and professed no desire to intrude upon the facts. "If I cannot make the portraiture of the scene itself sufficiently attractive without the false glitter of tapestry hangings, velvet table-cloths, and marble columns," he later wrote, "then I shall at least have the satisfaction of having failed in the cause of truth." The facts of the meeting were hard to recover (and as an unabashed Lincoln admirer, Carpenter was not the most objective party to be pursuing them). But he had an ally in Lincoln, who, as he sat for the artist, scoured his not-always-responsive memory for the details that Carpenter demanded.

The particulars of the scene, as recorded by Carpenter, were these: Seven members of Lincoln's cabinet—Welles, Seward, Stanton, Chase, Postmaster General Montgomery Blair, Attorney General Edward Bates, and Interior Secretary Caleb B. Smith—assembled with the president at 10:00 a.m. for a continuation of the cabinet session they had begun the day before. The setting was a room on the southeast corner of the second floor of the White House, which is today known as the Lincoln Bedroom, but which was then used by Lincoln as a private office as well as a meeting room for the cabinet. Blair arrived late, after Lincoln had already started, but all the others were there from the beginning.

The initial business was presidential orders to commanders in the field. The instructions, already introduced to the cabinet but not voted on, were essentially extensions of the disputed Confiscation Acts. One new order allowed Union troops to seize property needed to "subsist"; that is, to carry on their work while in Southern territory. A second allowed commanders to hire "persons of African descent" as laborers, including slaves who had been taken from their masters under the acts (but none, free or slave, was to carry arms). And a third, peculiarly, required a full accounting of all appropriated property with "such degrees of certainty as would enable compensation to be made in proper cases." Lincoln was hedging his bets on whether the federal courts would eventually invalidate the Confiscation Acts as inconsistent with the Constitution and force the government to offer just compensation to the slaves' former masters. The alternative—that they would be returned to their masters—was repugnant to him.

The president's introduction of the new measures seemed to suggest that he was shifting his long-skeptical approach to the Confiscation Acts, and perhaps to emancipation in general, but, if so, how far was he willing to go? And how much of it was against his will? Had the Radical Republicans—those who had long been frustrated by Lincoln's refusal to pursue a quicker, braver path to emancipation, to make it the primary mission of the war—finally won him over? Was he ready to respond to charges such as that by Michigan senator Zachariah Chandler, who called Lincoln "timid, vacillating, and inefficient," by taking some bold step?

The cabinet had been protective of Lincoln and his careful methods. Even those such as Seward, who had long been counted among the Radicals, had become more conservative. Once engaged with the responsibilities of his office, Seward had pulled back from any claim to urgency on the issue of slavery. Salmon Chase, a reliable antislavery beacon while governor of Ohio, had also shifted. He'd discovered a new respect for the Constitution and those in the slave states who "verily believe otherwise than I do." As Lincoln's treasury secretary, Chase now proclaimed that he was "not at liberty to substitute my convictions for theirs."

This audience listened, no doubt with trepidation, as the president turned to his main purpose for the meeting: the proclamation. As in his initial conversation with Welles and Seward on the way to James Stanton's funeral, the president made it clear that he was not asking those gathered before him *whether* he should issue an emancipation proclamation—that much he had decided—but only to put the subject on the table for conversation. He acknowledged that the men present had differing opinions on the slavery question, but he hoped for a "free discussion." Then, holding two pages of lined notepaper, 12½ by 7⅞, Lincoln read the proclamation aloud.

Other than the opening, which referred to the passage of the second Confiscation Act just five days earlier, the rest of the text was, presumably, what Lincoln had been drafting in the telegraph office—dull, careful, lawyerly, precise. The first part was a warning that those who insisted on aiding the rebellion should return to their proper allegiance to the United States "on pain of the forfeitures and seizures" of private property. The second was an outstretched hand, reminding all in rebellion that it was his intention "on the next meeting of congress to again recommend the adoption of a practical measure for tendering pecuniary aid to those who voluntarily adopt, gradual abolishment of slavery."

There followed a momentary though crucial departure where Lincoln reiterated the mission of the war as the reuniting of the rebellious states with "the general government," but then came the trumpet flare: ". . . as a fit and necessary military measure for effecting this object, I, as Commander-in-Chief of the Army and Navy of the United States, do order and declare that on the first day of January in the year of Our Lord one thousand, eight hundred and sixty-three, all persons held as slaves within any state or states, wherein the constitutional authority of the United States shall not then be practically recognized, submitted to, and maintained, shall then, thenceforward, and forever, be free."

Dull, yes, yet brilliant. In 325 words Lincoln had gone so much further than Congress had gone in the constitutionally suspect Confiscation Acts and done so legally (at least in his judgment) by tying his action to the war effort. He had given the rebellious states an opportunity to avoid the fate that now appeared to be their future by reminding them of his wish to compensate them for the freeing of their slaves and of his intention that the process would be—*could* be—gradual, but only if they laid down their arms and rejoined the Union. Finally, he had indicated in the one dramatic flourish to an otherwise leaden document that the freeing of the slaves, while proclaimed to serve a war effort, would not expire with the war. The freed slaves were not simply the spoils of battle. Once executed, the proclamation would render them then, *thenceforward*, and *forever* free.

In a sense, the document assumed the quality of a lab experiment. The slaves were to be "seized," legally, as "property." That, after all, was what the South and the Constitution considered them to be and what Lincoln now also considered them to be *for the purposes of this act* (even though he thought the *Dred Scott* decision declaring them property was an improper reading of the Constitution). Then, once "seized," the slaves, by the power of the same order, would become free, rights-holding human beings, as if law could, with the flash of pen, work the magic of biology. And Lincoln had done all of this—all of it—while still maintaining the soon-to-become-obvious fiction that the war was being fought *only* to save the Union; for freeing the slaves, in the way that the proclamation did it, was a tactical measure used to serve that one strategic mission. It was not the Radical Republicans' version of how emancipation should be achieved, and as he soon discovered, it was not the way that most of his more careful cabinet members wished it to be won either. But one can only imagine how this conjunction of codependent ideas and formulations, pronounced aloud by the president in his (by most accounts) reedy tenor voice, lingered in the air of the room.

Bates was the first to respond. A Virginian by birth, he had made his professional career in Missouri first in state politics, then as a US congressman. Like Seward and Chase, he had been Lincoln's rival, albeit a reluctant one, for the 1860 Republican presidential nomination. Older than the others, he had appealed to some as a welcome, conservative choice, a candidate with moderate views who could hold the country together, particularly since he had essentially sat out the 1850s, uninvolved in national politics, and was therefore untouched by the vicious partisanship of that decade.

While he came from a slaveholding family, Bates had emancipated his own slaves and held strong to the Republican position on the future of slavery—restricting it to where it was already established. He had also shown considerable courage nearly twenty years earlier when, in 1844, he argued for the freedom of a fourteen-year-old slave child, Lucy Berry, whose mother had been abducted, held in the free state of Illinois, and then sold to slaveholders in Missouri. In a separate suit, Berry's mother had earned her own freedom on the reasoning that once she was taken to free Illinois, she could no longer be legally held as a slave (the argument that was later overturned by the Supreme Court in *Dred Scott*). In his plea for Berry's daughter, Bates had taken the reasoning one step further by arguing that the child of a free woman is, by virtue of her mother's status, free as well.

Still, as with so many others in this time, Bates's opposition to forced human servitude did not equate with a belief in the equality of the races. So, on this day, reacting to Lincoln's reading, he announced that he supported the proclamation but wished that it had been accompanied by a plan for the compulsory deportation of the freed slaves to Africa or somewhere else outside the United States, for their future presence here was certainly unacceptable.

In Bates's mind, the only way that the races could coexist would be through gradual "amalgamation"—the contemporary term for interbreeding—and since this could not happen without the "degradation and demoralization of the white race" (Welles's words describing Bates's attitude, but supported by Bates's own writing), it was an impossibility. Even with the "disgusting process of mixed breeds," which he saw as "repugnant to nature and to our moral and better instincts," blacks could not be "elevated" to a position equal to that of whites. But Bates did make a distinction between "colored people who have been long free" and the slaves on the plantations of the South, who "have been long degraded by the total abolition of the family relation, shrouded in artificial darkness, and studiously kept in ignorance." He could tolerate the former, whom he recognized as having developed from the experience of freedom, but the latter? No, without a plan for forced deportation, Lincoln was risking a social disaster.

The fear that Bates attached to the commingling of the races was not unusual for his time. All manner of what we would today consider bizarre, primitive theories about race and human development carried sway in the mid-nineteenth century. Most significant were those contained in the works of several leading anthropologists who, rejecting the unity or "Adam and Eve" theory of the origins of mankind, claimed that man had a plural origin, with each of the races growing from its own creation point and developing its own physiology and anatomy. As the debate over slavery gained momentum in the 1840s and 1850s, so, too, did the argument over whether mankind was a single brotherhood, with the various races sharing a common origin, or, as these anthropologists believed, a collection of species, differentiated by a hierarchy ranking one as superior to another.

Harvard zoologist Louis Agassiz was the high priest of the pluralist argument. Swiss-born, he had already developed a reputation in Europe when he was invited to give a series of lectures at the Lowell Institute in Boston in the winter of 1847. Touring the United States in the months before his talks, Agassiz first encountered "men of color" at a Philadelphia hotel on its waitstaff. "As much as I try to feel pity at the sight of this degraded and degenerate race, as much as their fate fills me with compassion in thinking of them as really men," he wrote his mother back in Europe, "it is impossible for me to repress the feeling that they are not of the same blood as us. Seeing their black faces with their fat lips and their grimacing teeth, the wool on their heads, their bent knees, their elongated hands, their large curved fingernails, and above all the livid color of their palms, I could not turn my eyes from their face in order to tell them to keep their distance, and when they advanced that hideous hand toward my plate to serve me, I wished I could leave in order to eat a piece of bread apart rather than dine with such service. What unhappiness for the white race to have tied its existence so closely to that of the negroes in certain countries! God protect us from such contact."

With his Boston talks, Agassiz became a nineteenth-century sensation. Thousands in large assembly halls listened in agreement as Agassiz laid out his theory that in fetal development the embryo moves through various stages to maturity with each race arriving at a comparatively different end point at birth. The Negro was the lowest form of human being, the Caucasian the highest. "The brain of the Negro," he told one audience "is that of the imperfect brain of a seven-month's infant in the womb of a White." Shortly after his success in Boston, Harvard gave academic heft to his "discoveries" when it offered Agassiz a position as the head of its Lawrence Scientific School.

Agassiz's ideas pleased—indeed, inspired—Southern slaveholders, who saw in the plural-origin theory an opportunity to divide mankind into those (whites) who qualified for protection under the Declaration of Independence and those ("Negroes") who did not. They then squared this idea with American history by arguing that Jefferson's "created equal" phrase, when examined through a scientific lens, should properly be understood as referencing only those men who shared the same racial origin point as the Founders, while men of other races were to be excluded.

If that did not capture the original intent of Jefferson's phrase, said Alexander Stephens, the vice president of the Confederacy, in his Cornerstone Address—delivered in Savannah, Georgia, a few weeks after secession and a few weeks before the initiation of hostilities at Fort Sumter—it was only because Jefferson was unexposed to the nineteenth-century discoveries of men such as Agassiz and Samuel George Morton, the American anthropologist whose studies in the 1830s and 1840s of the relative sizes of the craniums of the races (his collection of six hundred or so skulls, nicknamed American Golgotha, now resides at the University of Pennsylvania) were an inspiration for those committed to scientific racism. "The prevailing ideas entertained by [Jefferson] and most of the leading statesmen at the time of the formation of the old Constitution," pronounced Stephens, "were, that the enslavement of the African was in violation of the laws of nature; that it was wrong in principle, socially, morally and politically. . . . Those ideas, however, were fundamentally wrong. They rested upon the assumption of the equality of races. This was an error. . . .

"Our new Government," Stephens went on, referring to the Confederacy, "is founded upon exactly the opposite ideas; its foundations are laid, its cornerstone rests, upon the great truth that the negro is not equal to the white man; that slavery, subordination to the superior race, is his natural and moral condition. This, our new Government, is the first, in the history of the world, based upon this great physical, philosophical, and moral truth." By Stephens's reading, then, slavery was not some relic of a pre-Enlightenment age; it was the embodiment of a new, scientific understanding of nature's rules, and the maintenance of slavery was not some side issue to the war, subservient to "states' rights." It was the "cornerstone."

Ironically, Agassiz himself was against slavery—he made that clear. "The defenders of slavery forget that for being black these men have as much right as we do to the enjoyment of their liberty," he wrote. But he was equally against affording blacks full

political rights, seeing abolitionists as naive do-gooders ("philanthropists" was the patronizing term he used) and, like Bates,
worrying about what he felt was the real danger inherent to
emancipation, the threat of interbreeding.

If the Creator (in whom he still claimed to believe) established each race according to a hierarchy of difference, then respect for that plan, argued Agassiz, was essential to the future
of humanity. In this, his ideas complemented the work of two
authors popular in the South, Josiah Nott and George Gliddon,
whom Agassiz soon befriended. Nott and Gliddon, who fancied
themselves the leaders of a field of study called niggerology, argued that, in the same way that the breeding of a horse and a
donkey will produce a sterile mule, the progeny of an interracial
couple could only be sterile. Interbreeding could then in time
only lead to one result: the extinction of the human race. Unlike
Agassiz, Nott and Gliddon believed in no benevolent God, not
even as a master of the hierarchy of race; to them it was science
versus nature, and science was on the side of slavery.

One might assume that Lincoln and Agassiz would be natural antagonists, but in his description of Bates's response to Lincoln's first reading of the Emancipation Proclamation, Welles
says Bates's views on race and intermarriage were also Lincoln's;
and while that is an oversimplification, there is some truth to it.
One of Stephen Douglas's favorite arguments, and one of his
most racist, was to suggest that the goal of the abolitionist movement was not simply to free the slaves, but to "amalgamate" with
them. In a speech before the Illinois State House in 1857, Lincoln took this argument on, accusing Douglas of an attempt to
"fasten the *odium of that idea* upon his adversaries" (italics added).
It is "counterfeit logic," Lincoln argued, to conclude that "be-

cause I do not want a black woman for a slave I must necessarily want her for a wife. I need not have her for either. I can just leave her alone."

His reasoning was irrefutable and rooted in the language of liberty and choice. But this exchange leaves the awkward notion that like so many less enlightened people of his time, Lincoln considered interbreeding to be repellent. It was still a far cry from the "disgust" and "repugnance" for relations between the races that Bates expressed privately (Bates's private comments being accepted here as more sincere than Lincoln's public ones), and both men were a long way from the attitudes of Morton and Agassiz and especially Nott and Gliddon. To Bates, it was only because slaves had lived in a degraded state imposed upon them by their masters that they had been rendered inferior; by his thinking, freedom was not only a moral right, but a civilizing act with the potential for bringing the race to a higher plane, presumably deep into the future. Given that laws prohibiting miscegenation were in force until 1967, when the Supreme Court in *Loving v. Virginia* overturned that state's 1924 Racial Integrity Act, it may be too much for us to expect that Bates or Lincoln, or even most Radical Republicans pushing to end slavery in the mid-nineteenth century, sought a society that blended races into a vast reproductive melting pot. They had probably not even thought that far, and they could never have imagined that less than 150 years later the nation would elect a president who was a product of interracial marriage.

Lincoln met Agassiz in 1865, but the record of their encounter is slight and wryly amusing. A congressman from Massachusetts, Samuel Hooper, arranged the visit. In his sketchy account, Noah Brooks, the California journalist who was particularly close with Lincoln and who sat in on the meeting, wrote that the two men were like little boys warily checking each other out, offering bland questions to hide a mutual suspicion. Lincoln first asked Agassiz how to properly pronounce his name ("Won't you give me a little lesson at that, please?"), then asked if Agassiz was of Swiss or French origins, to which Agassiz said a bit of both, one "amalgamation" that presumably met with his approval. A discussion of languages and words sharing common roots followed (perhaps a veiled reference by Lincoln to the unity theory of human origins). Lincoln asked a few questions on Agassiz's methods of lecturing and then reflected briefly on his own lecture on science and invention, which he considered unfinished and which Agassiz urged him to take up again. Then it was over. Brooks wrote that when he later asked Lincoln why he had spent such time discussing banalities with the renowned scientist and propagator of racial theories, Lincoln observed, "What we got from him isn't printed in the books; the other things are."

Next to speak in the 1862 cabinet meeting was Chase. He offered "cordial support" to Lincoln's proposal, but without enthusiasm. He said he preferred a "quieter" method to emancipation, worrying that something as bold and authoritarian as a presidential proclamation would lead to "depredation" and "massacre"—the much-feared race war—and, through that, perhaps a wave of sympathy for the Confederate insurrection. Why not simply have the various Union generals "organize and arm the slaves" and then declare emancipation in their departments when "practicable"? he asked. Chase's proposal recalled a time earlier in the war when Major General John Charles Frémont, serving as the commander of the Western Department, which included Missouri, declared martial law in that state, confiscating private property and emancipating the slaves of Confederate agitators. That move—by an inexperienced and incompetent officer (Frémont, an explorer and politician, had been the Republican Party's candidate for president in 1856 and was ill suited to the role of a general)—infuriated Lincoln, who ordered it reversed. Then, a few months after General Frémont's bold act, General David Hunter, commander of the Department of the South, did something similar. Hunter was a more experienced soldier. A graduate of West Point, class of 1822, he was older than most officers in the war, and he was in charge of what was at once the smallest and the most vulnerable department, comprised of parts of South Carolina, Florida, and Georgia that remained in Union control. In March 1862, frustrated by not having sufficient numbers of soldiers to face his Confederate enemies, Hunter took the bold move of issuing General Order No. 11, which declared that since the three states of the Department of the South were officially under martial law, and since "slavery and martial law in a free country are altogether incompatible; the persons in these three States—Georgia, Florida, and South Carolina—heretofore held as slaves, are therefore declared forever free." But Lincoln forced him to rescind this order as well.

Blair, the nation's postmaster general, spoke up in strong opposition to the proclamation. Like Bates, he had an antislavery pedigree, having been the attorney who argued for Dred Scott before the Supreme Court. But he saw dark political repercussions for the Republicans if the proclamation went forward. The freed slaves, he told the group, would be seen as a threat to jobs in the North, and that resentment would mean a Republican defeat at the polls in the midterm elections that fall.

The last person to respond to the reading was Seward. In

private correspondence, he had seemed to show some of the same interest as Chase in letting the troops, not some presidential edict, carry out the liberation of the slaves. "Proclamations are paper without the support of armies," he had written. He had also, like Chase, been worried about a race war, "a social revolution, with all its horrors, like the slave revolt in Santo Domingo." Along with so many others, Seward was concerned that extremists on both sides were now forcing the worst of all possible outcomes. Earlier this month, in a letter to Charles Francis Adams (son of John Quincy and grandson of John), he had shown frustration with both the rebels and the abolitionists, "the former [for] making the most desperate attempts to overthrow the federal Union, the latter by demanding an edict of universal emancipation as a lawful and necessary, if not, they say, the only legitimate way, of saving the Union."

Some accounts cite Seward as raising concerns in the cabinet meeting over whether emancipation might be frowned on by foreign governments who relied upon the South's cotton for European fabrics. But according to the artist Carpenter, the secretary's primary contribution to the discussion that day was a note of caution. He approved of the emancipation move, he said, just not the timing. With the Union Army in stark defeat throughout the Virginia peninsula that summer, would an emancipation proclamation not look like an act of desperation, "the last measure of an exhausted government, a cry for help; the government stretching forth its hands to Ethiopia, instead of Ethiopia stretching forth her hands to the government"? Wait, he said. Wait "until you can give it to the country supported by military success instead of issuing it, as would be the case now, upon the greatest disasters of the war." That argument struck

Lincoln "with very great force," and it convinced him to put the proclamation aside "as you do your sketch for a picture" not yet completed, he told Carpenter.

Over the next few weeks, Lincoln would pull the draft out from time to time and touch it up "here and there," he remembered later, while he waited for the progress of events. But how much "wait" could the nation endure? A "profound gloom" had settled across the country with "the great mass of the people . . . discouraged and disheartened," reported the *New York Times.* "They have poured out their treasures and their blood like water; and they do not see the fruits they were promised for such sacrifices. They have given their confidence without stint to the men who wielded the weapons they had placed in their hands,—and they do not find that confidence justified by success. They have waited patiently week after week, month after month, through the slow revolving seasons of a whole year, for victories, brilliant and decisive, promised them from day to day; and though every home mourns its dead, and every heart grieves for friends who will return no more forever, the victories are yet delayed and seem indeed further off than when the war began."

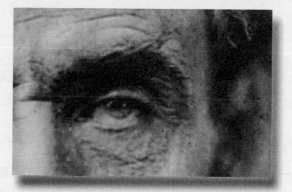

V.

SEND THEM AWAY

THE PRESIDENT'S SCHEDULE for the first few days of August 1862 was an odd mixture of the superficial and the grave. On Sunday, the third, he summoned his cabinet for an early-morning meeting. Lincoln described his concerns over a new treaty between the Cherokee Indians and the Confederates. He asked for the secretaries' opinions on whether the army should attack the Cherokees in response. Lincoln mentioned that the *Louisville Daily Democrat* had come out for "disunion" since, as their editorialist put it, "the federal government was now in the hands of Abolitionists." He then listened to Chase reiterate his feeling that the time for suppressing the rebellion without interference with slavery had passed, how the bitterness had united the Southern whites "against us," and that "the loyal whites remaining, if they would not prefer the union without slavery, certainly would not prefer slavery to union." The treasury secretary again described a plan that fit his desire for a "quiet" introduction of emancipation, without a proclamation, but the president seemed unimpressed.

On August 4, a delegation from Indiana visited, offering to lead "two colored regiments" in the fight. Lincoln informed them that he was not ready "to go to the length of enlisting negroes as soldiers," that "he could not afford to lose Kentucky," and that the plan they proposed would, in his opinion, "turn fifty thousand bayonets from loyal Border States against us." On the seventh, the president went to the Navy Yards and inspected the newly invented Rafael Repeater, a machine gun that could fire forty shots in twenty seconds, and on the eighth, he sent a note of congratulations to the British queen, Victoria, on the marriage of her "beloved" daughter, Her Royal Highness, the Princess Alice Maud Mary ("Feeling a lively interest in all that concerns Your Majesty's August Family, I participate in the satisfaction afforded by this happy event"). That same day he issued orders to Secretary of War Stanton to arrest all protesters who discouraged enlistments.

On August 9 came news of the battle at Cedar Mountain, Virginia, another defeat for the Union, and Lincoln penned a note to John Clay, son of the legendary senator Henry Clay of Kentucky, thanking him for the gift of the senator's beloved snuffbox. Finally, on the fourteenth, Lincoln, having consulted with none of his top advisers on the subject, sat down with a delegation of "colored men" and encouraged them to begin a movement to take their race abroad.

What had happened between July 22 and now? It was almost as though, having written the proclamation and then tested the idea on his closest colleagues and then tested it again on his cabinet, Lincoln still felt the need to test it on himself, to mold it and turn it like a whittler might turn a piece of wood, to press the idea in his hands until it felt welcome and right. Was this why he had so peremptorily told Welles and Seward and the cabinet as well that he had made up his mind and that they should not try to persuade him otherwise, because in fact he had not yet made up his mind and did not want to risk being swayed from what he regarded as the more courageous act (emancipation) for the more expedient act, which was—what? To not act at all, to hide his real intentions (what *were* his real intentions?) behind a mission to restore the Union and nothing else? In the way that we may seek a reason not to do the thing we fear to do even if it may be the right thing, Lincoln appeared to have taken Seward's advice to delay action more because it put off emancipation than because he was impressed by the logic that the proclamation should only be issued at the right moment, when some undeniable victory put the Union in a position of strength.

But if not emancipation, then what alternative was there for this intractable war that now claimed 147,753 Union casualties, 147,747 Confederate? And what if battlefield defeat continued to follow battlefield defeat, as indeed it would through this awful month and the beginning of the next, the anticipated moment of victory that was to have triggered the proclamation proving more and more elusive? Would Lincoln be content to watch young men die while he sat inert, leaving this particular object of his struggle, whether it was his primary object or his secondary object, unspoken or, worse yet, denied? What alternative, what middle ground between emancipation and the continuance of slavery, was there that could end the war, keep the Union intact, and at the same time address the moral wrong that he and so many others believed slavery to be?

That last question had an answer, unsatisfactory as it may have appeared to Lincoln at the time, and loathsome as it was to so many more progressive minds of the day: colonization. Free the slaves and then send them away along with all other free members of their race, send them to some far-off place so that the dreaded race war would never materialize, so that the end of slavery would not mean the beginning of equality, so that Negro and white man would not need to find peace with each other, so North and South would end their blood-spattered quarrel, so America could remain a white, Anglo-Saxon nation—and all as the ghastly and merciless institution that had started it all was brought to an end.

This was hardly a new idea. Plantation owners and religious groups (an odd pairing, to say the least) had founded the American Colonization Society in 1816 on something like this very premise, that free blacks should be encouraged to leave the United States and settle on the west coast of Africa, where they could enjoy liberties denied them here and perhaps even bring there, to the savage world, some of the enlightenment of Christian civilization that had rubbed off on them in America (while they were being, well, abused). That would have described the religious leaders' point of view. For the plantation owners, the motivation for colonization was not so "benevolent." They wanted colonization because they worried that free blacks, whom

Virginia congressman John Randolph, an early supporter of the ACS, referred to as "promoters of mischief," had begun to foment unrest among their slave populations and that they served as a temptation to slaves by putting "ideas" in their heads, by demonstrating that a life cut free from the chains of their masters was possible. It was a fascinating dichotomy: while the religious leaders saw colonization as a way of eventually *ending* slavery, plantation owners saw it as a way of *protecting* slavery from those who sought to subvert it. Yet both converged on the same plan.

In the early decades of the nineteenth century, colonization had the support of President Andrew Jackson, of the Senate statesmen Henry Clay and Daniel Webster, and of George Washington's nephew Bushrod Washington, who, while an associate justice of the US Supreme Court, signed on to be the first president of the ACS. Colonization also had the backing of Congress, which in 1819 provided $100,000 in federal funds ($2.3 million in 2013 dollars) to the society to begin its work.

The result was a first outpost at Cape Mesurado just south of the British colony of Sierra Leone. It was already home to the descendants of black American Loyalists who, having fought on the side of the British in the American Revolution in exchange for their freedom, escaped with the British army and eventually resettled there. Now the ACS pioneers proposed a new settlement there to be called Monrovia, after the sitting president, James Monroe, an ironic decision when you consider that in 1800, while serving as governor of Virginia, Monroe had violently put down a plot organized by a slave blacksmith named Gabriel Prosser. Prosser's scheme was to lead a group of runaway slaves in a raid on Richmond, kidnap Governor Monroe and other civic leaders, then hold them hostage until the rebels could be provided with a ship and safe passage out of the United States. Hearing of the plot within days of its planned implementation, Monroe called out the state militia, which tore through slave quarters on a dozen local plantations, capturing Prosser and thirty or so others. All were hanged, but to send a message, Prosser's death was made into a piece of dark theater. He alone was denied the executioner's snap of the neck that allows for a mercifully quick strangulation and was left instead to flail in agony from the rope, dangling in the wind until the life was slowly squeezed out of him. (It only took a little more than two hundred years for Virginia to officially acknowledge this wrong. In 2007, Governor Tim Kaine pardoned Prosser, saying that the slave had been inspired by "the ideals of the American revolution" when he risked death "to secure liberty.")

By the 1830s, the ACS mission had gained traction, particularly in Maryland, where the overcultivation of tobacco had sapped the soil of the necessary nutrients for that plant, forcing the introduction of crops such as wheat, which required fewer hands to farm. From this development, Marylanders could see that their future would not carry the same demand for slave labor as it had in the past, yet where would all the former slaves and free blacks among them now go? What would they do? How should they be treated? The state already had more freemen than any other; indeed, for every slave in Baltimore in the 1830s, there were four free blacks.

Colonization provided a solution. The Maryland legislature went so far as to establish its own West African colony, the Republic of Maryland—an unconstitutional act (a state with its own foreign colony?) that went unchallenged in American courts. Within fifteen years it was joined by privately funded colonies such as Kentucky in Africa and others originating in Louisiana and Mississippi. By 1847, the country of Liberia, cobbled together from these beginnings, had declared its independence. Still, the colonization movement never had the impact that its founders intended; opposition from abolitionists at home and from African tribes in Liberia, who were resentful of the intrusion on their shores, kept the numbers of repatriating blacks low.

For Lincoln, who during these years was a practicing lawyer, a member of the Illinois General Assembly, and finally a congressman, the key figure supporting colonization was Henry Clay. In a career ranging from 1803 to his death in 1852, Clay was a politician of unique standing, serving, variously, as Speaker of the House, secretary of state, senator, founder of the Whig Party, and as a three-time candidate for president. That would include 1824, when Clay, in a deadlocked presidential contest that was eventually decided by the House of Representatives, threw his votes to John Quincy Adams, the eventual winner; 1832, when he was defeated by Andrew Jackson; and 1844, when he narrowly lost to James K. Polk.

Clay had three valuable gifts: a voice that could enthrall an audience, an actor's sense of timing and movement, and a talent, known to only a few who have walked the Capitol's corridors, for finding that narrow sliver of common ground between two seemingly incompatible positions and staking his claim for history there. This last skill earned him the title the Great Pacificator. But he had other honorifics, including the Great Compromiser, Harry of the West, the Gallant Star, and Prince Hal. In what is regarded as the historical high point of American political oratory, Clay, Massachusetts senator Daniel Webster, and South Carolina senator John C. Calhoun were known as the Great

Triumvirate, three senators, possessed of the same Roman flair, whose debates held the nation rapt during the intense sectional crises of the mid-nineteenth century that threatened to erupt into fratricidal war. If ever there was an argument for the power of words to quell the fevered primal dispute, it is the seventy-two-year-old Clay standing before his fellow lawmakers in an effort to gain their support for what we now call the Compromise of 1850. Frail, consumptive, raising his bony fist for emphasis, Clay stood addressing the chamber for two days, entreating his colleagues to "repress the ardor of these passions, to look to their country, to its interests," and when something is proposed they deem not worthy of their acceptance, "not to denounce it, but to improve it . . . so as to accomplish the object which I indulge the hope is common to all and every one of us, to restore peace and quiet, and harmony and happiness to the country." Thanks to him, the nation, barely half a century old and still considered by many to be an experiment more likely to fail than not, was once again pulled back from the precipice of collapse, making it all the sadder to reflect on his having died less than two years later under the illusion that the work of the Great Triumvirate had spared his country from a civil war.

Clay was a master of the political straddle, which he effected by walking the Senate floor from side to side—a silk handkerchief in one hand, a snuffbox in the other—holding forth as if in permanent soliloquy, but he struck a particularly delicate balance when it came to the subject of slavery. While his was a forceful voice for abolition, as a slaveholder himself his bonds with human chattel and the society that protected it made him reluctant to act too quickly. Instead, he adhered to the Whig position that acknowledged the institution as an abomination but

saw immediate abolition as a cure that could be worse than the
disease, havoc heaped upon blasphemy. Clay based his judgment
on the some three hundred thousand freemen throughout the
country, whom he regarded as the "most corrupt, depraved, and
abandoned" class of humanity anywhere. Yet, like Bates, he felt
"it is not so much their fault as the consequence of their anoma-
lous condition. Place ourselves, place any men, in the like predicament, and similar effects would follow. They are not slaves,
and yet they are not free. The laws, it is true, proclaim them
free; but prejudices, more powerful than any laws, deny them
the privileges of freemen."

If slavery was abolished, it would increase tenfold the numbers of the "depraved" roaming freely, and it would be foolish,
he argued, to think that this would do anything but magnify the
problem. Not even time could cure the ills created by slavery
and bigotry. The effects of the blacks' "predicament" were far
too ingrained in their character, and the prejudice against them
for their "depravity" was far too ingrained in American society.
To Clay, there was no way to rise above the past. "No talents
however great, no piety, however pure and devoted, no patriotism, however ardent can secure their admission" as equals in a
white world. The only sensible choice was colonization, which
Clay pushed throughout his life, becoming president of the ACS
in 1836. There he made it clear that the organization's program
was intended only to address the futures of those already free,
that it had no intention of disturbing the "domestic tranquility"
of Southern society, of weakening the "obligations of obedience," having "neither . . . the power nor the will to affect the
property of any one contrary to his consent." Leaving little doubt
as to which of the two ACS constituencies—the religious and

the slaveholding—he belonged to, Clay asserted that the "execution of [the ACS] scheme would augment instead of [diminish]
the value of the property left behind."

Clay was revered, more popular in his day than anyone else
who could not claim the title of president. It was said that when
he spoke before audiences back home, the crowds were so large
he briefly "depopulated the fields and forests of the West." When,
in 1852, he died, a period of national mourning followed and he
became the first American to lie in state in the rotunda of the
Capitol. His body was then transported by train to Lexington,
Kentucky, for burial, following a twelve-hundred-mile route
that allowed mourners in Philadelphia, New York, Albany, Buf-
falo, Cleveland, Cincinnati, and Louisville to pay their respects.
In New York, his casket was paraded up Broadway to City Hall,
where more than twenty thousand passed before it, and in Philadelphia a torchlight procession led it to Independence Hall, a
symbolic statement that captured the feeling that Clay was a
prized member of a "second generation" of American founders.
In death, Clay remained true to his convictions (qualified as they
may have been). The phrase inscribed on his headstone at the
Lexington Cemetery read, "I know no North—no South—no
East—no West," and in his will he called for the gradual emancipation—and colonization—of the children of his slaves.

A few days after Clay's passing, Abraham Lincoln rose from
his seat in the Illinois statehouse to pay tribute to the man he
later referred to as his "beau ideal of a statesman." The two had
never met, but Lincoln had long been an admirer from afar and
saw something of his own story in Clay's climb to prominence:
a self-educated Kentuckian, who rose from humble beginnings
to the profession of the law, and who remained throughout his

career both nationalist in spirit and practical in his actions. Clay may never have reached his ultimate goal of the presidency, said Lincoln, but while "with other men, to be defeated was to be forgotten . . . to him, defeat was but a trifling incident, neither changing him or the world's estimate of him." Something more than respect was in Lincoln's tone; there was affection. Many have noted that Clay was like a father figure to Lincoln, as in the wished-for father that he never had. Clay's eloquence and grandeur, his life of purpose and love of learning, his command of the English language, was in direct contrast to Lincoln's acknowledged father, Thomas, an illiterate who scolded the young Abe for his intellectual ambitions and saw his love of reading as "lazy" in a backwoods life that valued brawn over brains.

As an adult, Lincoln had so drifted from Thomas Lincoln that in 1851, when the older Lincoln was on his deathbed, Abe declined the opportunity to visit him, saying, somewhat mysteriously, "If we could meet now, it is doubtful whether it would not be more painful than pleasant." Their incompatibility helped feed the theories that Tom Lincoln was in fact not Lincoln's father, and predictably, in the 1920s, when an avalanche of popular (and suspect) histories were written about Lincoln, among the many great men put forward as candidates to have sired the sixteenth president was Clay. After all, the senator was, like Lincoln, tall, the right age, from the right state, and he had a reputation for infidelity. (However, as the author of an article in H. L. Mencken's *American Mercury* magazine wrote at the time, that description could have fit a large portion of the male population of Kentucky.)

Lincoln noted that Clay had been born of "undistinguished parents" in 1777 "while the bloody struggle between those resolute rebels, and their haughty would-be-masters, was still waging" in the War of Independence. Clay was therefore as old as America itself, which seemed to suggest that Clay *was* America and that his ideas represented the maturing and developing of the Founders' original impulses. Lincoln went on to describe Clay's eloquence as rooted not in logic or reasoning, but, rather, in "that deeply earnest and impassioned tone" that "touches the chords of sympathy." (On this, Lincoln and Clay parted comparison, as Lincoln's words were always deeply embedded in reason and analogy.) Finally, Lincoln laid out a defense of Clay's position on the critical subject of the day: "Cast into life where slavery was already widely spread and deeply seated, he did not perceive, as I think no wise man has perceived, how it could be at once eradicated, without producing a greater evil, even to the cause of human liberty itself. His feeling and his judgment, therefore, ever led him to oppose both extremes of opinion on the subject. Those who would shiver into fragments the Union of these States; tear to tatters its now venerated constitution; and even burn the last copy of the Bible, rather than slavery should continue a single hour, together with all their more halting sympathisers, have received, and are receiving their just execration; and the name, and opinions, and influence of Mr. Clay, are fully, and, as I trust, effectually and enduringly, arrayed against them. But I would also, if I could, array his name, opinions, and influence against the opposite extreme—against a few, but an increasing number of men, who, for the sake of perpetuating slavery, are beginning to assail and to ridicule the white man's charter of freedom—the declaration that 'all men are created free and equal.'"

Lincoln then turned to Clay's support for colonization. He confirmed that the senator thought it "no demerit" that colonization "tended to relieve slave-holders from the troublesome presence of the free negroes," but quoted the senator, approvingly, that there "is a moral fitness in the idea of returning to Africa her children, whose ancestors have been torn from her by the ruthless hand of fraud and violence. Transplanted in a foreign land, they will carry back to their native soil the rich fruits of religion, civilization, law and liberty." This convinced Lincoln to overlook the incongruence of Clay's abolitionist rhetoric and his ownership of slaves: he was only holding them because he wanted to ensure that they were sent to a place where they would flourish. This was not only the Kentuckian's considered plan but "one of the great designs of the Ruler of the universe (whose ways are often inscrutable by shortsighted mortals) thus to transform an original crime, into a signal blessing to that most unfortunate portion of the globe."

Among the many advocates for colonization that Lincoln met during this time was the Reverend James Mitchell, a Methodist minister and abolitionist from Indiana. Lincoln remembered Mitchell years later when in June of 1862 he appointed him "commissioner of emigration" in the Department of the Interior. With the failure of the ACS's West Africa plan, Interior Secretary Caleb B. Smith had encouraged Lincoln to establish a colony in the coal-rich Chiriquí region of Panama, which at the time was part of Colombia, and Mitchell had been assigned by Smith to pursue that plan. To begin his work, the minister reached out to black churches in the District of Columbia and asked them to send representatives to a meeting in which emigration would be discussed. The group then gathered to hear Mitchell at a Washington church.

Mitchell requested their cooperation on a plan that would encourage free black Americans to emigrate to Chiriquí. After a silence, the group, while unmoved, agreed to send a five-member delegation to meet with the president and continue the conversation. On August 14, 1862, in what Mitchell described later as the first time that an American president had hosted "colored men" at the White House, Lincoln, his draft of the Emancipation Proclamation still known to only the cabinet and a few close friends and advisers, entertained five black American leaders with the purpose of encouraging them to start a mass exodus from America and rid the nation of its "race problem" forever. (In fact, this was not the first time an African-American had visited the Executive Mansion; Lincoln had met earlier in the year with a black religious leader over the emancipation of slaves in the District of Columbia, but that was not as public a moment as this, where the exchange between Lincoln and the delegation was reported in depth in the newspapers.)

To make its position clear in advance of the meeting, the black group, which was composed of well-educated members of the nation's small but significant black elite, issued a statement describing the proposed policy as "inexpedient, inauspicious, and impolitic." They did not want their willingness to meet to be read as an endorsement. Then, in what is certainly one of the more bizarre episodes of Lincoln's time in office, the members of the delegation, led by Edward Thomas, who was the president of the Anglo-African Institute for the Encouragement of Industry and Art, and including John F. Cook Jr., who had attended Oberlin College in Ohio, Benjamin McCoy, who had founded the Asbury Methodist Church in DC, Cornelius T. Clark, a member of the anti-emigration group known as the Social, Civil, and Statistical Association (SCSA), and John T.

Costin, a noted Freemason, were brought into the presidential office, where they sat quietly and listened to their president tell them, essentially, to leave the country.

"You and we are different races," Lincoln said. "Even when you cease to be slaves, you are yet far removed from being placed on an equality with the white race. . . . It is better for us both, therefore, to be separated." Lincoln told the group that it was their presence in a white society—not slavery, not Southern secession—that was the root cause of this terrible war, and that slavery had done this to the white race. Oh, just look at what slavery has done! "See our present condition—the country engaged in war!—our white men cutting one another's throats, none knowing how far it will extend." Sounding like a suspiciously interested travel agent, he then waxed on about the beauty and opportunities they would discover in Central America if only they would give it a try. Lincoln even invoked George Washington and the deprivation suffered by American troops during the Revolution as a lesson from which black Americans could learn. That effort had required the suffering of hardships for the greater good; so, too, should this one. It was up to them to show their race the path to a more promising future in a far-off land even if that required them to forgo some of their "present comfort" and resist the "selfish" urge to stay here. The carnival pitch then became a challenge. "Could I get a hundred tolerably intelligent men, with their wives and children . . . ? Can I have fifty? If I could find twenty-five able-bodied men, with a mixture of women and children, good things in the family relation, I think I could make a successful commencement."

Once news of Lincoln's remarks got out, the reaction was dismay. It was "disgraceful," "either a piece of charlatanism or the statesmanship of a backwoods lawyer." A Republican senator from New Hampshire called it "one of the most absurd ideas that ever entered into the head of man or woman." Lincoln's plan struck Treasury Secretary Salmon Chase as a policy of cowardice. "How much better," he told his diary, "would be a manly protest against prejudice" (Was he referring here to emancipation? Did he presume that Lincoln had abandoned that plan for this one?) and "a wise effort to give freemen homes in America!" Chase then continued, "A Military Order, emancipating at least the slaves of South Carolina, Georgia and the Gulf States, would do more to terminate the war and ensure an early restoration of solid peace and prosperity than anything else that can be devised." He may have been convinced that this was the right action, but was Lincoln?

Among the most vocal critics of the emigration plan was the former slave Frederick Douglass. In 1838, while posing as a free black seaman, he had hopped the "colored car" trailing a train out of Havre de Grace, Maryland, switched to a steamboat in Wilmington, Delaware, and then boarded another train in Philadelphia as he escaped to the home of black activist David Ruggles in New York City and a life of freedom. Douglass was an intellectual. He had learned to read while still a slave and had taught other slaves to read the New Testament, a brazen act for which he had faced severe punishment. For decades as a freeman he had commanded a forceful voice for abolition, especially since, unlike others, he spoke from experience, having endured the sting of his master's whip. While Lincoln's enemies had long accused of him of associating with Douglass (the contemporary term was *niggerism*), the two had never met (they would, three times, starting in 1863, and develop a qualified mutual respect).

Douglass had publicly supported Lincoln, both in his 1858 Illinois US Senate campaign and in his 1860 run for the presidency, but he had found Lincoln, as president, to be a disappointment. As recently as July, Douglass had expressed his exasperation with a cutting description of Lincoln and McClellan. "The one plays lawyer for the benefit of the rebels, and the other handles the army for the benefit of the traitors. We should not be surprised if both should be hurled from their places before this rebellion is ended," he wrote, the reference to "playing the lawyer" here being a nod to Lincoln's strict enforcement of what Douglass had once referred to as the "slave-hunting, slave-catching, slave-killing" Fugitive Slave Act of 1850.

A month later, after Lincoln's peculiar pitch on emigration, Douglass exploded. "Mr. Lincoln assumes the language and arguments of an itinerant Colonization lecturer," read the opening essay in the September 1862 edition of *Douglass' Monthly*, one of four abolitionist periodicals Douglass edited during the war, "showing all his inconsistencies, his pride of race and blood, his contempt for Negroes and his canting hypocrisy."

Douglass seized upon Lincoln's claim that the slaves were responsible for the war. "A horse thief pleading that the existence of the horse is the apology for his theft or a highway man contending that the money in the traveler's pocket is the sole first cause of his robbery are about as much entitled to respect as is the President's reasoning at this point. No, Mr. President, it is not the innocent horse that makes the horse thief, not the traveler's purse that makes the highway robber, and it is not the presence of the Negro that causes this foul and unnatural war, but the cruel and brutal cupidity of those who wish to possess horses, money and Negroes by means of theft, robbery, and rebellion."

Lincoln's assertion on this issue was at least ambiguous ("But for your race among us there could not be war"). The president probably intended his words to convey that *but for your race being forcibly brought here to serve in slavery*, there could be no war. But Douglass's attack on Lincoln's assertion of the incompatibility of the races was on firmer ground. Not only Lincoln, but Clay, too, and even many headstrong abolitionists, despaired over the chances for the races to ever live in harmony. With the historical shadow of slavery lingering over all future interactions, blacks and whites would never be able to live together in peace, at least not *here*, not in *America*. According to some who embraced this argument, it was only just that those who had been torn from their homeland and brought here against their will in chains should be returned to where the sin began, in a sense, to the natural state from which they were so violently wrenched.

Douglass had little patience with any of this. On the thought that the races were incompatible because one was superior to the other, he blamed history: "If the colored people instead of having been stolen and forcibly brought to the United States had come as free immigrants, like the German and the Irish [and] never thought of as suitable objects of property, they never would have become the objects of aversion and bitter persecution, nor would there ever have been divulged and propagated the arrogant and malignant nonsense about natural repellancy and the incompatibility of races." In Mexico, Central America, and South America, wrote Douglass, many "distinct races" were living "peaceably together in the enjoyment of equal rights."

As to Lincoln's argument that it was only right to return African-Americans to their country of ancestral origin, he, and so many others, had miscalculated the degree to which African-

Americans saw America as their country, too. The slaves "are as much the natives of the country as any of their oppressors," argued the author of an essay in William Lloyd Garrison's abolitionist paper, *The Liberator*. "Here they were born; here, by every consideration of justice and humanity, they are entitled to live; and here it is for them to die in the course of nature." In a letter to the president, New Jersey freeman A. P. Smith challenged Lincoln: "Pray tell us, is our right to a home in this country less than your own, Mr. Lincoln. . . . Are you an American? So are we. Are you a patriot? So are we." There was simply no way to reconcile the leader of a country founded on the principles of liberty lecturing an entire race of people on their duty to return to an ancestral past with which they had little, if anything, in common. Hadn't Jefferson himself settled this question when he wrote about earth belonging to the living, that they and they alone should be the determiners of their fate, not the crippling legacy of some fossilized past? Then again, Jefferson, was a man of contradictions; he, too, advocated for a gradual end to slavery by (guess what?) colonization.

To Douglass, the colonization plan laid bare Lincoln's true character. "Illogical and unfair as Mr. Lincoln's statements are, they are nevertheless quite in keeping with his whole course from the beginning of his administration up to this day, and confirm the painful conviction that though elected as an anti-slavery man by Republican and Abolition voters, Mr. Lincoln is quite a genuine representative of American prejudice and Negro hatred and far more concerned for the preservation of slavery, and the favor of the Border Slave States, than for any sentiment of magnanimity or principle of justice and humanity."

Others who had put so much hope in Lincoln echoed Douglass's critique. On August 20, journalist Horace Greeley, writing in his influential *New York Tribune*, provided a challenge with a full-page editorial he titled "The Prayer of Twenty Millions," referring to the population of the Northern states. Greeley, writing as one of them but for *all of them*, described himself as "sorely disappointed and deeply pained by the policy you seem to be pursuing with regard to the slaves of the Rebels." The president was "strangely and disastrously remiss in the discharge of [his] official and imperative duty" (to enforce the second Confiscation Act), "unduly influenced" by politicians from border slave states, and showing "mistaken deference to rebel slavery." Greeley implored him to change course.

Lincoln's response, issued two days later, through a letter to Washington's *Daily National Intelligencer*, remains one of the most famous passages he ever wrote: "As to the policy I 'seem to be pursuing' as you say, I have not meant to leave any one in doubt. . . . If I could save the Union without freeing any slave I would do it, and if I could save it by freeing all slaves I would do it; and if I could save it by freeing some and leaving others alone I would also do that. What I do about slavery, and the colored race, I do because I believe it helps to save the Union; and what I forbear, I forbear because I don't believe it would help to save the Union. I shall do less whenever I shall believe what I am doing hurts the cause, and I shall do more whenever I shall believe doing more will help the cause. I shall try to correct errors when shown to be error; and I shall adopt new views so fast as they shall appear to be true views. I have here stated my purpose according to my view of Official duty: and I intend no modification of my oft-expressed personal wish that all men everywhere could be free. Yours, A. Lincoln."

VI.

GOD KNOWS

WHETHER HE INTENDED to be opaque or merely political, Lincoln's response to Horace Greeley and "The Prayer of Twenty Millions" was all things to all people and nothing to anyone. He had left every conceivable option open: freeing no slaves, freeing some slaves, freeing all slaves, hinging everything on what would "save the Union." For those Northerners who did not want to see emancipation directly linked to the war effort, who did not want their young, white men to die defending the rights of an "inferior" race, it was a satisfactory answer, for Lincoln did put the Union first. For those on the other side of the question, for the increasing number of people who wanted emancipation to be the war's primary mission, that Lincoln had actually mentioned the option that they had been waiting to hear—freeing all the slaves—and that he had referred to the saving of the Union as only his paramount objective, meaning that there were other objectives, was a sign that the president had shifted ever so slightly in their direction. But the language of obfuscation employed by Lincoln here was dazzling. He had joined with all sides and committed himself to none. He had seemed forceful but had established no course of action. And all this while his draft of the Emancipation Proclamation, the one he had worked on so assiduously in the telegraph office, the one where he chose the option of freeing some of the slaves and not freeing others *because he did not see any other viable option*, lay pulsing imperceptibly in the drawer of his desk.

In his succinct response (227 words) to Greeley's loquacious "prayer" (2,204 words), Lincoln also saw fit to include the gratuitous line of self-declaration "I have here stated my purpose according to my view of Official duty: and I intend no modification of my oft-expressed personal wish that all men everywhere could be free." This can be read in several ways. The most obvious is that the passage shows Lincoln, the lawyer, asserting that as president he had a formal "legal self" that was separate from his "private self," and his private self was with Greeley and the "twenty millions." That was not insignificant, either, since it was the first time that Lincoln as president had voiced any opinion about slavery. Another, albeit similar reading, detects Lincoln, the straddling politician, pronouncing, *In spirit, I am always with those who would abolish slavery, but I cannot free people with a wave of my hand or the stroke of a pen. Emancipation can only be a legislative initiative, and there are states whose elected representatives do not believe as I do and a population in rebellion that would sooner die than be subjected to what I believe. I am the president of all the people, not just those who think as I think.* Yet by far the most peculiar expression in the sentence was the word *could*, as when Lincoln wrote, "I intend no modification of my oft-expressed personal wish that all men everywhere *could* be free."

If he had written *should be free*, then he would have been using a verb of advocacy. If he had written *must be free*, then he would have been using a verb of conviction. If he had written *will be free*, then he would have been using a verb of personal commitment or at the very least establishing a historical imperative. But Lincoln chose *could*, a word that divorced him from responsibility, pledged him to nothing, a word that has the quality not of action but of passive observation, suggesting a conditional state, as in all people *could* be free, but for . . . what? He does not say.

Maybe the passive phrasing was radical enough for this moment. Perhaps he was saying, "Look, the slaves *could* be free and the world would not end!" Or maybe it was an expression of desire: "If only they *could* be free, as they deserve to be!" But whatever his intentions, the words he used to respond to Horace Greeley did not form a statement of direction or energy. Yet how could he reconcile them with the plans he was making in private? Was he now abandoning the proclamation? Had he lost his passion for it? Or was he merely being coy, testing the idea by floating all choices and getting a glimpse at the public's reaction to each?

The accepted wisdom among those who have examined this period is to rely upon the artist Francis Carpenter's recall of his conversations with Lincoln two years later (again, a dubious source) and from the impression left by his secretaries John Hay and John Nicolay, who concluded in their own *Abraham Lincoln: A History* that the president always had a "fixed purpose" of issuing the proclamation and his hesitation was therefore purposeful, that it served as a way of preparing the North, that his words were indeed a tease intended to spark a response. He knew he would not free all the slaves—he was firm in his belief that he did not have the constitutional power to do so—and yet he had already freed some of the slaves through the Confiscation Acts, which he had signed (even though he had not supported them because he thought these, too, were unconstitutional). Slavery had been abolished in the District of Columbia through a legislative act signed by Lincoln in April. And he knew that as an act of war he was prepared to free the slaves in the states in rebellion very, very soon. It was his way of saying that he had other, even more radical, options so that if he chose to reveal the limited emancipation that was contained in the proclamation, it would seem as though he had opted for a middle ground. Waiting for the battle victory that would put him in a position to act, he was paving the way for the proclamation's eventual success. "Many of my strongest supporters urged Emancipation before I thought it indispensable," Carpenter recalled Lincoln saying, "and, I may say, before I thought the country ready for it. It is my conviction that, had the proclamation been issued even six months earlier than it was, public sentiment would not have sustained it." To underscore the point, Lincoln used an analogy: "A man watches his pear-tree day after day, impatient for the ripening of the fruit. Let him attempt to force the process, and he may spoil both fruit and tree. But let him patiently wait, and the ripe pear at length falls into his lap! We have seen this great revolution in public sentiment slowly but surely progressing, so that, when final action came, the opposition was not strong enough to defeat the purpose. I can now solemnly assert that I have a clear conscience in regard to my action on this momentous question."

Was it really that easy? Ripe fruit dropping on its own from a tree? Or is this comment a reflection of a triumphant Lincoln's self-congratulation after the fact, safe now from his doubts, guilt, and anxiety, or is it maybe even the fantasy of his adoring fan Carpenter, recording something he wished to hear rather than what he actually heard? We do know that throughout the summer, Lincoln was continuing to polish his draft of the emancipation document, trying it out on more ears and leaking news of its existence or the possibility of its existence, yet still holding it in reserve, presumably for that "special moment." Nicolay and Hay describe this process as a "species of self torment," for, as they claim, he was so "conscientious" that "he made the complaints and the implied reproaches of even his humblest petitioner his own . . . from which he found relief only by a most searching analysis of his own motives in self-justification," growing "irritable" and "overstrung."

In late July, six days after he had read the proclamation to his cabinet, Lincoln had sent the document to the staunch Kentucky Republican lawyer James Speed, the brother of Lincoln's childhood friend Joshua Speed, and the man whom Lincoln would install as attorney general in his second term. Speed told him, "It will do no good; probably much harm." He urged Lincoln to "banish the idea . . . that the negro can be set free or benefitted by mere paper proclamations." It could only fail. For one, it would be the federal government imposing its will on the states.

For another, it struck Speed as an ironic twist on the immorality of human bondage for the white man to be "freeing" the black man. Where was the slave himself in all of this? For "if he has not the spirit to strike for freedom, he has not the pride of character to make him keep it when given to him." No, wrote Speed, "if the negro is to be free he must strike for it himself."

Sometime, probably in late August, Lincoln summoned his friend Leonard Swett, an Illinois lawyer, to the White House to sit with him while he read from letters he had received containing all manner of arguments for and against emancipation. (Lincoln loved to read aloud, for "when I read aloud I hear what is read and I see it" and thereby "catch the idea by two senses.") The president then responded, also aloud, to each argument, both for and against, while Swett remained silent, his reactions never even sought by Lincoln nor provided. Swett later told a friend that, for Lincoln, it appeared to be "an instance of stating conclusions aloud, not that they might convince another, or be combatted by him, but that [Lincoln] might see for himself how they looked when taken out of the region of mere reflection and embodied in words." Lincoln's approach was so careful and "judicious" and so absent of any will to persuade, Swett felt his presence was less as a "hearer of Lincoln's views" than "as a witness of the President's mental operations."

On August 18, Lincoln let Robert J. Walker, a former senator from Mississippi who had broken with the South to support the Union cause, know of the proclamation, and as he did, he cleverly included journalist James R. Gilmore in on the conversation. Gilmore, with Lincoln's approval, then passed the scoop on to Greeley. In fact, Greeley heard about the proclamation on the day that he published his "prayer." But even as Lincoln continued to whisper his plans to others, he remained "cautious, dilatory, reticent," Greeley later wrote. On emancipation, Lincoln "hesitated, and demurred, and resisted," perhaps still hoping that the war would take care of the subject without his having to do anything, that the situation for the Union Army would take enough of a dramatic shift for the better so that emancipation would fall naturally—like a fruit from a tree, again—from the enemy's diminished sense of its chances.

On September 2, 1862, Lincoln convened a cabinet meeting. Only days before, the Union Army, under the direction of General John Pope, had suffered a particularly frustrating defeat, this at the same site of another devastating defeat fourteen months earlier—Manassas Junction, Virginia, home to a critical Union supply depot. Lincoln had harbored high hopes for Pope. He was the anti-McClellan—a Republican where McClellan was a Democrat, a risk taker where McClellan was restrained. Lincoln also felt that he knew Pope, the general having spent many days sitting next to Lincoln in the telegraph office, reading the recalcitrant messages from McClellan that so irritated Lincoln and reinforcing the president's reactions with his own educated military judgments. But Lincoln soon learned that Pope had his own set of liabilities. He was ambitious, conniving, and arrogant. He curried favor with Lincoln by speaking ill of his rivals. His reputation had been built in the Western Theater, so here, in the East, he was greeted as an outsider. There was also the long shadow of the soldiers' general. Men who had served under Little Mac loved him. The same men did not like Pope.

Long before they became rivals in this war, McClellan had formed his own unfavorable image of Pope, so, when Pope's army got in trouble at the Second Battle of Bull Run (the North's name for Manassas—the Confederacy named battles for towns, while the Union named them for the nearest river or creek), McClellan, sensing a defeat that could mar his reputation if he joined in, refused to send reinforcements, even suggesting that it was best "to leave Pope to get out of his scrape." Thousands died while McClellan and his army camped outside the capital, pampering his worries that this war, or at least this battle, was too dangerous for his soldiers to fight. "I am in charge of the defenses of Washington," he wrote in a telegram to colleagues now under Pope's command, "and I am doing all I can do to render your retreat safe should that become necessary." Lincoln, Seward, and Stanton were outraged.

Torn over what to do, his plan to attach his war strategy to a more aggressive military leader a failure, Lincoln sank into despair. "There was a more desponding feeling than I have ever witnessed," wrote Gideon Welles of the September 2 cabinet meeting. Humiliated, and under the objections of the rest of those in attendance, Lincoln announced that he would turn again to McClellan. "He is a good engineer, all admit; there is no better organizer," said the president, sounding himself unconvinced. "He can be trusted to act on the defensive." Defense being the exact opposite of what Lincoln wanted in a general, the words must have been hard for him to pronounce, but with Lee now free to move deeper into Maryland, defense was exactly what he needed. Bates heard Lincoln say that he was "almost ready to hang himself."

While the date remains in question, it has long been believed that sometime this same week, Lincoln sat down and penned an extraordinary note of frustration, as mysterious as it is compelling. It was found among his effects shortly after his death in

1865. "In great contests each party claims to act in accordance with the will of God," he writes in strong cursive across a single sheet of lined paper, a painful acknowledgment—to whom, only himself?—of the limits of human reasoning. "Both may be, and one must be, wrong. God cannot be for and against the same thing at the same time." Yet if God is neither a Unionist nor a Confederate, precisely what does he will by tolerating all this death and destruction? "In the present civil war it is quite possible that God's purpose is something different from the purpose of either party; and yet the human instrumentalities, working just as they do, are of the best adaptation to effect his purpose. I am almost ready to say that this is probably true; that God wills this contest, and wills that it shall not end yet. By his mere great power on the minds of the now contestants, he could have either saved or destroyed the Union without a human contest. Yet the contest began. And, having begun, he could give the final victory to either side any day. Yet the contest proceeds."

As if on cue, a group of Chicago clergymen visited Lincoln at the White House on September 13 to press him on emancipation. They told him that the military failures of the summer were "tokens of divine displeasure," which the president should read as the God of the weak and the downtrodden telling him to act now. Lincoln responded sarcastically by suggesting that if God intended to show his will "on a point so intimately connected with the president's duty, it might be supposed that he would reveal it directly to me." No, he expected no such "miracle" to happen. And, anyway, "what good would a proclamation of emancipation from me do, especially as we are now situated?" It would be, he said, "like the pope's bull against the comet," a reference to Pope Calixtus III, who upon seeing the "apparition" we now refer to as Halley's Comet, thought it an omen of ill will toward Christians and took the futile gesture of issuing an edict (a bull) "excommunicating" it.

The ministers touched a nerve with Lincoln and he gave them the full argument of why he should not issue an emancipation proclamation, including parts of the critique that has continued to challenge the proclamation's greatness throughout history. "Would my word free the slaves, when I cannot even enforce the Constitution in the rebel States? Is there a single court, or magistrate, or individual that would be influenced by it there? And what reason is there to think it would have any greater effect upon the slaves than the late law of Congress [the Confiscation Act], which I approved, and which offers protection and freedom to the slaves of rebel masters who come within our lines? Yet I cannot learn that that law has caused a single slave to come over to us. And suppose they could be induced by a proclamation of freedom from me to throw themselves upon us, what should we do with them? How can we feed and care for such a multitude?"

Almost cocky in his initial rebuke of the ministers, dismissive, it seemed, of God's part in the struggle, Lincoln grew defensive and analytical, as if working out his inner conflict in front of them. "I admit that Slavery is at the root of the Rebellion, or at least its *sine qua non*," he told the clergy. ". . . I will also concede that Emancipation would help us in Europe, and convince [the Europeans] that we are incited by something more than ambition. I grant, further, that it would help somewhat at the North, though not so much, I fear, as you and those you represent imagine. Still, some additional strength would be added in that way to the war. And then, unquestionably, it would weaken the rebels by drawing off their laborers, which is of great importance; but I am not so sure we could do much with the blacks. If we were to arm them, I fear that in a few weeks the arms would be in the hands of the rebels; and, indeed, thus far, we have not had arms enough to equip our white troops."

He then turned to his stated mission as if to ask the clergy why this goal was not sufficient. "I think you should admit that we already have an important principle to rally and unite the people in the fact that constitutional government is at stake. This is a fundamental idea, going down about as deep as anything." Deep, yes, but it was not the moral correction that the men of God sought.

Lincoln's parting comments had the quality of an apology. "Do not misunderstand me because I have mentioned these objections," he implored them. "They indicate the difficulties that have thus far prevented my action in some such way as you desire. I have not decided against a proclamation of liberty to the slaves, but hold the matter under advisement. And I can assure you that the subject is on my mind, by day and by night, more than any other. Whatever shall appear to be God's will, I will do. I trust that, in the freedom with which I have canvassed your views, I have not in any respect injured your feelings."

God's will. Our ears might hear the expression as little more than an appropriate toss-off for this audience as the president parted from their company. But the reference carried more weight than mere ceremonial deism. Religion was never far from the story of the Civil War. Soldiers on each side saw themselves in the midst of a holy war, a clash between the godly and the unrighteous. The ministers believed Lincoln had been chosen to lead this charge and that he would be forsaking God if he did not accept divine direction. To them, *God's will* meant, well, "God's will."

But what did *God's will* mean to the one who spoke of it here, to Lincoln himself? *Whatever shall appear to be God's will, I will do* suggests that his plan would be to try to determine God's preference and then commit himself to it. Yet Lincoln believed something else. Like so much about Lincoln, his thinking about God and the divinity of Christ, about sin and redemption, about free will and Divine Providence, about the literal truth of the Bible and the nature and purpose of God's grace, all of this, is the subject of considerable debate. That is in part because so many have wanted to claim Lincoln as one of their own (Republicans and Democrats, Christians and agnostics, nationalists and universalists), beginning with his earliest biographers (the largely discredited Josiah Gilbert Holland's 1866 *Life of Abraham Lincoln* claimed through disreputable evidence that Lincoln was a devout, though private, Christian), and because Lincoln's religious attitudes are so hard to identify according to most readily available definitions. He was not the unquestioning follower of one particular faith. If anything, he appears to have been fluid in his thinking on religion, his beliefs subject to persistent reassessment.

Lincoln's parents were devout Baptists—*hard-shell Baptists* was the wonderfully evocative term of the day, referencing those who resisted the fracturing of the church in the early nineteenth century into all manner of derivative sects, each with its own defined rituals and beliefs. The hard-shells held to the old-school faith even as it came under assault during this Second Great Awakening, the religious movement that, lasting from roughly 1800 to 1840, led to the democratization of American religion, to a new emphasis on the individual religious experience as opposed to that of the community of faith, on the importance of good works and the "purification" of society, a man-centered Christianity as opposed to a God-centered Christianity. Religion to these reformers was not something you were born to, but something you tried on, that you adopted, that became an element of self-definition. In the early nineteenth century, itinerate lay preachers were everywhere, pitching tents and leading revival meetings where they would hawk their new brands of faith, looking for converts by the power of persuasion, and wrenching society from its bonds with long-established religious orthodoxies. These new forms of an evangelical Protestant faith emphasized the ability of man to earn God's grace, while traditionalists, such as Tom and Nancy Lincoln, held firm to the Calvinist principle of predestination and to a belief in an innate human depravity that could never be overcome. God had predetermined who would be granted salvation and who would be sent to burn in the fires of hell, and there was no disturbing that plan. *God's will* was "God's will."

Growing up in this era, Lincoln did not choose to actively part from his parents' faith, but he didn't exactly embrace it either, nor did he embrace any of the emerging faiths of the Second Great Awakening. He did not join any church (then, or afterward) and, according to his law partner Herndon, spent his young-adult years in New Salem, Illinois, among a group of liberal thinkers reading the provocative American writer Thomas Paine, author of *The Age of Reason* ("of all the systems of religion . . . there is none more derogatory to the Almighty, more unedifying to man, more repugnant to reason, and more contradictory in itself than this thing called Christianity"), and the French philosopher

Comte de Volney (especially his *Ruins of Empires*), two authors who, to put it mildly, cast doubt on religious certainty.

While Lincoln loved to read, he does not seem to have cared for books as a material possession, keeping only a small personal library, which in the New Salem days included the Bible, Shakespeare, and the works of William Cowper and Thomas Gray, two of the so-called Graveyard Poets, whose obsession with death and remembrance, soaked as it was in the Christian tradition, brought them considerable fame in eighteenth-century England. Cowper's hymn "God Moves in a Mysterious Way" and Gray's "Elegy Written in a Country Churchyard" sealed their respective places in literary history. Yet Lincoln's favorite poet would appear to have been the satirist Robert Burns. He had memorized many of Burns's works and would recite them aloud, adopting the Scottish brogue in which they were written (what a sight that must have been). Lincoln particularly took to Burns's "Holy Willie's Prayer," which mocked the predestination doctrine of Calvinists and old-line Baptists. The Scottish bard "helped Lincoln to be an infidel," his friend James Matheny told Herndon, ". . . he found in Burns a like thinker and feeler."

Much like his idol Thomas Jefferson, who was contemptuous of the religious establishment and was so impressed by Volney's attacks on the faithful he personally translated *Ruins of Empires* from the original French (anonymously, though, as he feared the political consequences of religious skepticism), Lincoln found the more fantastic elements of the Christ story unmoving. "As to the Christian theory that Christ is God or equal to the Creator," recalled one friend to Herndon, Lincoln "said that it had better be taken for granted; for by the test of reason we might become infidels on that subject."

Lincoln was "enthusiastic" in his religious "infidelity," and to one observer he even "bordered on atheism." But as he grew older, he either became more discreet about this skepticism, recognizing, like Jefferson, the political liability to being seen as a freethinker, or, just as likely, began to see that religious certainty was only as problematic as unreligious certainty.

The political sensitivities seemed to be at work in 1848 when Lincoln was running for Congress and his opponent accused him of being "an open scoffer at Christianity." Lincoln responded with a carefully worded defense—so Lincoln!—in which he said one thing and then another and in the end never answered the underlying charge that he was a nonbeliever, even as the cadences of his statement make it seem as though he had satisfied all doubt. In his "Handbill Replying to Charges of Infidelity," distributed to voters, Lincoln admitted that he was a member of no church, "but I have never denied the truth of the Scriptures" and "I have never spoken with intentional disrespect of religion in general, or any denomination of Christians in particular." (That's right; it was the Christian *story* that he had found imaginary, not the religion itself.) "It is true that in early life I was inclined to believe in what I understand is called the 'Doctrine of Necessity'—that is, that the human mind is impelled to action, or held in rest by some power, over which the mind itself has no control; and I have sometimes (with one, two or three, but never publicly) tried to maintain this opinion in argument." ("Tried" makes it sounds as though he believes his argument did not prevail, and since he dates this inclination to youth, it begs the question *What does he believe now?*) "I do not think I could myself, be brought to support a man for office, whom I knew to be an open enemy of, and scoffer at, religion. Leaving the higher matter of eternal consequences, between him and his Maker, I still do not think any man has the right thus to insult the feelings, and injure the morals, of the community in which he may live." Religion, then, is a private affair, and he intends to keep his religion private, too. Lincoln won the election.

David Davis, another fellow Illinois lawyer whom Lincoln later nominated to the Supreme Court, told Herndon that Lincoln may not have had any faith "in the Christian sense of the term" but he "had faith in laws, principles, causes and effects." That fits with the Lincoln we may think we know—a scientific rationalist at heart. Still, surprisingly, the mature Lincoln was also given to frequent expressions of piety, even when it would not seem to have been politically necessary. The note he wrote in 1851, upon hearing news of his father's impending death, contained not only that cold reference to some mysterious split between the two of them. Lincoln also beseeched his father to "call upon and confide in our great and good and merciful Maker, who will not turn away from him in any extremity," who "notes the fall of a sparrow, and numbers the hairs of our heads . . . and . . . will not forget the dying man who puts his trust in him."

Maybe this was Lincoln's kind gesture to his believing father in an otherwise unkind note, but Lincoln made other such statements of seeming faithfulness. At his celebrated 1858 debates with Stephen Douglas, Lincoln frequently called upon biblical, including Christian, imagery to support the Declaration's principle that "all men are created equal." This countered the oft-repeated slaveholders' claim that the Bible supported slavery (Abraham had slaves; the apostle Paul returned a slave to his master; though, as Lincoln pointed out, these were white men enslaving white men), and so perhaps even this could be seen less as the language of belief than the language of persuasion aimed at an audience that might want to ground its antislavery leanings in Scripture. "I shall be vindicated," Lincoln once told his friend Newton Bateman, an Illinois school superintendent, "and these men will find that they have not read their Bibles aright."

As the nominee for the Republican Party in 1860, Lincoln was the subject of more than a dozen party-produced campaign biographies. In what some have called the most trustworthy of these, the one written by Chicago journalist John Locke Scripps and based on an interview with Lincoln, the candidate is said to be a "regular attendant upon religious worship, and though not a communicant, is a pew-holder and liberal supporter of the Presbyterian church in Springfield, to which Mrs. Lincoln belongs." Other press claims included the observation that Lincoln "always held up the doctrines of the Bible, and the truths and examples of the Christian religion, as the foundation of all good." (In the Scripps biography Lincoln is famously quoted describing his early life by referencing one of his beloved Graveyard Poets: "It can all be condensed into a single sentence, and that sentence you will find in Gray's Elegy: 'The short and simple annals of the poor.'") This, too, might seem like campaign rhetoric, but if he did not really believe, then why was Lincoln so taken with making references to the Almighty, more, one might add, than any president before him? "I now leave, not knowing when, or whether ever, I may return, with a task before me greater than that which rested upon Washington," he said to those gathered at a Springfield train station to see the president-elect off. "Without the assistance of that Divine Being, who ever attended him, I cannot succeed. With that assistance I cannot fail. Trusting in Him, who can go with me, and remain with you and be everywhere for good, let us confidently hope that all will yet be well. To His care commending you, as I hope in your prayers you will commend me, I bid you an affectionate farewell."

By the time of his inaugural, it appeared as though Lincoln had assumed the posture of a casual believer (if that is not a contradiction) or a public believer (if that is not too cynical), which may not be the same as saying he was a true believer, but is more than one might have expected after his New Salem days. Appealing to the rebel states, he asked for patience: "Intelligence, patriotism, Christianity, and a firm reliance on Him who has never yet forsaken this favored land are still competent to adjust in the best way all our present difficulty." Lincoln and Mary declined the offer of a pew at the First Presbyterian Church, "the church of the presidents," where Jackson, Polk, Pierce, and Buchanan— all Democrats—had worshipped because he sought a church that would be "aloof from politics." He finally settled on the New York Avenue Presbyterian Church, which had experienced a schism between Old School Presbyterians and New School Presbyterians, much like the schism of the Baptists. Here, under the direction of Dr. Phineas Densmore Gurley, the Old School had prevailed. While Gurley was against slavery and against secession, he confined his preaching "to the great central doctrines of the cross." Lincoln and Gurley maintained a friendly, though never close, relationship. Their separate approaches to religious devotion may have created a gap too large to bridge. Still, the president once told Gurley and several other Presbyterian ministers, "I have often wished I was a more devout man than I am."

Noah Brooks, a California journalist who had almost daily access to Lincoln from late 1862, remembered the president's reading habits as being eclectic—the Bible (especially the Old

Testament, from which he frequently quoted), English philosopher Joseph Butler's *Analogy of Religion*, and the works of the English political philosopher John Stuart Mill forming a "queer companionship" with the comic writings of David R. Locke, the popular poetry of Thomas Hood, Oliver Wendell Holmes Sr.—especially "September Gale," about the 1815 hurricane that struck New England—and Henry Wadsworth Longfellow's "Birds of Killingworth," which Brooks said Lincoln found printed in a newspaper, cut out, and "carried in his vest pocket until he had committed it to memory." That memory was often on display, both in his ability to quote chapter and verse on Scriptural passages and to "repeat from memory whole chapters" of his favorite humorists before his staff, "preserv[ing] his own gravity" while his audience was convulsed in laughter. Lincoln had little patience for anyone who lacked a sense of humor, once commenting of Salmon Chase that "it required a surgical operation to get a joke into his head."

However, if, during these White House days, Lincoln's secular fascinations had a prime outlet, it was likely to have been the theater. While evangelicals still held suspicions about the morality of the stage and its stories, even looking upon them as competitors for the souls of the religiously unattached, Lincoln spent dozens of evenings in the audience of Washington theaters watching both stage plays and operas. He found drama, particularly Shakespearean drama, among the greatest of human artistic achievements, and he thrilled to the performances of the best actors of his day, which included the Booth brothers Edwin and John Wilkes. Once, after watching a particularly stirring performance by the latter in Charles Selby's *The Marble Heart* (Booth, presaging his place in history, played the villain), Lincoln invited the actor to come visit him in the presidential box, but he was rebuffed.

"He was not a technical Christian," Mary Lincoln explained to Herndon years after Lincoln's death, a strange term that seems to suggest that Lincoln was indeed Christian, just some other kind of Christian, some "nontechnical" Christian, which may also have been her way of saying that while Lincoln was not inspired by the dogma of the faith, he practiced grace, forgiveness, and humility, virtues that could be described as elements of a Christian life. In what sounds like a sentiment straight out of the Gospel of Luke, Mary recalled that Lincoln's response to his harshest of critics was to "do good to those who hate you and turn their ill will into friendship."

Mary recognized these qualities as Lincoln's "poetic" nature, and others who knew the president similarly described him as possessed of a special gift, a kind of "natural religion" appropriate for a historic figure we tend to believe arose from the earth unschooled, unrefined, yet essentially human in his yearnings for understanding and guidance. By this thinking his was a simple, vulnerable faith, eschewing ritual and tradition, doctrine and dependency, yet embracing a fundamental generosity of spirit. It was also a very American religion in that it was personally crafted by Lincoln in the here and now, borrowing something from reading, from insight, and from experience, realizing the relationship with God anew, realizing it singularly for himself, and yet at the same time framing this relationship in philosophical terms applicable to the national situation. Lincoln's personal God was not the personal God of the evangelicals. They, too, believed in a "present" religion, but unlike the evangelical, Lincoln did not act to gain God's grace. He did not pray for favors or assistance for the missions of his life. He acted because he thought it right by the laws of reason to act, and if he prayed— the journalist Noah Brooks claimed, in a dubious account, that Lincoln regularly prayed—it was likely for nothing more than the strength to see God's plan through, for Lincoln believed God's grace was God's to give, not his to earn and certainly not his to request. Confident though he might be in his perception of right, he was humbled to think that he could also be wrong, that life was made up of both reasonable forces (those we understand) and unreasonable forces (those we do not). "What is to be will be," Herndon remembered him often saying, "and no *prayers* of ours can reverse the decree."

Lincoln's religious views have a core contradiction: we must act as if we have free will and yet finally accede to powers that would deny it. That is why his parting words to the Chicago ministers who had been demanding that he emancipate the slaves are now so intriguing. When he says, *Whatever shall appear to be God's will, I will do*, what he really means is, whether he succeeds or fails in his own intentions, God's master plan will be at work. Or, reframing his words, *Whatever I do shall appear to be God's will*. This statement was no toss-off. He meant what he said.

Curiously for his time, religion did not seem to provide Lincoln comfort, not that he appears to have sought comfort from it. Mary Lincoln told Herndon that only after the sudden death of their son Willie had Lincoln "seemed to think about the subject," which is not true unless what she meant was that only after the death of his favorite child did Lincoln's exploration of religion become an impassioned search for meaning instead of his more detached intellectual or philosophical pursuit of before. It is tantalizing to consider what Lincoln did, alone, on the Thursdays he was said to set aside for grieving for his dead son, but even if he spent that time in prayer, he would probably not have expected an appeal to the Almighty to change his awful personal loss any more than a hands-clasped entreaty could be expected to stop the ghastly carnage in Virginia. Reflecting the Calvinist fatalism of his parents, Lincoln appeared to accept that if God set the plan, he had set a particularly devastating one for Lincoln. " 'There's a divinity that shapes our ends,'" Lincoln would often say, quoting *Hamlet*, " 'rough-hew them how we will.'"

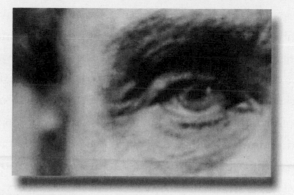

VII.

ONE DAY:
SEPTEMBER 17, 1862

EVERY NATION HAS a worst day at war. For America, it was September 17, 1862, the seventy-fifth anniversary of the writing of the Constitution, when nearly twenty-three thousand casualties were counted, including twice as many American deaths as were suffered in the entire course of the Mexican War. By percentage of the nation's population, the loss would be comparable today to 222,000 dead, wounded, or missing, and all on a stubborn tract of rugged cornfield in the western region of Maryland, sixty miles from the nation's capital. There were roughly sixty-six hundred American casualties in the invasion of Normandy in 1944. Imagine the losses of four Normandy invasions wrapped into twelve hours of one September day and you will have a sense of the blood that was spilled at Antietam. Yet even these numbers likely do not provide the full dimensions of the loss, for there was no adequate way to quantify the range of destruction, the missing who, like crippled animals, crawled off to die in some remote shaded wood, the diseased who expired months later from infection (more malaria, dysentery, and typhoid), and the injured who, though never healed, went on to fight elsewhere until one wound was compounded by a second and the second by a third, a life cruelly lost in stages. More than any other battle to that awful day, Antietam proved Lincoln's 1861 description of this Civil War as "a people's contest," for so many people—"plain people," as he called them—died here.

The battle was more like a natural disaster than a clash of armies, a cyclone ripping through the brush and the streams unannounced, leaving death in its wake. Yes, Antietam had a strategic importance. It was Lee invading Maryland to square off against McClellan, a turning point for the war, being the first time that Union soldiers were defending Union-held soil, but it all happened so quickly and with such explosive force that when the killing was over, and Lee, in what made it a qualified Union victory, had retreated back toward Virginia (unpursued by the ever-cautious McClellan, to Lincoln's great regret), surviving soldiers surveying the earth through the early-morning fog witnessed the gruesome sight of thousands of inert bodies, both Union and Confederate, many of them ripped apart to where they barely even resembled a human form. The scene was so littered with corpses and sections of corpses and *sections of sections of corpses* that, it was said, you could walk it without ever touching the ground. Nothing in the history of battle warfare compares with the single-day casualties suffered at the beginning of the Battle of the Somme in World War I, when thirty thousand died in the first twenty-four hours, twenty thousand of them British, but when historians write of the American Civil War as foreshadowing the Western Front, the images from Antietam are among those that animate their imaginations.

"Certainly the joy of conflict was not ours that day," wrote David L. Thompson of the Ninth New York, the anticipated thrill of killing and lying in fear of your own death being something that only soldiers who have never been in combat claim. ". . . As we rose and started all the fire that had been held back so long was loosed. In a second the air was full of the hiss of bullets and the hurtle of grape-shot." Thompson, whose justly famous essay on his experience was written twenty years after the fact, coined a memorable phrase there, which has come to be associated with Antietam. Borrowing from Goethe's description of a battle in the Napoleonic Wars (the Civil War was the first in which the fighting forces could both read and write, though a fluency with the writings of Goethe demonstrates something more than being simply "literate"), Thompson wrote, "The whole landscape . . . turned slightly red." To that, he might have added Goethe's description of the power of red: a "peculiar" color that "conveys . . . the dignity of age and the amiableness of youth" in the same hue.

The things one saw at Antietam challenged even the most battle-hardened soldier's sensibilities. A captain in McClellan's army observed bodies that were "already far advanced in putrefication, hideously swollen, and many of them black as soot."

Some, he wrote, were "so covered with dust, torn, crushed, and trampled that they resembled clods of earth, and you were obliged to look twice before recognizing them as human remains." The diary of another witness detailed a man "with a hole in his belly about as big as a hat and about a quart of dark-looking maggots working away." The business of dying was slow, even when consciousness had long ago slipped away, with blood and gas expelling from every orifice for hours. "Arms, legs, feet, and hands [were] lying in piles rotting in the blazing heat," wrote a surgeon from the 121st New York volunteers, "unburied and uncared for." The journalist Albert Deane Richardson observed dead bodies, piled "like cord-wood," and with blackened faces (and how ironic was that for a war over which the fate of the darker race hung?). "There were forms with every rigid muscle strained in fierce agony, and those with hands folded peacefully upon the bosom; some still clutching their guns, others with arm upraised, and one with a single open finger pointing to heaven. Several remained hanging over a fence which they were climbing when the fatal shot struck them."

The horror lasted long after that first morning, too, with the odor of decaying flesh filling the air around western Maryland for months, and the wounded occupying houses, barns, and churches over miles, turning the area, as a local newspaper reported, into "one vast hospital." Horse-drawn ambulances were trafficking throughout the area with "the wounded men hollering, 'Oh, Lord, Oh, Lord,'" recalled a witness, ". . . and the blood running down through the bottom of the wagons." Nearly a year later, when the soldiers of Lee's army marched back north on their way to their defeat at Gettysburg, a repugnant discovery awaited them: the Confederate dead from Antietam, having only hastily been buried in shallow graves, had been unearthed by foraging animals, the flesh picked off the carcasses, and the dry bones left to bleach in the sun.

A handful of images tell the story of Antietam. One is farmer David R. Miller's cornfield, abutting the Hagerstown Pike. Miller was preparing to harvest his thirty or so acres of crop, corn that he used as feed for his cattle, when the peaceful, rustic scene became instead a picture of hell: "The men are loading and firing with demoniacal fury," wrote Major Rufus Dawes of the Sixth Wisconsin regarding the cornfield assault, ". . . shouting and laughing hysterically and the whole field before us is covered with rebels fleeing for life, into the [adjacent] woods." One Texas regiment lost 82 percent of its men—hundreds—in just forty-five minutes. Union general Joe Hooker described the field after battle as having every cornstalk cut closely as if with a knife and the bodies of the slain "in rows precisely as they had stood in their ranks a few moments before."

Then there is the "sunken road," though it was not really a road at all, but a lane improvised through the fields by wagon wheels persistently eroding the earth as farmers looked to bypass the town of Sharpsburg. In this shallow trench, on the morning of the seventeenth, a Confederate division of twenty-six hundred faced off against a Union assault of more than twice that number. More than five thousand were killed or wounded in this spot in less than four hours. By the time the smoke had cleared, the sunken road had been rechristened Bloody Lane. More than seven hundred men—Confederate and Union soldiers both—were interred nearby in mass graves carved in the fields of William Roulette's farm.

The most famous image from Antietam is Dunker Church.

How ironic that the meeting place for a little German sect that had split from the Baptist Church and was nicknamed for its practice of dunking the whole body at baptisms should become the centerpiece of any battle. While the Dunkers were against the practice of slavery, they were also pacifists and refused on religious principle to serve in either the Union or Confederate armies. Those in western Maryland had met in a local home until 1852, when they proudly built their own modest prayer building. Worshippers there on September 14, 1862—the Sunday before the battle—recalled hearing the sounds of cannon fire coming from off in the distance, an omen of the fighting that would reach their churchyard three days later. On the day of the battle, the church became a focal point of the combat, its walls riddled with bullets, a mockery of the convictions held there. As the number of wounded began to mount, the structure was converted into a makeshift clinic, and then, when the number of dead competed with the number of injured, an embalming station. Not even God's house, such as it was, offered escape from the horrors of Antietam.

Finally, there is Rohrbach Bridge, after Henry Rohrbach, whose acres adjoined it. The graceful limestone and granite structure had been built by the Dunkers for transporting their produce and livestock over Antietam Creek on the way to Sharpsburg. But at roughly noon on the day of the battle, it became the scene of fierce, hours-long fighting between a small number of Confederates and the Union Army's Ninth Corps, under the command of General Ambrose Burnside, whose repeated attempts to take the bridge were resisted while McClellan refused Burnside's request for reinforcements. When the Ninth Corps finally broke through, it had cost the Union five hundred casualties, the Confederates, one hundred and twenty. Today, it is known as Burnside's Bridge.

Antietam was important not only for what happened there, but for its lingering effects. For weeks, a long stream of soldiers straggled through the arteries leading from the battlefield—a "caravan of maimed pilgrims," in the words of the writer Oliver Wendell Holmes Sr. ". . . delicate boys, with more spirit than strength, flushed with fever or pale with exhaustion or haggard with suffering, [dragging] their weary limbs along." Beside them were search parties composed of families and other loved ones looking through the detritus of battle for a sign that maybe, just maybe, while thousands of other soldiers had died, *their* soldier would be found among the limping.

Holmes himself was in search of his son Captain Oliver Wendell Holmes Jr., who, he knew, from a letter received back in Boston, had been hit in the shoulder—the intruder came in through the "central seam of coat and waistcoat collar" and departed on the other side, was the way the younger Holmes had described it—but the letter offered little else, leaving his father's considerable imagination to flights of fancy (Holmes Sr. was among the most popular writers of his day). This was Captain Holmes's second brush with mortality on a Civil War battlefield, having nearly bled to death from an injury at Ball's Bluff in 1861, and his father, who in addition to being a writer was a professor at Harvard Medical School, had equipped him with a bottle of laudanum—an opiate popular at the time as a painkiller and, when used in excess dosage, as a means of suicide—should the pain prompt him to hurry his own passing.

Walking through churches where the pews had been overlaid with boards, straw strewn on the boards, and the wounded laid on the straw, the older Holmes now looked from bed to bed for a recognizable face before he learned that his son—the future Supreme Court justice, who served with distinction until almost the time of President Franklin Roosevelt—was healing well and had been seen departing the area in the back of a milk cart on his way to the home of friends in Philadelphia. Many other search parties were not so lucky.

Captain Holmes made a full recovery and returned to fight in the Battle of Chancellorsville eight months later, but his experience at Antietam stayed with him. While he was on the Supreme Court, he carried his lunch in a painted tin ammunition box saved from his days in battle, and every year he privately toasted his dead comrades on the anniversary of the Antietam fighting. Upon Holmes's own death in 1935, the two musket balls that had been removed from his body were found preserved among his personal effects and two Civil War uniforms were discovered hanging in his closet. On one was pinned an explanatory note, almost defensive in tone, as if to leave no doubt as to the centrality of this event in his life: "These uniforms were worn by me in the Civil War and the stains upon them are my blood."

Photographers recorded the scene at Antietam, most notably the Scottish immigrant Alexander Gardner, who, working for the legendary photographer Mathew Brady (until late 1862, when Gardner struck out on his own, Brady's name is on most all of Gardner's work), rushed from Washington, arriving in time to see the aftermath of the fighting. Had he reached there the day of the battle, Gardner would have been frustrated by the speed of the action. Camera exposures took ten or more minutes to complete, and subjects needed to hold still during that time, which is one reason no one is ever seen smiling in a nineteenth-century photographic portrait (metal head braces employed for the purpose of keeping the subject still only made the experience more grim). But the dead turned out to be cooperative subjects. Wandering the battlefield, Gardner took multiple pictures of corpses, seventy pictures in four days, most of them focused on inert bodies, each contorted in some pathetic final gesture of surrender. They are the images that have burnished Antietam into our national consciousness. It is our Somme.

The first war photographs were the work of British photographers in the Crimea in the 1850s, most importantly Roger Fenton. But these were documentary only in the most formal, sanitized way, showing portraits and stark landscapes where one could well imagine that battle had once occurred, but imagine it only. Fenton was a friend of the royal couple, Victoria and Albert, and he had either been instructed, or it was simply his well-mannered British instinct, not to show the real devastation of war. His task was essentially that of a propagandist: to confirm for British society the rightness of the conflict and the heroism that attended the English soldier in battle. Most important, he was to avoid any image that might challenge war policy by joining it with a dose of reality. War was good and noble and worthy.

That left it to Gardner a decade later to show war's human sacrifice, to suggest something substantive about the business of war, which is the business of slaughter. ("Organized murder" is the phrase one historian used to describe this war.) Given the newness of the medium, the stark challenge that such work posed to accepted norms of journalism and the patriotic fervor that still gripped the nation on both sides of the conflict, Gardner's work, although he did not consider himself a journalist, represents a remarkable act of reportorial bravery.

Gardner's boss, Brady, was the era's celebrated portraitist. His 1850 set of plates *The Gallery of Illustrious Americans* had brought him attention for its pictures of Andrew Jackson, Daniel Webster, John J. Audubon, and John Calhoun, among others (actually, they were lithographs made from his daguerreotypes, which was the only way at the time of reproducing large quantities of "prints"). But Brady, it could be said, was a painterly photographer. He had learned his craft from, of all people, Samuel F. B. Morse—the artist-turned-telegraph-pioneer we met in chapter 3 (how history sometimes appears as but the story of a handful of intimates). Morse was among the first to dabble in the new technology of the daguerreotype in the 1840s, but in the way that new technologies, until they explain themselves to us, are usually defined according to the norms and traditions of an existing medium, Morse referred to his output as "photographic paintings," and he taught Brady that the camera was an extension of the artist's brush.

By the time of the Civil War, most photographers—and many were roaming the battlefield with the sketch artists, in excess of three hundred at some times attached to the Army of the Potomac—followed the predictable, and financially rewarding, approach of the portraitist, tacking up a cloth backdrop in camp and snapping proud poses of soldiers gleaming in their finery, then printing them in a hastily constructed on-site darkroom so they could be offered up as *cartes de visite* to loved ones back home. Gardner, too, did his fair share of these—he needed the money—but in his other work he separated himself from the crowd, especially in the way that he, with prescience, began to work to the new medium's strength. Morse was wrong. Photography was not simply a quicker and more profitable method by which to do a painting. With photography, art was secondary to the magic of truth-telling, to the way that this new tool could "capture" reality, alter time and space by sealing the imagistic details of a scene so that it lived on forever. "Fast seeing" is how the American modernist Alvin Langdon Coburn is said to have cleverly described this quality of photography in 1918. But that was after the phonograph and the automobile and the airplane had been invented. The camera was the first of these miracle machines. When we think of Gardner's "fast seeing," we have to understand the wonder it appeared to be in an era still driven by the horse and buggy.

The more he explored this truth-telling potential, the more Gardner became photography's dark and brooding messenger. If Brady's shots of well-turned-out senior officers made war look like heroic work, the stuff of manly righteousness, Gardner's shots put the lie to all that, his pictures displaying big, wide swaths of battle landscape where the bodies of the fallen soldiers appear not as the sacrifice of virtue, but as the inanimate debris of savage encounter. No war painting ever did what Gardner's pictures did; here there was no myth of grandeur, only fact. They were "so nearly like visiting the battlefield . . ."—Holmes Sr. again, reacting to Gardner's work in the *Atlantic Monthly*—"that all the emotions exerted by the actual sight of the stained and sordid scene, strewed with rags and wrecks, came back to us, and we buried them in the recesses of our cabinet as we would have buried the mutilated remains of the dead they too vividly represented."

Through Gardner, and others who began to work like him, Morse's camera-as-brush equation was reversed, photography leading painting now instead of the other way around. The greatest American artist working during the Civil War was Winslow Homer, who shunned the war-art tradition of set scenes, battle-field charges, and parades in favor of private moments recorded as he saw them—a sharpshooter perched in a tree, an army doctor tending to his patient, a farmer swinging a scythe through a wheat field that presumably was once a scene of battle. There were no corpses or blood but there was no manipulative veneer either. These were snapshots rendered in paint.

War is a private affair, as any veteran of combat will tell you. Since the beginning of time, this has separated the soldier—especially the infantryman—from the rest of us, making it impossible for him to find comfort anywhere but in the company of those who have seen what he has seen (*intimate violence* is the term sometimes used in psychiatric research) and done what he has done (kill or run from being killed, neither of which provides comfort to the soul). This private hell is, perhaps, the root of what we today call *post-traumatic stress disorder,* and what the post–Civil War medical community called, alternately, *irritable heart* or, simply, *nostalgia*, wildly innocent terms for something we now understand to be lonely, grave, and irreversible. Simply put, it is the terror that is experienced when the mind cannot discard a memory because there is no satisfying narrative to explain it away (that would be the "irritating" bit) and no way to reconcile it with the life that one understood before one had to go to war (there's the "nostalgia"). It is lonely precisely because no words, when used to describe this mental anguish, can break its grip. "How shall I speak?" says the war-hardened soldier in Herman Melville's *Battle-Pieces.* "Thoughts knot with thoughts, and utterance check." Melville wrote the poem in 1866.

Yet now, for the first time, pictures—pictures!—afforded a

peek into the soldier's hell. A month after the fighting, when Gardner's images were shown at Brady's New York gallery under a starkly descriptive title, *The Dead at Antietam,* a *New York Times* reporter wrote that the experience was as if the cameraman had "brought bodies and laid them in our dooryards and along the streets" for all to see. He noticed "hushed, reveren[t] groups standing around these weird copies of carnage . . . chained by the strange spell that dwells in dead men's eyes." For the first time, they had gazed behind the soldier's private curtain.

A writer from *Harper's Weekly* demonstrated the same voyeuristic fascination for Gardner's pictures. They showed, he wrote, "beautiful stretches of pastoral scenery, disfigured by the evidences of strife," the "dead grouped in every imaginal [*sic*] position, the stiffened limbs preserving the same attitude as that maintained by the sufferers in their last agonies." It all had an almost morbid attraction for him. "Minute as are the features of the dead, and unrecognizable by the naked eye, you can, by bringing a magnifying glass to bear on them, identify not merely their general outline, but actual expression. This, in many instances, is perfectly horrible, and shows through what tortures the poor victims must have passed before they were relieved from their sufferings." Before long, the magnifying glass would be unnecessary. In 1864, Gardner introduced his *Incidents of War,* a lantern slide show in which his pictures of the dead were projected on a six-hundred-square-foot canvas in a New York City theater, a prefigure of the motion picture. Patrons were charged twenty-five cents a ticket for the prurient thrill of watching a steady stream of suffering and death.

Gruesome though they may have been, these images, too, were reproduced on *cartes de visite* and passed around as social currency. Some of the fascination no doubt had to do with the way that such mangled corpses looked—young boys who met the soldier's sad end not with a simple peaceful closing of the eyes but with a dismembering episode of mechanized violence. Few had witnessed the results of such butchery ever before. "The dead of the battlefield come up to us very rarely, even in dreams," continued the *Times* reporter. "We see the list in the morning paper at breakfast, but dismiss its recollection with the coffee. . . ." There was also something supernatural about a photograph of the dead, something akin to the fascination with the séance and with spiritualism that Mary Lincoln and others had shown. A painting is so clearly a representation of life—no one would confuse it for life itself—but the photograph was something very different. Many thought the camera to be a paranormal contraption capable of lifting the "ghost" from a body, be it a portrait or, as here, a shot of the lifeless body. Lincoln, who sat for Brady many times, once described the experience as having his "shaddow" taken, and looking at pictures, many people shared the feeling of a reviewer of Gardner's lantern slide show, who found the depictions of the dead, ironically, so "life-like" that it appeared as though they were "almost to speak" to him.

Finally, from a different point of view, perhaps the one that lingered, the images of the dead had to have prompted a reassessment of the relationship between war and those for whom the war was being fought. For Gardner was showing not simply a record of war but also the human price of war, and where one recognizes a price, questions of value are raised. Was it worth it? Did the preservation of the Union justify all the young death dreadfully portrayed, the bodies twisted and contorted into odd shapes, frozen for all time, all the dark indignity? Despite the centuries of literature and art glorifying the martyred warrior, there is no assured nobility to a battle death except that which we apply afterward when we say, yes, he died, but he died for *this; this* freedom, *this* idea, *this something*. Those of the Confederacy could say, "He died defending his homeland from invasion," to ignore the defense of slavery per se and adhere instead to the idea that he had been sacrificed to protect the loamy soil of Southern tradition and culture, what was often summed up in the code as the "Southern way of life." But what could be said about the Union soldiers who perished here? That they died so sons of Virginians would be required to call themselves Americans, that the people of South Carolina and Alabama would be compelled to accept a national kinship with those from Maine and New York? Was "union" an ideal that stirred such feelings of justifiable sacrifice? Could a war, or, more precisely, *this* war, this ruthless war, really be fought on such terms?

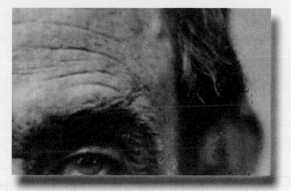

VIII.

PRELIMINARIES

During the battle of Antietam, Lincoln spent his hours—where else?—in the War Department telegraph office waiting for news. He had hoped for a more commanding victory than the one that McClellan gave him. He had told the general he wanted him to not merely repel Lee. Lincoln wanted him to destroy the rebel army or, at the least, not let Lee get off "without being hurt." But McClellan continued to be the same cautious, timid operations chief he had been in the humiliating Peninsula Campaign earlier in the year. He claimed that he didn't have enough soldiers (in fact he had eighty thousand, while Lee had just thirty-seven thousand), he felt that there wasn't enough time to get ready (actually, he had squandered the time he had, allowing Lee to gain a more favorable position), and perhaps most important, he had begun to sniff out Lincoln's emancipation plan and didn't like it. Some among McClellan's staff had said that they should refuse to engage with Lee and simply countermarch to Washington, where they would confront Lincoln himself until he backed down on his plan to interfere with slavery. Even as he was fighting one of the bloodiest battles in American history, it appeared as though McClellan liked the idea of a limited success, one in which he let his enemy live another day. And this, while Union casualties, bloated by the Second Battle of Bull Run, by Harpers Ferry, by a handful of smaller battles, and, of course, now by the battle at Antietam Creek, had reached 212,249.

Antietam was certainly not the victory that Seward was thinking of back in July when he warned Lincoln to pause, to put his proclamation in his pocket, and to wait for better timing, for a moment when he could issue emancipation from a position of strength so that it would appear not as "the last measure of an exhausted government," but as a triumphant flourish to a Union surge. No matter. It was good enough to serve as the trigger for his long-awaited act. Lincoln had planned it this way, or so he claimed, almost boastfully. "When Lee came over the river, I made a resolve that when McClellan drove him back—and I expected he would do it sometime or other—I would send the Proclamation after him," the president told George S. Boutwell, the former Massachusetts governor who served under Lincoln as the nation's first commissioner of Internal Revenue. "The battle of Antietam was fought Wednesday, and until Saturday I could not find out whether we had gained a victory or lost . . . [so] I fixed [the proclamation] up a little Sunday, and Monday I let them have it." But his comments here came several weeks after the fact. When he was in the moment, when he stood before the cabinet on September 22, 1862, the Monday after the terrible carnage at Antietam Creek, where once again his general had let him down, and told them—anxiously, it would seem, from all indications—that he was ready to issue an executive order of emancipation, Lincoln said that it was not so much his idea as a sign from the Almighty that prompted him to commit to this new, and potentially dangerous, policy now. He had made a covenant with God, he told the men assembled before him—Chase and Stanton to his right; Bates, Blair, Welles, and the others to his left—none of whom was familiar with Lincoln's speaking so reverently. If Lee were driven back to Virginia, he would look upon that as a sign of divine intention, a message that God himself "had decided this question in favor of the slaves." And since Lee had indeed been driven back, well, now Lincoln was ready to carry out God's wishes.

Knowing the conclusion of their July meeting, and knowing that reports from Antietam had indicated a qualified Union victory, and then hearing that Lincoln, after spending the weekend at his Soldiers' Home retreat, had returned to the White House early on Sunday morning the twenty-first and locked himself away to work, both Chase and Lincoln's secretary, John Milton Hay, had been thinking that the proclamation was in its last bits of preparation. But they had no notion that the future of slavery hung on a "covenant with God." Chase could not believe his ears when Lincoln told of the promise he had made "to myself"—here, all agree, he hesitated a bit as if he anticipated the shock—

"and to my Maker." Chase asked the president to repeat himself, just to be certain there was no mistake.

Had Lincoln, the religious skeptic, been transformed, enlightened by the light of the heavens, or was this claim just another sign—there were so many in these months!—that this man of character and principle was susceptible, no less than those around him, to the fear and confusion that attended this searing crisis? Was he God's instrument or *was God Lincoln's instrument*, the president using this convenient handoff as a way of distancing himself from the awful responsibility, not only of a constitutionally suspect policy that could lead to slave riots and a deeper war, to a loss of the Border States, and maybe even to a loss of the Union, but of an act no mortal should think his to make? Freeing people? It was our nature to be free, something endowed by our Creator. God could free people, but a country lawyer? "He liked to think he was the attorney of the people," wrote Noah Brooks of Lincoln, "not their ruler."

The men were equally surprised by Lincoln's approach to the topic that morning, which began with, of all things, a humorous story. The nation had just suffered its worst day at war on top of its worst summer at war, the air throughout Virginia and Maryland perfumed with the fetid odor of death, the landscape strewn with fragments of innominate victims, bereavement now the central binding national emotion, yet Lincoln opened this first cabinet meeting after such unprecedented bloodshed not with an expression of the commonality of grief or with the requisite gesture of memorial, but with a reading from the work of Maine humorist Charles Farrar Browne. It is hard to fathom, but Abraham Lincoln appeared to have decided on an "icebreaker" before announcing that 4 million would be released from the chains of bondage.

"Gentlemen," he began, "did you ever read anything from Artemus Ward?" Ward was Browne's pen name and comic persona, a country bumbler who spoke the language of satire in a dialect we might associate with Mark Twain, and indeed Twain apparently looked upon Browne-Ward as an inspiration for his own work, though the author of *Huckleberry Finn* and *Tom Sawyer* was an infinitely better writer, evidenced, interestingly, by Twain's description of Browne himself when he saw him performing as Artemus Ward onstage: "He looked like a glove-stretcher. His hair, red and brushed well forward at the sides, reminded one of a divided flame. His nose rambled on aggressively before him, with all the strength and determination of a cow-catcher, while his red moustache—to follow out the simile—seemed not unlike the unfortunate cow."

While Ward's farcical vignettes took a run at a few sacred institutions and the Mormon Church (his *Artemus Ward Among the Mormons* was penned 150 years before Broadway's *Book of Mormon*), and gently mocked wilderness simplicity, most of them do not translate well across the generations, certainly not as satire, not even as humor. The story Lincoln chose that morning, "High-Handed Outrage at Utica," was no exception. "Let me read you a chapter that is very funny," said the president. Lincoln then recited Ward's inane scene of a man in "Utiky, a trooly great sitty in the State of New York," who put on a display of wax figures of the Last Supper. Suddenly, a "burly feller" walked up, grabbed Judas Iscariot, and pounded him as hard as he could while demanding to know what Ward had brought this "pussylanermus cus here fur." Shocked, Ward told the man that it was a mere wax figure and not the real Judas, whereupon the attacker showed that this made no difference to him, for "Judas Iscarrot can't show hisself in Utiky with impurnety by a darn site." (As I said, it doesn't travel well.)

When Lincoln finished, there was silence in the room. Seward smiled to acknowledge the "humor," and Chase may have as well. But Stanton was particularly offended at the president's inappropriate tone and wrote about it in his diary. Then Lincoln shifted to a "graver" subject (what wouldn't be graver than Artemus Ward?), the proclamation. Welles remembered Lincoln again repeating his stipulation that the act and its consequences were his ("His decision was fixed and unalterable"), but he wanted them to know what he was doing and to invite their criticism, by which he meant an analysis of the language and details. As to his having looked to God as the final determining force, he acknowledged in what Welles described as a "subdued tone" that this may have seemed "strange" but that "the way was not clear to his mind" and so it appeared more convenient to submit "the disposal of the subject to a Higher Power," and then abide by the "Supreme Will." Lincoln then read the document aloud.

Welles described the discussion as long, earnest, and "harmonious," with few objections raised. (If God and not Lincoln had made this decision, what objection *could* be raised?) The only substantial voice of caution came again from Bates, who now worried that the proclamation would push the Border States to the secessionists and that it would encourage the rise of an opposition party in the North. Lincoln responded that he had of course considered the potential for both outcomes, but that he had still deemed it better to act than not to act.

This document and the one Lincoln had presented to the cabinet in July differed. Like the July draft, this Preliminary Emancipation Proclamation (as it was known) began by reasserting the mission of the war as the restoration of the constitutional relation between the states. Lincoln did not want to sound an alarm otherwise. Yet from there, the rest of the document was framed, essentially, as a threat. The rebel states had until January 1, 1863, to cease their hostilities or the provisions of the proclamation would be enforced. Again, as in the July draft, Lincoln softened that threat by offering compensation to those states that quit the rebellion now and decided to outlaw the practice of slavery, whether that process was gradual or immediate. But in this version, picking up on Bates's suggestion from July to "send them away," Lincoln added that "the effort to colonize persons of African descent . . . upon this continent, or elsewhere," would continue. The difference was that Bates had wanted compulsory deportations of the former slaves, while Lincoln, though only after taking a suggestion from Seward, stressed that any such moves had to be with the consent of those being colonized. (Seward's handwritten corrections can be seen on the document itself.) The whole atmosphere—the drama, the sudden religiosity, the awkward attempts at humor—as well as these little shifts and emendations in the document reflected Lincoln's preoccupations ("perplexities" was the evocative word that Nicolay and Hay used) during the two months since he had first introduced his proclamation plan: concerns that the races could never live together in harmony; puzzlement over faith and questions as to why God would so test him and his nation; an increasingly brutal war that he had once thought would be short and decisive; and a futile wish that somehow he would not have to do this, that he would wake up one day and the rebel states would have magically decided to end their secessionist adventure, rejoined the Union, and begun the gradual eradication of slavery.

Other differences in the September proclamation were critical. Embedded within Lincoln's dense legal linguistics was a calculated attempt to blunt the obvious criticism that he was assuming powers outside the Constitution. He had been enduring such criticism since the outset of the war when, after a mob of rebels prevented the passage of Union troops through Baltimore, he suspended the writ of habeas corpus, that bulwark of English law that protects against the arbitrary use of power by requiring a court to review the arrest of any person—the phrase is literally translated as "you have the body," meaning the detainee's body—and upon an argument for his or her custody either approve it as legal or deny it, setting the person free. Because the habeas right is such a time-honored practice dating back to the days of the Magna Carta (if not before), the Constitution allows for its suspension only in the most extreme instances, "when in Cases of Rebellion or Invasion the public safety may require it." But it is unclear as to who actually gets to do the suspending— Congress or the president. Lincoln decided it was his power to wield, and he assigned Secretary Seward to oversee the arrest and detention of all Southern activists. Seward—in what may be an apocryphal story dreamed up to discredit the administration—is reported to have bragged to a British minister, "I can touch a bell on my right hand and order the arrest of a citizen in Ohio. I can touch a bell again and order the imprisonment of a citizen in New York, and no power on Earth but that of the President can release them. Can the Queen of England, in her dominions, say as much?"

Naturally, many voices objected to this reading of the Constitution, but the most important of these belonged to Roger Brooke Taney, chief justice of the Supreme Court. Taney was a tall, sallow-cheeked Marylander who served as US attorney general, secretary of the treasury, and, for the last twenty-eight years of his life, as chief justice. He was a Jacksonian Democrat—Andrew Jackson appointed him to his cabinet and then to the Court—and once practiced law with "Star-Spangled Banner" author Francis Scott Key. Taney was married to Key's sister. In the surviving pictures of him, he looks like an aged Oscar Wilde, a long, dramatic shock of hair careening across his forehead. But where Wilde's face had an impish quality (he was, after all, Oscar Wilde), Taney's supported a perpetual scowl. He is justly famous for his simply awful decision in *Dred Scott*, but before that banner headline was applied to his career, Taney was something of a political moderate whose tenure on the Court was distinctive for his work on whether the Constitution's Commerce Clause gave the federal government exclusive power to regulate corporations or whether that power was shared with the states (Taney's Court said it shared this power). Even on slavery, Taney was initially more flexible than his reputation acknowledges. As a young man, he freed his own slaves and publicly described the practice as immoral. But he was no believer in racial equality and had, since his youth, grown increasingly protective of Southern culture and traditions. Remarkable though it may seem, Taney thought that by settling the question against black citizenship and declaring Congress powerless to legislate on the legality of slavery in the new Western territories, *Dred Scott* would solve the bitter sectional conflict that threatened to devolve into civil war. He could not have been more wrong.

Born in 1777, Taney was older than the Constitution itself, and when, on March 4, 1861, his withered shape rose to the East Portico of the Capitol, where he administered the oath of office to Lincoln, he was about to serve with his tenth president, seven of whom he had sworn into office. Yet even at eighty-four, the chief justice remained a robust and formidable opponent, which he showed only a few days later. After John Merryman, a wealthy Maryland landowner and rebel sympathizer, was seized from his bedroom at 2:00 a.m. and imprisoned at Fort McHenry for his part in riots that resulted in the destruction of railroad bridges and telegraph wire, Merryman's lawyers petitioned for a writ of habeas corpus. Taney responded by ordering that the general in charge of Fort McHenry deliver Merryman before his court the next day. (Not the Supreme Court; as was the practice in that day, Taney and other Supreme Court justices would, in addition to their high-court duties, "ride the circuit," hearing cases in lower courts around the country.) But the next day arrived and there was no general and no Merryman. Instead, a lower-ranking aide from Fort McHenry arrived to convey the message that Merryman was being held for treason and that he would not be brought before the court because President Lincoln had suspended the writ of habeas corpus. When Taney tried again the next day, he was again rebuffed, whereupon he issued a statement asserting that the president's suspension was itself illegal.

News of the dramatic standoff spread throughout the country, with Southerners cheering on Taney as a courageous hero to their cause and Northerners condemning him for conspiring, wrote a reporter for the *New York Times*, to "throw the weight of the judiciary against the United States and in favor of the rebels." The tottering justice—he entered and departed the courtroom supported on the arm of his grandson—appeared a little too eager for the challenge. "The fact that Taney, old and infirm as he is, volunteered to go to Baltimore to issue a writ in favor of the rebels," continued the *Times* reporter, "shows the alacrity with which he serves the cause of rebellion." But the chief justice was popular in his home state and Lincoln, well, not so much. The president had carried less than 3 percent of Maryland's voters in the 1860 election (more than 45 percent voted for the secessionist Southern Democrat John Breckinridge), hence his worry that if Maryland fell to the Confederacy, the District of Columbia would be cut off from the rest of the Union and rendered essentially defenseless. The crowds outside the courthouse greeted Taney with a silence of respect, the men holding their hats aloft to him as he passed, and in the midst of the confrontation, when George William Brown, the mayor of Baltimore, congratulated the chief justice for his fortitude, Taney was heard to reply, "Mr. Brown, I am an old man, a very old man, but perhaps I was preserved for this occasion."

Taney issued his opinion a week later, and it argued that since the authority to suspend the writ is contained in Article I—which deals exclusively with the powers of Congress (the executive powers are outlined in Article II, the judiciary in Article III)—only Congress can suspend the writ. Taney reiterated the Framers' well-documented fear of executive power and charged that Lincoln was moving dangerously close to the policies of a tyrant. If the executive could deprive citizens of due process and civil liberty "upon any pretext or under any circumstances," then the people, he claimed, would no longer be living under a government of laws, but "at the will and pleasure of the army officer in whose military district [they] may happen to be found." In a letter to former president Franklin Pierce of New Hampshire, who supported Taney's decision on Merryman, Taney went even further. He depicted the nation's capital as in a state of "delirium" (describing not the rebels, but the power-hungry president and his followers) and warned of an approaching "reign of terror." He could only hope, Taney wrote, that "sober thoughts" would lead to the conclusion that a peaceful separation of the North and the South "with free institutions in each section is far better that the union of all the present states under a military government." In a civil war in which the central issue was secession, the chief justice of the United States had just shown himself to be on the side of the secessionists.

Lincoln did not directly respond to Taney, and his administration did not appeal the decision on Merryman's habeas petition; it simply ignored it. The strategy of the government was to choose survival over righteousness, to first quell the rebellion and then later, wrote Seward to a friend, "cast ourselves upon the judgment of the people." But in a July 4, 1861, address to a special session of Congress, an exasperated Lincoln finally injected his voice into the controversy. Refuting Taney's claim that the power to suspend habeas corpus was reserved exclusively to Congress, Lincoln noted that suspension, according to the Constitution, is reserved to emergencies, to cases of "rebellion" and "invasion." Surely the Framers did not intend that such calamities would have to await the convening of Congress, "the very assembling of which might be prevented, as was intended in this case, by the rebellion," before the rebellion itself could be addressed. And even if it was not his power to suspend—which Lincoln firmly believed it was—"are all the laws, but one, to go unexecuted, and the government itself to go to pieces, lest that one be violated? . . . Would not the official oath"—the presidential oath to preserve and defend the Constitution of the United States—"be broken if the government should be overthrown, when it was believed that disregarding the single law would tend to preserve it?" This, said Lincoln, was not only a question for the United States now, it was a question for "the whole family of man" as to "whether a constitutional republic, or democracy—a government of the people by the same people—can or can not maintain its territorial integrity against its own domestic foes. . . . Must a government of necessity be too strong for the liberties of its own people, or too weak to maintain its own existence?"

Still, it would be wrong to underestimate the effect these charges of tyranny likely had on Lincoln. He was a man of the law and had a profound respect for its authority. The writ of habeas corpus is the most crucial of all civil liberties—the one right upon which all other rights depend—and no president had suspended the writ before (only one has since, Ulysses S. Grant). Even as he acknowledged in his July 4 address that some of his decisions might fall short of being "strictly legal," defensible only on a claim of "public necessity," it had to weigh on him that he, a lawyer, was twisting and pulling the fabric of the law to get what he wanted. Respect for the law was a hallmark of Lincoln's political oratory going all the way back to his justly famous Lyceum speech of 1838, when he warned abolitionists to seek their goals not through violence but through "legal enactments." A few months after Merryman, in that aforementioned episode when Major General Frémont imposed martial law in the state of Missouri, spontaneously confiscating secessionist property, and issuing his own order emancipating that state's slaves, Frémont's abuse of the law riled Lincoln. He described the orders as having the quality of a "dictatorship" and, sounding more like Taney than Taney, asked if "it is any longer . . . a government of Constitution and laws wherein a General *or a President* [emphasis mine] may make permanent rules of property by proclamation?" All of which brings us back to September 22, 1862, for here was Lincoln, *a president*, alerting his cabinet that he was about to issue a historic document "making permanent rules of property by proclamation." No wonder he wanted to start with a joke.

According to Gideon Welles, whether Lincoln should seek legislative support for the initiative had already been discussed individually with the cabinet members. Congressional agreement would at least have tempered the appearance of executive overreaching. But to a man they were agreed that Congress had no more authority to legislate the taking of private property without due process than the president did to take it without enabling legislation, while the president alone, by virtue of his war powers, did have the authority to free the slaves as a method of prosecuting the war. Lincoln had already determined this path would be the safest, most constitutionally sound, approach to emancipation, the very same reasoning that he had expressed to Welles and Seward back in July. The best that Lincoln could do now to lighten the appearance of an executive power grab was to incorporate quotes from legislative acts that, while superfluous to the proclamation, at least suggested that the Congress had expressed its will in similar terms—that it, too, was inching toward emancipation even if it did not have the constitutional power to grant it. He included the text of the Article of War, for instance, passed in March, which had finally ended the practice of Union soldiers returning fugitive slaves to their rebel masters. He also included the text of the second Confiscation Act. There, Congress had declared the slaves of Confederate civilian and military officials involved in the rebellion (and those "who shall in any way give aid or comfort thereto") "forever free of their servitude." That phrasing—"forever free"—was significant here because in the meat of the Preliminary Proclamation Lincoln used the same phrase to apply to all slaves being held in rebel states: "That on the first day of January in the year of our Lord, one thousand eight hundred and sixty-three, all persons held as slaves within any State, or designated part of a State, the people whereof shall then be in rebellion against the United States shall be then, thenceforward, and *forever free.*" Lincoln seemed to be suggesting that he was only doing what Congress wished it could do but could not by the dictates of the Constitution.

Thanks again to Seward's suggested edits, this Preliminary Proclamation had teeth. The language of the document that Lincoln had originally brought the cabinet only pledged to "recognize" the freedom of the former slaves. Seward changed that to recognize *and maintain*, meaning that the freedom of the former slaves would be protected by military authority and, critically, that no attempt would be made to "repress . . . efforts they may make for their actual freedom," which meant that the Union Army would do nothing to stop the dreaded slave insurrection from being carried out. The president had also, curiously, put a time limit on the proclamation's freedoms, limiting them to "the continuance in office of the present incumbent." Did Lincoln mean to admit the opportunity for those whom he had freed to be enslaved again upon the election of a successor? Or was this just yet another sign of his modesty, his doubt, his insecurity, his awkwardness? Nothing in the record refers to cabinet discussion on this point, other than that Seward and Chase convinced him to delete the language, which he did, saying—in a statement remarkable for any lawyer to make, even more, *this* lawyer—that he "did not care much about the phrases he had used."

Who knew if the subtleties Lincoln did bake into the Preliminary Proclamation, those intended to diminish its authoritarian rhythms and those aimed at bleaching all reference to moral purpose, would be recognized and, after that, appreciated? Such carefulness gave the document an aura of mystery and even disguise, as if Lincoln was hiding something behind his tightly wound prose, which of course he was. Lincoln, who had spoken out forcefully against slavery for decades, had just authored a proclamation of freedom without mentioning the most forceful argument for doing it, *which is that it was the right thing to do.* Just as odd, he had written a proclamation ostensibly removing 4 million people from the clutches of their masters, yet among his greatest concerns was that he, in his own position of power, not be seen as acting undemocratically, as forcing his will on others, a slave master of a different sort. And yet there was no denying that he was indeed acting undemocratically, and this from the same man who in Peoria in 1854 had quoted the Declaration of Independence not only for its expression of the equality of all men, but for its expression that governments derive their just powers "from the consent of the governed."

The whole situation was like one of those Russian nesting dolls with this irony encased within another irony and that inside one more. Yet was it also possible that there was, for Lincoln, *no* irony? For if we are to believe the 1862 date Hay applied to Lincoln's "Meditation on the Divine Will," then it would be reasonable to determine that Lincoln had become less assured that the moral issue was his to argue and had instead reduced his ambitions to a simple recognition that "God wills this contest, and wills that it shall not end yet." Would that be so unusual an interpretation when he had started off this day by saying that God alone willed this act of his, this proclamation—that he, Lincoln, was only responding to the mystical sign of the Almighty that he had asked to be shown to him? By this point of view, the argument for the Emancipation Proclamation was not a moral one at all; it could *only* be as a war measure, as a way for the contest that God willed (for whatever reason he willed it) to continue until he willed it to end.

Whatever was going through Lincoln's tortured mind, those in the room with him seemed to recognize that they were part of no ordinary cabinet meeting, that they were witnessing a historic moment that could be the opening salvo of a second American revolution. Absent the Jeffersonian flourish for words, this proclamation was as brave a gesture as the Declaration of Independence that had inspired it, for, as with the Declaration, no one knew what would happen next, whether this bold expression might be the saving of the Union or lead to its certain destruction, whether it would render them heroes for their courage or autocrats for their brazen and unwarranted use of authority. Welles reflected privately on the extraordinary exercise of power he was witnessing—calling it "arbitrary" and "despotic," though not in a tone of objection. This unprecedented exhibit of executive power, he acknowledged, "would never have been attempted but to preserve the national existence." Still, like others in the room, he thought it unlikely to shorten the war. If anything, it would lengthen it. There was little probability that the rebels would accept the terms and cease their rebellion, and now, more than ever before, the North's mission was what so many in the South always thought it secretly was, and what so many in the North increasingly felt that it rightly should be, providing "emancipation to the slave." No matter the obfuscations of the president's public statements, or the density of his legal prose, the war was now down to its essential issue.

Seward, too, privately had more reservations about the proclamation than he let on in the cabinet meeting. Don Piatt, a former diplomat and Union officer who expressed enthusiasm for the act, wrote that the secretary of state privately told him it was nothing more than "a puff of wind over an accomplished fact" and that the "Emancipation Proclamation"—by which he meant, broadly, the opportunity to end slavery—had been "uttered in the first gun fired at Sumter and we have been the last to hear it." Seward struck at the act's most vulnerable point when he told Piatt that "we show our sympathy with slavery by emancipating slaves where we cannot reach them, and holding them in bondage where we can set them free." That Lincoln had waited to issue the document largely because Seward himself had urged Lincoln to wait seems to have been lost here. But is that any surprise? With so much on the line, anyone in the room had to be hedging his bets. Depending on whom Seward was talking to and when, the proclamation was either too late and too little or too much and too soon.

The cabinet meeting ended with Lincoln handing the amended proclamation to Seward for its publication, and Seward in turn passing it off to Lincoln's private secretary, John Nicolay, and Nicolay then turning the document over to the assistant secretary, William Stoddard, whose job it was then to make copies, by hand, one each for the House and the Senate. Years later, Stoddard described what was going through his mind as he considered the enormity of this simple task: "Here it is. Mr. Lincoln's own hand. His draft of the Proclamation of Emancipation. Read it carefully through before you take up your pen, and think of what it means to the future of your country, and to the future of the bond men whom it liberates. You try to, but you cannot. You are not nervous, but you spoil a sheet or two of paper in beginning your copy. No wonder, for you cannot but think while writing."

Outside the White House on the evening of the twenty-fourth, a group of revelers serenaded Lincoln. Upon hearing news of the proclamation, they had gathered at Brown's Hotel and moved up Pennsylvania Avenue, "keeping time to the music of the Marine Band," wrote John Hay, and then abruptly stopped "before the white columns of the portico of the Executive Mansion, standing lucid and diaphanous . . . like the architecture of a dream. The crowd flowed in and filled every nook and corner of the grand entrance as instantly and quietly as molten metal fills a mold," before Lincoln, startled, emerged and deflected their tribute. "What I did," he told them, "I did after a very full deliberation and under a very heavy and solemn sense of responsibility. I can only trust in God I have made no mistake." He then begged off any further dialogue, out of respect to the soldiers. "I will say no more upon this subject. In my position I am environed with difficulties. Yet they are scarcely so great as the difficulties of those who upon the battlefield are endeavoring to purchase with their blood and their lives the future happiness and prosperity of this country. Let us never forget them."

The crowd dispersed and made its way to Chase's three-story town house at the corner of Sixth and E. There, the Ohioan and the abolitionist crusader Cassius Clay, so long a critic of Lincoln's for not declaring emancipation earlier, appeared before them. Someone called for a gas light, to which Chase responded that all the light that was needed would be that emanating from this great act of the president's. The proclamation was, Chase said, "the dawn of a new era," one baptized by blood yet grounded in justice and humanity. Clay added a few words of his own, and then the men, joined by Hay and a few other diplomats— "old fogies" was Hay's affectionately descriptive term for the group—retired inside, where they enjoyed wine and conversation. "If the slave holders had stayed in the Union they might have kept the life in their institution for many years to come," Chase speculated to the group, sounding like a man who was already enjoying victory. "They all seemed to feel a sort of new and exhilarated life," wrote Hay of the gathering. ". . . The President's Proclamation had freed them as well as the slaves. They gleefully and merrily called each other and themselves abolitionists, and seemed to enjoy the novel accusation of appropriating that horrible name."

IX.

DISSENT

We have no opinion polls to provide us with concrete information on how the Preliminary Emancipation Proclamation was received, whether it increased the Northern verve for battle with the South, or frustrated it, but going by the reactions in private letters, in newspaper accounts, in editorials, and in orations from the soapbox, it appears to have been greeted with mixed feelings. That would make sense. Like Lincoln's "all things to all people" response to Greeley's "Prayer of Twenty Millions," there was something here for everyone and nothing for anyone. For the abolitionists, it was what they had long been

clamoring for, or was it? It was indeed a proclamation of freedom, and many hailed it as such. "From this date to the 1st of
January," wrote an editorialist in the *National Republican*, a Washington daily, "will be the last Hundred Days of Slavery on the
American continent. So mote it be." Greeley's *Tribune* declared
it nothing less than "the beginning of the end of the rebellion;
the beginning of the new life of the nation." Frederick Douglass
deemed it an occasion to "shout for joy," a first chapter for a new
America, though he added, with alarming insight into the president's tortured and ambivalent path, that Lincoln had arrived
at this long-awaited moment "in his own peculiar, cautious,
forbearing and hesitating way." For Douglass, all was forgiven.
Despite Lincoln's slow gait to the obvious, the president would
not look back, Douglass comforted his readers. No, not Lincoln.
"His word has gone out over the country and the world, giving
joy and gladness to the friends of freedom and progress wherever those words are read, and he will stand by them, and carry
them out to the letter." Douglass did not yet know that Lincoln
would spend the bulk of his next cabinet meeting arguing for the
colonization plan that Douglass and every other abolitionist so
despised.

Some antislavery activists bemoaned the lack of a moral assertion within the proclamation, or any reference to the essential justice of the act. If indeed Lincoln addressed himself to
justice in this effort (did he?), if it had any motivation beyond
a war measure (did it?), if this was a proclamation of freedom
and not simply some cynical act of political manipulation, why
was it "preliminary"? Why did it not take effect right away? Why
was there this grace period in which those in the slaveholding
states could simply stop their rebellion and return to the Union,

agreeing, yes, to some gradual and compensated end to slavery, but who knew how long that might take—decades?—or even if the promise of emancipation might be forgotten once the guns went silent and the country was whole once again? After all, Lincoln opened the Preliminary Proclamation by reiterating his professed mission, that "hereafter, as heretofore, the war will be prosecuted for the object of practically restoring the constitutional relation between the United States" and the states in rebellion. The *restoration of the Union*—and not a permanent end to slavery—was still the official goal of this slaughter.

The document seemed to raise so many more questions than it answered. For even in the unlikely instance that the states in rebellion were to succumb to the demand that they voluntarily end slavery as a precondition for rejoining the Union, in what form could this end be "gradual" and "compensated"? Was "gradual" to mean that those already in slavery would continue in slavery but children born to them after a certain date would be deemed to have been born into freedom (what a mockery of freedom!), and if so, how could the federal government decide that a debt was "owed" to these slaveholders for having relinquished—what?—their hold on the lives of the *next* generation? That, a writer in the *National Republican* had opined, "would be to admit an imaginary interest in persons not yet in existence."

Those less concerned with abolition, or even opposed to it, those who may have been vulnerable to the first patriotic stir to battle until it lost its luster and who may have been excited about fighting for some inchoate sense of country, but who did not want to see their young men die in what more than a few were beginning to indelicately describe as a "nigger-freeing" mission or a "damned abolition war," still had quite a bit to hold on to.

There was not only Lincoln's reiteration of the primary war aim as being the restoration of the Union, but also his constitutionally necessary assertion that this new freedom he was declaring was limited to those slaves being held in areas belligerent to the federal government. All of that would seem to underscore that this was not a war for equality; *it indeed was a war for union.* But who believed that? How could slavery be ended and then not be ended all in the same event? How could it be abolished for some and not for others residing in the next plantation, the neighboring district, the adjacent state? Surely Lincoln, when he spoke of Union, was engaged in a lofty distraction hiding his true intentions, or did he really expect mothers to continue to watch their boys die for something so abstract, cerebral, and unstable as the American idea of a continental union resting on first principles? "The Union is unnatural," wrote the novelist Nathaniel Hawthorne at the beginning of the war, "a scheme of man, not an ordinance of God. . . . How can you feel a heart's love for a mere political arrangement?" Hawthorne certainly didn't, nor did his emotions run strong for abolition. He felt the whole enterprise to end slavery to be foolhardy, meaningless, the ideal of emancipation one of "misty" philanthropy, the war itself a venture where young men (the term *infantry* being derived from the French *infante*, for "youth") were dying for old men's stale ideals. As the killing continued, many Northerners seemed to be examining the war in the same way.

For many white Southerners, the Preliminary Proclamation was confirmation of what they had always believed about Lincoln, that he was by nature a tyrant, his soldiers nothing more than little "Lincolnites" intent on carrying out his authoritarian wishes. The rebels were right to secede from a nation that intended to deprive them of their personal property, of their constitutional liberties, of the freedoms upon which this nation, *their* nation—the true embodiment of the Founders' vision!—was established. It was also a stark picture of what awaited them if they did not win this war: a forcible end to their "peculiar institution," a radical change for their economic and political prospects, a subjection of their will to the will of their neighbors to the north. Only one population greeted the news of the Preliminary Emancipation Proclamation with unrestricted joy: the slaves themselves, to whom the news was passed orally—most all slaves were illiterate—yet reached them, in some cases, before it had reached the newspapers of their masters. The enthusiasm even extended to the Border States such as Kentucky, where the rush of slaves ready to assert their freedom prompted the *Louisville Journal* to request that leaders in the black community explain the technical details of the proclamation, including how the freedoms granted there did not yet belong to them.

The white Southerner's view of Lincoln as a despot, hell-bent on achieving some unnatural vision of "equality," was shared by Northern Democrats, some of whom thought the president was now possessed by a "religious fanaticism." This was the same trumpet of self-righteousness, of frothy Christian zealotry, that had propelled the abolitionist movement up to this point, only now, where abolitionists were ranting from the outside, Lincoln and his allies were on the inside with their hands on the instruments of power. From this point of view, the Preliminary Proclamation was nothing less than a fiat, an arbitrary command issued from the armchair of power. It was, said one Lincoln opponent, "Robespierrian," yet another reference to the French Revolution, which was as close in years to 1862 as the early days of the Cold War are to ours. Surely no American Reign of Terror was being plotted in the Executive Mansion, nothing to match the fanaticism and wanton violence of the French revolutionaries, but then again, what *was* being plotted in the Executive Mansion? No one could be sure. The 1798 Alien and Sedition Acts—John Adams's repressive restrictions on political dissent and on immigration that Thomas Jefferson referred to as the "Reign of Witches"—were no further from the memory than the Jacobins.

The image of Lincoln as a religious fanatic was matched by the image of Lincoln as a racial fanatic, consumed with this "nigger business," as one Ohioan put it to the Democratic congressman Clement Vallandigham. Vallandigham was a favorite of the Copperheads (the Northern "Peace Democrats"), whom he led, famously, with the slogan "To maintain the Constitution as it is, and to restore the Union as it was." Lincoln himself may once have agreed with that platform, at least in so far as the text goes (remember, he long argued that he intended no challenge to slavery *where it is existed*, only that it not be allowed in the territories acquired in the Mexican War), but Vallandigham meant something very different by these words. In his version of recent history, a sectional rivalry had developed not so much between the North and the South as between the Northeast and the West. The Southern states had not seceded of their own accord. No, New England, with its fanatical abolitionists, had driven the Southern states to secede, and now that it had done so, it expected the West—meaning Ohio, Illinois, Indiana—to fight side by side with it in a cause, emancipation, that Westerners should rightly find wholly objectionable. In declaring his contempt for the abolitionists, Vallandigham made it clear that

he saw Lincoln as one of them, wielding the hard hand of executive power to coerce the South to abide by his personal laws
and, in so doing, move the nation dangerously away from the
once-stable past. Lincoln, Vallandigham claimed, was not out to
save the Union, but to reinvent it, and not through the constitutional processes that the Founders had established for orderly
change, but through the sinister practice of self-aggrandizement.
Lincoln's approach was pure despotism.

Such anti-Lincoln fervor was strong in Ohio, both because
the acerbic and vocal Vallandigham was there, encouraging such
dissent, and because the state's substantial population of Irish-
American workers feared that emancipation would lead to a
flood of cheap labor that would threaten their jobs on the docks
of the Ohio River. In March, the abolitionist Wendell Phillips
had been stoned, egged, and run from the stage at the Cincinnati Opera House, where he had been giving a lecture. In July,
after word that former slaves freed by the Confiscation Acts
were being hired as "strikebreakers" and "scab labor," Irish- and
German-American stevedores had mounted small-scale riots in
Cincinnati and Toledo. Among these Northerners, a new cry
was heard, expanding on Vallandigham's "old" one: "The Constitution as it is, the Union as it was, and *the niggers where they
are.*" And all of this tension had been building *before* Lincoln announced the Preliminary Proclamation.

Whether it was in Ohio, Illinois, New York, or anywhere else,
the prospect for Northern unrest, for what Lincoln would later
call "the fire in the rear," worried the president and his cabinet
so much that on September 24, just two days after he issued the
Preliminary Proclamation, Lincoln issued a second order, Proclamation 94, suspending habeas corpus for the entire nation.

One might think on the face of it that Lincoln had declared a dramatic and provocative new policy—emancipation—and then declared, posthaste, his intention to squelch the voice of opposition to that policy. Yet the strategy was more specific than that. It was to enforce the first federal military draft in American history and silence anyone who tried to speak out against it.

Lincoln didn't yet know if he would need a national draft (he would, and it would come with the controversial, and paradoxically named, Enrollment Act of 1863), but after the initial enthusiasm that accompanied the attack on Fort Sumter and the call for seventy-five thousand volunteers, it had become harder and harder to fulfill the army's manpower needs. The failure of McClellan's Peninsula Campaign and a feeling that the war was now dragging on much longer than expected—the Union confused in its mission, hesitant in its leadership—had made the situation even worse. If recruitment didn't pick up quickly, a draft would be the only way to populate the army. But a draft, all knew, would be highly *un*popular.

When the Constitution was ratified, it was generally assumed that the power of Congress to "raise and support armies" meant armies of *volunteers*. Yes, the various states could draft men into their state militias, and some did, but the notion of a national draft to build a federal army was looked upon with disfavor, first because the idea of *any* national army was looked upon with disfavor (the Founders, particularly Thomas Jefferson, feared that it could be used as an instrument of tyranny against the states), and then because the drafting of citizens of the various states into federal military service seemed to preempt the spirit of federalism. The state militias—not the federal army—were seen as the core unit of defense, to be called upon to supplement the stand-

ing army in the suppression of "insurrections" and "invasions."
If anything, the militias—formed of ordinary citizens ready to
grab a gun and go—were intended to be a democratic check on
the professional army of the federal government. It ensured that
no war could be fought that was not a "people's war." Indeed,
when Lincoln asked for volunteers after Fort Sumter, his request
went not to the broad population but to the individual states to
provide men from their various militias. A national draft would
change all that and therefore could be challenged as unconstitutional. When Secretary of War James Monroe proposed a draft
in the middle of the War of 1812, the great orator and future
senator Daniel Webster—no states' rights champion, he—had
risen in the chamber of the House of Representatives to con-
demn it as such: "Where is it written in the Constitution . . . that
you may take children from their parents, and parents from their
children, and compel them to fight the battles of any war which
the folly or the wickedness of government may engage in?" he
asked. "If the Secretary of War has proved the right of Congress
to enact a law enforcing a draft of men out of the militia and into
the regular army, he will at any time be able to prove, quite as
clearly, that Congress has the power to create a dictator." Roger
Taney agreed with that sentiment. As he watched Lincoln plot a
Civil War draft, the chief justice secretly readied an opinion invalidating the act should the subject ever come before his Court.
It didn't, and Taney's unpublished opinion was discovered lying
inert in his desk after his death.

Another tantalizing theme hung over this discussion. When
Daniel Webster implored his fellow congressmen to reject conscription for the War of 1812, he described the power to draft
men into military service as the authority to wield "chains" and

hold free men in "bondage." It had no place, he said, in a free society. It was a "solecism"—an error, an incongruity, a paradox, a contradiction—and only through "an exercise of perverse ingenuity" could one decide that such "slavery"—he used the word—could coexist with free institutions. Webster intended no irony, though he had opposed the real, chattel slavery of the South even then. Still, the notion that slavery could describe the relationship between the federal government and its citizens, that undemocratic demands in the form of forced military service represented another kind of bondage, was in the air nearly fifty years after Webster's address. By that way of thinking, Lincoln was using a form of slavery to fight a war to end slavery.

Still, the Civil War draft was constructed with an answer to critics who argued that the draft was coercive and unconstitutional. While all able-bodied men were required to make themselves available to the draft, those who wished could pay a fee rather than serve (the going rate was $300). That meant that the draft was, technically speaking, a tax, and service was not forced—it was not "slavery"—since there was a way to not serve, but that would not be tested in the courts until 1918, when the Supreme Court declared that the Thirteenth Amendment, abolishing slavery, which was adopted in 1865, did not prevent the federal government from compelling a citizen to public service.

For now, Lincoln used only the threat of a draft, not a draft itself, but to ensure that the threat was credible, the clampdown on dissent became very real. No reliable records exist as to the number of civilians who were arrested during the Civil War, though the accepted estimate is fourteen thousand. Most of those were likely deserters and draft dodgers responding to the real draft in 1863 (which set off violent demonstrations in New York City), but the clampdown on dissent began much earlier, earlier even than September 1862, and it included the punishment of what we would today regard as tame expressions of opinion, not an incitement to break the law. A Democratic politician in New Hampshire was seized for interrupting a recruitment rally to say that three-quarters of those signing up would likely die and go to hell. A vocally anti-Lincoln Democrat was arrested for interfering with another rally with "hooting and noise." The editor of the *Dubuque Herald*, Dennis A. Mahony, was arrested for publishing material deemed to be obstructing the enthusiasm for enlistment. This last one, in particular, would come back to haunt Lincoln. With the assistance of the Catholic archbishop, Mahony was released, whereupon, in freedom, he published a scathing book, *Prisoner of State*, lambasting Lincoln for claiming that the "emergency" required him to curb civil liberties. The Caesars in Rome, the Bourbons and Napoléons in France, and the Stuarts in England all claimed the same pretext for their abuse of power, wrote Mahony.

Federal marshals, working with little guidance from the judge advocate general, were left to decide what expressions met the standard of "disloyalty" and what did not. Terrible inconsistencies thus resulted from state to state, and, as is the case when crime is left up to personal judgment, corruption was fierce. As the war went on, Lincoln, it is said, came to regret the arrests his government was making for disloyal speech, but apparently not enough to stop them.

The war's most famous arrest for dissenting speech would come in 1863 when Clement Vallandigham himself was seized for giving verbal aid to the enemy. By then, the Ohioan had expanded his critique of Lincoln to take note of the administration's assault on civil liberties. In frequent speeches before Ohio audiences, he declared the Union Army to have been unsuccessful to the point where the paucity of volunteers forced the adoption of a "French conscription law." He referred to the president as "King Lincoln," and while he stopped short of recommending resistance to the draft (a key distinction), he urged his listeners to use the ballot box (also key) to "hurl the tyrant from the throne." General Ambrose Burnside—the Antietam hero—who was by then the commander of the Department of Ohio, ordered Vallandigham's arrest. He was seized in the middle of the night at his Dayton, Ohio, home, where he first resisted the authorities and, perched by a bedroom window, fired a pistol three times into the air so as to alert his friends. While the civil and criminal courts were open and available for trial, Vallandigham's case was heard instead before a military tribunal, which the prisoner, once again asserting the comparison to France, referred to as a "military bastillle [*sic*]." When the judge asked if he wished to have counsel present, Vallandigham refused, believing that this would be a sign that he had accepted the legitimacy of the trial, which he did not. Instead, he chose to defend himself. Convicted, he was sentenced to prison for the duration of the war, but then Lincoln injected himself into the case.

The president, along with many of the members of his cabinet, had been disappointed by Burnside's decision to arrest Vallandigham, but apparently Lincoln was uncomfortable with overruling a subordinate and so sent Burnside a message pledging his "kind assurance of support." Still, determined not to let his enemy assume the status of a martyr—large crowds had been building in support of Vallandigham—Lincoln adjusted the sentence, banishing him to the Confederacy instead, where his speech, the president reasoned, would not have the same injurious effect.

Many developments in the fall of 1862 suggested that the war had taken on a different character, and it had, or more precisely, it was about to. In addition to restricting dissent, making preparations for the first national military draft, widening the suspension of habeas corpus, and issuing the Preliminary Emancipation Proclamation, Lincoln traveled to the battlefield at Antietam for a three-day visit with the battle-worn troops and their commander, George B. McClellan. It would be Lincoln's final meeting with the general, but neither man knew it just yet.

Lincoln arrived with several others in tow: Ward Hill Lamon, a big, bulky figure who had been a law partner with Lincoln back in Illinois but was now, essentially, his bodyguard and occasional entertainer (Lamon, who regularly regaled Lincoln with jokes and songs, remains chiefly famous for his mysterious absence on the night when Lincoln was murdered); General John McClernand, an ambitious and conniving officer who was once a protégé of Stephen Douglas's and who was exploiting this opportunity to get Lincoln's ear and maybe a promotion; John W. Garrett, who was the president of the Baltimore and Ohio Railroad and who had been instrumental in arranging for his trains to deliver troops to put down John Brown's raid in 1859; and the only Republican among the president's guests, Ozias Mather Hatch, Illinois's secretary of state, whose office had served as the first meeting place for those exploring Lincoln's run for the 1860 Republican nomination. While Lamon, McClernand, and Garrett were Democrats, they were also Unionists. They continued to harbor Southern sympathies, but were loyal to Lincoln and against secession.

McClellan surmised (correctly) that the president was coming to Sharpsburg to push him to advance his troops across the Potomac in pursuit of the now-long-departed Lee. The general believed that his men were weary from battle—"the old regiments are reduced to mere skeletons. . . . The new . . . are not fit for the field"—and he intended to show his displeasure when Lee's pursuit came up in their conversations. "These people don't know what an army requires, and therefore act stupidly," he wrote to his wife, referring not only to Lincoln, but also to Secretary of War Stanton and General in Chief Halleck, both of whom McClellan despised as inferiors. He mocked Halleck's reputation as Old Brains—a title the general earned for his considerable pedigree as a scholar—finding him "hopelessly stupid," and objected to Stanton's lack of principle, for "[he] would say one thing to a man's face and just the reverse behind his back."

While the consensus in Washington was that McClellan had missed an opportunity to settle the war when he did not pursue Lee (more than that, it was said McClellan let Lee get off with nearly every caisson, tent, wagon, and piece of artillery that he arrived with), McClellan continued to strike the pose of a self-appointed "genius" misunderstood by his own feeble times. Friends, he puffed to his wife, had informed him that Antietam was nothing less than a complete victory, "a masterpiece of art." He could not imagine its outcome to be anything but that the villain Stanton would be sacked and that Halleck would step aside for McClellan to be restored to his rightful place as general-in-chief, saying, "Unless these conditions are fulfilled, I will leave the service." Yet even if such terms *were* met—they wouldn't be, they couldn't be—the awkward fact was that Lincoln had just changed the mission on him, moving it to what McClellan referred to as the "accursed doctrine" of emancipation, which he felt was little more than an encouragement to "servile insurrection." The general had considered addressing his soldiers on the subject and also on Lincoln's suspension of habeas corpus, which he saw as transforming "our free institutions into despotism," but on the counsel of others he instead issued General Order No. 163, reminding his men that their duty was to support the actions of their civil authorities and, in a not so subtle message of rebuke to Lincoln, that "the remedy for political errors, if any are committed, is to be found in the action of the people at the polls." McClellan's decision to issue the order may have been inspired by the story of his army's Major John J. Key, who in late September was overheard describing why the Army of the Potomac had not pursued Lee after Antietam. "That is not the game," he told a fellow officer. "The object is that neither army shall get much advantage of the other; that both shall be kept in the field till they are exhausted, when we will make a compromise and save Slavery." When Lincoln heard of the comment, he told John Hay that if it was true, Key's "head should go off." Lincoln summoned Key to Washington and, once convinced that the words had been reported correctly, promptly dismissed him from the nation's service.

The president arrived at camp on October 1, and by that afternoon he and McClellan were reviewing the troops together, Lincoln dressed all in black with his trademark top hat, the general crisp in his parade finery. The strain between them was palpable, as photographs show. Upon hearing that Lincoln had left Washington to visit Antietam, Alexander Gardner rushed to capture the visit on film, and the images he recorded are of Lincoln and McClellan locked in a painful stare.

To journalist Albert Deane Richardson, the president looked "weary and careworn," and as he toured the troops, he showed little emotion, the disappointment with McClellan combining with a feeling of urgency about their impending talk to distract him from the array of dedicated warriors before him. Lincoln did not wish to minimize what the troops had done at Antietam. He was even willing to defer to McClellan's judgment that it was indeed a "victory"—why argue?—but the president could not abide how the man whom he still considered to be his best general continued to see this as a defensive war, how McClellan, again, as in the Peninsula Campaign, wanted "more time," and not only to rest his exhausted army but to build fortifications, repair bridges and railroad tracks, and all that to combat further Confederate incursions into Maryland and Pennsylvania. To Lincoln, this was a wasted effort. The moment was ripe to chase after Lee now, while he was in retreat, to disrupt his communications with the capital in Richmond and engage him in one final battle supreme. The war could only be over when the Confederate Army was defeated. Why, Lincoln wondered, did the general not get this?

After reviewing the troops, Lincoln retired to his tent. Then, early the next morning (or it could have been the morning after that, the record is not clear), he reportedly woke Ozias Hatch and asked him to come with him on a walk. The camp itself had yet to rise, and while the two came upon an occasional guard on their path, there was no one else to see them. As they moved, Lincoln did not speak to Hatch, nor did Hatch speak to Lincoln. Only the sound of their feet moving through the morning dew marked the silence of the dawn. The two made their way to the top of a summit where they looked over the expanse of tents. No one could not have missed the grandeur of the scene, a wearied army sleeping off wounds from America's worst day at battle, as well as the pathos: that battle represented a nation fighting with itself, brother against brother, and all on a piece of real estate unknown to them even days before. Yet if his mind did wander to such despairing thoughts, Lincoln quickly reverted to the frustration of the task at hand. "Hatch, what is all this?" he asked in an exchange that has been quoted frequently in histories ever since. "Why, Mr. Lincoln, this is the Army of the Potomac." Lincoln looked at him. "No, Hatch, no. This is General McClellan's bodyguard."

The visit went on, with more reviewing of more troops—Sumner's corps, Burnside's corps, Fitz John Porter's corps—and in between, enough conversation between McClellan and Lincoln to break the chill. To his surprise, the general found Lincoln warm and supportive, flush with enthusiasm for the recent victory. (Was McClellan's ego imagining this or was Lincoln using flattery to get his way?) Walking the battlefield with the president, the general remembered Lincoln saying that he would defend McClellan against all his Washington critics, that he should not move until ready, and that he was the best man for the job. McClellan had no doubt that Lincoln meant what he said.

Near the end of the visit, the men abandoned their horses and climbed into an ambulance for the several-miles journey to yet another camp. The ambulance quarters were tight, particularly with the rotund Lamon along for the ride, so tight that one soldier who saw them remarked upon how Lincoln's "long legs doubled up so that his knees almost struck his chin." The mode of travel appeared undignified for a president, the same soldier judged, and he looked like a "baboon"—that favorite image among Lincoln critics—laughing through the window. But Lincoln had more than executive decorum on his mind. He had spent three days touring the camps and battlefields, putting faces and lives to the reports that he had received back at the telegraph office, and he had felt the atmosphere to be unfriendly. He had visited the makeshift hospitals where the sick were being crudely treated and seen the freshly dug graves of young boys on a mission that he was still struggling to frame. He knew more young death was coming, likely much more. As they traversed the bumpy path, Lincoln turned to Lamon and asked him to sing a favorite song, a "sad song." Lamon launched into the verses of "Twenty Years Ago." He had long sung this ballad to Lincoln, going all the way back to their time together on the Illinois circuit, and many times Lamon had watched it bring Lincoln to tears. "I've wandered to the village, Tom" went the simple, almost maudlin, verse, "I've sat beneath the tree. / Upon the schoolhouse playground, / That sheltered you and me. / But none were left to greet me, Tom, / And few were left to know, / Who played with us upon the green, / Some twenty years ago."

Perhaps the sentiment was too raw, too harsh, for the moment, an unforgiving light cast across the rough-hewn burial grounds before them. Lamon noticed that the song had only deepened Lincoln's sadness, so, as Lamon had done on many other occasions when he saw the need to pull Lincoln "from the pit of melancholy," he followed with "two or three little comic things," including a gently ribald Negro song called "Picayune Butler." The men soon arrived at camp, reviewed the troops, and the next morning Lincoln was on his way back to Washington. But two years later, when he was running for reelection

against, of all people, the now-former-general George B. Mc-
Clellan, who was atop the Democratic Party slate, this episode
would come back to haunt Lincoln. The Democratic press reported that he had committed a sacrilege by making light of the
scene before him. "Abe may crack his jolly jokes / o'er bloody
fields of stricken battle, / While yet the ebbing life-tide smokes /
from men that die like butchered cattle."

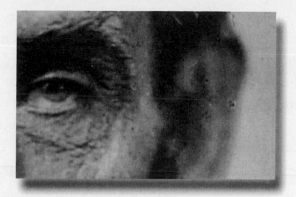

X.

A DIFFERENT WAR

DESPITE THE SIGNS of harmony that accompanied the end of their Antietam visit, Lincoln and McClellan soon reverted to style. Whatever pledge of patience the president may have made to the general (and who knows if he really did), Lincoln displayed none. Immediately upon his return to Washington late on Saturday, October 4, he dispatched an order to McClellan to move, however tired his troops. In return, whatever promise McClellan had made to pursue Lee across the Potomac (did he?), the general now paused, and even when he began the much-awaited journey, he adopted a pace that would ensure the strategy's failure. "It was eleven days before he crossed his first man over the Potomac," Lincoln complained later. "It was eleven days after that before he crossed the last man." Lee, by contrast, had covered the same distance with his entire army "between dark one night and daylight the next." To Lincoln, time was the central issue. If Lee was able to get back to Richmond while McClellan sat like an "inert mass"—Halleck's phrase—well, then, an opportunity to cut him off would be lost, and who knew when another would arrive?

Unlike many in his administration, Lincoln still did not regard McClellan as a "traitor or an officer without capacity," preferring to believe that he had "bad counselors" upon whose judgment he depended. But the time for goodwill had long passed. This most recent display of intransigence was, for Lincoln, "the last grain of sand that broke the camel's back." The war could not be fought this way, not with his military chiefs refusing to follow their civilian superiors. Lincoln had "tried long enough to bore with an auger too dull to take hold" and was ready to try something else.

On the evening of November 7, 1862, three days after the midterm elections, Brigadier General Catharinus P. Buckingham arrived at the headquarters of the Army of the Potomac with two letters, one addressed to McClellan, ordering him to relinquish command and return home to Trenton, New Jersey, where he was to await further orders, the other ordering Ambrose Burnside to assume command from McClellan. Secretary Stanton had sent a general on what was essentially a messenger's task because he feared that McClellan might reject even this order. But he didn't. At 11:30 p.m., in the presence of Burnside and Buckingham, the general silently read the letter dismissing him, and while he later wrote that he had been surprised at his sacking, in the moment he remained proud, determined that "not the slightest expression of feeling" would be "visible on my face" for the others to see. The troops were devastated. As he rode before them in a gesture of farewell, the ovation was deafening. Soldiers, wrote one reporter, "rushed out from their campground and thronged the road side, anxious to take another look at their beloved general. Many of them were melted to tears; and after cheering him again, joined in the universal supplication: 'Come back to us, come back to us, McClellan!'" But soon McClellan was on his way north, back to his wife and baby, a fine mist of self-pity dampening the journey. "Alas, for my poor country," he wrote. "I know in my inmost heart she never had a truer servant."

Lincoln had stuck so long with McClellan for a reason. The general may have had his flaws, but the president—no man of arms—needed a schooled soldier to lead the war, and McClellan was the best of a bad lot. We today, so used to a militarized federal government, find it hard to imagine how paltry the country's defenses were in 1861 and how unprepared the nation was for a war. It was particularly unprepared for *this* war, a rebellion where some of the best soldiers bolted to serve the other side. When Lincoln assumed the title of commander in chief, the army of the United States consisted of just sixteen thousand men—about a third of them Southerners—and the South claimed a disproportionate representation within the officer corps. The nation's general-in-chief, the gout-plagued, seventy-four-year-old Winfield Scott—Old Fuss and Feathers—was himself from Virginia (though his loyalties were decidedly with the North), and the superintendent of West Point was the Louisiana-born, soon-to-be Confederate general Pierre Gustave Toutant Beauregard. Even the nation's most recent secretary of war, John B. Floyd, who had overseen the building of the army that Lincoln would inherit, was a Southerner (Virginia) who harbored strong rebel sympathies. Floyd spent the time between Lincoln's election and Lincoln's inauguration shipping large quantities of arms to arsenals in the South, "so as to be on hand," as Ulysses Grant put it in his memoirs, "when treason wanted them." Two months after Lincoln arrived in Washington, Floyd was a brigadier general in the Confederate Army.

Floyd was a lawyer playing a soldier and acted like one, too, suffering a humiliating defeat to Grant at Fort Donelson, Tennessee, in February 1862. But the Union had far more such "political generals" than did the South, men rewarded for their loyalty with a uniform and bars. Most of the officers with any military experience were West Point alumni, and they could be found in positions of power on both sides. Along with Beauregard, the South boasted Thomas "Stonewall" Jackson, James Longstreet, and, of course, the former West Point superintendent Robert E. Lee; the North had Halleck, George Meade, Joseph Hooker, and the taciturn Grant. Roughly 250 federal army officers (around a quarter of the entire force) resigned from the US army to join the Confederacy. In the middle of the war, Congress considered shuttering the Academy, so concerned were its members that the federally funded facility was schooling officers who were then leaving in large numbers for Southern state militias, ready to fight the very army that had trained them. "I am prepared to vote to abolish the West Point Academy," pronounced Zachariah Chandler of Michigan on the floor of the Senate in December 1861, ". . . upon the ground that [it] has

produced more traitors within the last fifty years than all the institutions of learning and education that have existed since Judas
Iscariot's time. I state that, and I believe it."

Unlike the new president of the Confederacy, Jefferson
Davis, who was himself a West Pointer and a former secretary of
war in the administration of Franklin Pierce, Lincoln had no war
experience, though he had served a short stint as a militia captain
in the 1832 Black Hawk war, a skirmish with Native Americans
in Illinois where the only action he encountered was, as he described it, with "wild onions" and "musquetoes." Now, by jet-
tisoning McClellan, Lincoln had made the war, more than ever
before, his own, and yet what did Lincoln know about the profession of arms; about tactics and maneuvers and strategies; and
what made him so sure that McClellan's cautious approach was
timidity or paranoia and not the shape of a careful methodology
developed from the lessons of military history, a plan set to the
standards of a profession that is as old as man himself?

Shortly after becoming president, Lincoln decided to educate
himself in the principles of war, or at least that is what his secretaries Nicolay and Hay later wrote. He read "strategical works"
on battle and conferred with generals and other military experts
to learn their craft. Soon he began to speak in the special language
of the schooled warrior, leaving his better-educated military advisers "astonished," wrote Nicolay and Hay, "by the extent of his
special knowledge and the keen intelligence of his questions."
We do not know exactly which books Lincoln read—he did not
refer to them ever in his letters or speeches nor do his secretaries
tell us—but we do know that his library could not have included
Carl Philipp Gottfried von Clausewitz's *On War*, the seminal
work by the early-nineteenth-century Prussian soldier and theo-

rist who is today regarded as the greatest thinker on the subject of battle. Clausewitz's work, first published in 1832, was not translated into English until a decade after the Civil War. Still, we do know that Lincoln spent considerable time with Henry Halleck's own *Elements of Military Art and Science*, a volume built from lectures Halleck gave at the Lowell Institute in Boston in 1845 (the same lecture venue that would host Louis Agassiz a few years later). Lincoln checked the book out of the Library of Congress on January 8, 1862, and held it for over two years, but since he never made reference to it, one wonders if his extended possession was because he found it so valuable or because he never picked it up. The book is important because it would have explained to Lincoln at least some part of McClellan's thinking, if not his behavior. Indeed, with the critical exceptions of William Tecumseh Sherman and Grant, Halleck's work would have explained the way that many West Point officers serving in the war thought about their work.

At West Point, Halleck had been a favorite student of Dennis Hart Mahan's, and from Mahan—a legendary engineering instructor who had studied war theory in Europe—Halleck learned the ideas of Baron Antoine-Henri Jomini, a Swiss war theorist who had done a careful analysis of the campaigns of Frederick the Great and Napoléon and derived from them a series of lessons for military strategists. Halleck's lectures and his book were essentially extensions of the ideas of Jomini, and the ideas of Jomini were essentially extensions of the ideas of several seventeenth- and eighteenth-century European authors, including the Welsh writer Henry Lloyd, the Prussian Dietrich von Bülow, and, especially, the French military engineer Sébastien Le Prestre de Vauban, all of whom sought to devise predictable methods and strategies for the conduct of war. Together, they have been described as representing a kind of "Military Enlightenment," determined as they were to show that success did not depend simply upon waiting for a talented officer to respond to the charge—the ineffable element of military genius that was the stuff of so many heroic legends—but on the mastery of a series of immutable principles "which are by their nature invariable." War, they believed, was like any other human activity, something that could be improved upon with study and practice. Follow the rules and it would be quick and decisive; ignore them and war will remain the arena of indiscriminate blood and bluster that it had been for most of human history. Theirs was a civilized approach to battle, one extending from the kinds of fortifications one built to the sorts of maneuvers an army conducted to (well, at least with the French) the style of uniforms soldiers wore, and all in the interest of making war orderly, logical. These men saw war as a transaction between consenting parties or, better yet, a systemic process, which, when understood, became reliable as a method for achieving intended results. War, as von Bülow wrote, was nothing more than "the impulsion and repulsion of physical masses," so why shouldn't it simply follow the well-established laws of physics?

Vauban was, as one historian describes him, the "Palladio" of siege warfare. His designs for fortifications were informed by geometrical calculations that he used to shape walls and corners at precisely the right angle so as to maximize the impact of defensive gunfire, making an attack upon the fort little more than a gesture of futility. Before Vauban, traditional fort design emphasized height, to prevent invading armies from scaling the walls and penetrating the interior. But the popularity of the mobile field artillery cannon, capable as it was of piercing the average fortification surface, dramatically changed the approach to defensive engineering. With height less of an advantage, Vauban's designs emphasized depth, both in the thickness of the walls and in the design of the fortification itself, which was more likely now to be built low and extend deep across the landscape (the American fort at Ticonderoga and the Pentagon in Virginia are, one could say, Vauban-inspired designs).

Vauban's structures were beautiful in their geometrical perfection. They were also built to last. Indeed, three centuries later, they continued to form the defense of France, the citadel at Verdun occupying a central place in the battle fought there during World War I; and the fort at Ypres, in Belgium, serving as home to British Tommies defending the city in that same war—that is, until German artillery leveled the town and provided history with its first breath of poison gas.

But Vauban's contribution did not end with the designing and building of forts. He took the same considered approach to offense as he did to defense, developing a strategy for the taking of a defended fortification, with the invading force burrowing through zigzagging trenches (another Vauban legacy, one that became the defining image of the Western Front) laid out in a series of progressive lines moving closer and closer to the target. Vauban is even credited with inventing the fixed bayonet and the tactic of ricochet fire, a particularly brutal development when you consider that a multisurfaced fortification could forward a bullet in a variety of directions, multiplying its deadly force.

Jomini was born nearly a century after Vauban and came of age during the rise of France under Napoléon, but he proved to be a worthy successor to the earlier engineer's mission. Indeed, his aim was to do for troop maneuvers what Vauban did for fortification design: utilize math and other logical certainties in the service of efficiency and success. Jomini prescribed a line of operations that would lie at right angles to the base sustaining it. He recommended ignoring minor objectives in favor of applying massive force at one decisive point to break the enemy. That point could be geographical—a river or a mountain pass—or it could be related to the specific maneuvers of one's enemy, cutting him off from his base or from supply routes. The decisive point could also be political—a capital, such as Richmond, for instance—or it could be a supply-rich province that, if captured, would critically damage the enemy's chances to fight onward. Not all of these maneuvers would require engaging the enemy in combat, and even when the enemy was engaged, Jomini's methods were aimed at quick, conclusive results. This was war as a gigantic chess game where the mission was to push one's opponent from his fixed position and continue to apply pressure on him through one's own movements in the hopes of winning the battle without actually fighting. A war to end all wars.

Jomini did not discount the importance of military "genius." Much of his work is an effort to explain what he believed came naturally to great battlefield leaders, especially his hero, Napoléon, with whom he served (though Bonaparte, too, came under Jomini's criticism for moments when he let passion cloud his judgment). Then, too, even with his elaborate rules, Jomini saw the need for some element of individuality on the part of the field general. Jomini argued that his was a "simple theory," not an "absolute" rulebook. The field officer still needed to have "liberty of action," and to protect this autonomy he should be put in charge of his own fate, not merely execute the orders of a

distant authority. Still, the essential message of Jomini was con-
formity. Since neither genius nor individuality could be taught,
he saw himself as divining for posterity the lessons he saw in the
work of the greatest military leaders in history. (The shadow of
Napoléon clung closely to the era's imagination; not only did
McClellan pattern himself after the Corsican, but later in the
war Jefferson Davis publicly threatened Union general William
Tecumseh Sherman, saying that Sherman could not long perpetuate his march before "our people will harass and destroy his
army as the Cossacks did that of Napoléon." Sherman apparently enjoyed the challenge.)

It is hard to gauge exactly what Jomini's influence was on
the West Point strategists of the Civil War. McClellan never
mentions Jomini in any of his writings, nor do any of the other
major officers of the era. Grant dismisses Jomini, insisting that
he doesn't remember reading him, even though it is well docu-
mented that Jomini was taught at West Point when Grant was
there. (Grant graduated in the bottom half of his class.) When
Dennis Hart Mahan taught the Jomini-infused "Science of
War," which, tellingly, was sometimes called "The Art of War,"
he cautioned that "common sense" should accompany an appreciation of the rules (the cadets, mocking Mahan's nasal accent,
nicknamed him Old Cobbon Sense), and while Mahan's text on
the building of field fortifications was inspired by his visits to see
Vauban's work at Metz, it was Mahan the cadets read, not Vauban. Yet even if the names of Jomini, Vauban, and von Bülow
were not exactly on the lips of Civil War officers trained at West
Point, their ideas were. When McClellan, as a cadet, delivered
his departing address to the Dialectic Society of West Point (a
literary and debating group) in June 1846, he explained that in

the past "the passions of man had the mastery over his reason," but the wars of Napoléon had shown "the immense effects of science." It was now an officer's duty, he argued, "to impose that order and discipline without which it [would be] vain to hope for constant victory." (McClellan graduated *second* in his class.)

Though he may not have identified it as such, McClellan also showed the impact of Jomini in the way he conducted himself on the battlefield. His meticulous planning, his unwillingness to commit himself to a frontal assault of the enemy, his dependence upon crisp, carefully drawn lines of supply and communication, his abhorrence of unnecessary bloodshed, his resentment of civilian leadership distant from the battlefield—all of these are redolent of Jomini. One could argue that McClellan was a *bad* Jominian—that is, he took the rules of Jomini too literally and did not possess the "genius" to mold those rules to new situations, emphasizing some (such as the ones calling for cautious preparation) over others (such as the one that urged a hard and quick strike once the target had been identified)—but he was undeniably a Jominian.

Whether Lincoln had the sophistication in war studies to understand McClellan as such was irrelevant by late 1862, when the push to remove the general became too strong to ignore. All along, as the opposition to McClellan grew, it had carried a tone that rejected the professional in favor of the amateur, preferred pragmatism to bookish theories, heroism to utilitarianism, and the common soldier to the West Point officer. "Engineers are the incarnation of defensive warfare," wrote Adam Gurowski, a Polish émigré and minor State Department official whose diary, published to a sensation in late 1862, contained all manner of invective toward the Lincoln administration (Gurowski was the one person Lincoln feared could be his assassin). Gurowski mocked McClellan as a "mud mole," the "inventor of the bloodless strategy" that Gurowski suspected was little more than veiled cowardice. Others agreed. Writing in the *Deseret News* of Utah, one Union supporter ridiculed the mathematical war plans of "West Point boys" that would work, he feigned, only if "armies can be reckoned into blocks of stone, which will stand still to be measured, weighted, calculated, and then one to be lifted over another as if by cranes and pulleys." The impatience in Congress carried a similar tone. "You can never destroy [the enemy] by building fortifications and planting cannon in them and seeing how far you can throw a ball," said Senator Trumbull of Illinois, a few months after Antietam. ". . . We have had in the field more men than mortal man could marshal in battle array. . . . Let them with their eyes fixed upon the rebels, advance upon them with the power of a hundred thousand bayonets and you will . . . crush and destroy this rebellion."

Sometime in November, Lincoln expressed his own frustration to the members of the women's council of the Western Sanitary Commission who had paid him a visit. The tone of his words suggested that he had come to a similar conclusion. Looking drawn and haggard and approaching them in a "staggering gait," as if awoken from an uncomfortable sleep, the president replied to their request for encouraging news by telling them that there was none. "The military situation is far from bright; and the country knows it as well as I do. . . . The fact is the people haven't yet made up their minds that we are at war with the South. They haven't buckled down to the determination to fight this war through; for they have got the idea into their heads that we are going to get out of this fix, somehow, by strategy."

He was just gaining steam, his scorn for his recently departed general growing. "That's the word—*strategy*. General McClellan thinks he is going to whip the rebels by strategy; and the army has got the same notion. They have no idea that the war is to be carried on and put through by hard, tough fighting, that will hurt somebody; and no headway is going to be made while this delusion lasts."

It was a disheartening picture, this claim that all the bloodshed, all the painful loss, was being directed by nothing more than a "delusion," by men enamored of philosophies and arcane treatises, classmates from Academy studies, working their schemes against one another as though they were members of competing school debate teams, war as an academic exercise, student versus student, disinterested in the political mission. But what was the alternative, a return to mindless brutality? While Lincoln remained faithful—for the moment—to Halleck and to Burnside and their rich schooling, he was beginning to think like so many others, that war was best not left to the generals, that they lacked the simplicity of vision necessary. When he told the women's group that only "hard, tough fighting" would bring results now, what did he mean by this? That planning was useless, that there was no "science" to be relied upon, no calculation or theory, only the parries of fierce, unbridled competition with results unknown? A war of passion played to its natural conclusion?

Without knowing it, Lincoln was speaking the language of Jomini's chief rival in military theory, Carl von Clausewitz. Indeed, facile summaries of the Union approach to the Civil War often divide it between a Jominian phase and a Clausewitzian phase, with the break here, in the fall of 1862. It was not as clean as that might suggest, and the application of theory came not as a prescription, but as an explanation after the fact. Still, around this time the shift to a different war at the very least *began*, and when reading backward, it appears as though Clausewitz's approach was what Lincoln adopted.

Clausewitz was Jomini's opposite in so many ways. A Prussian soldier, he resented French aggression under Napoléon—indeed, Clausewitz commanded a battalion at the 1806 Battle of Auerstedt, when Napoléon forced the Prussian army into a humiliating retreat—and he studied war in earnest in part to thwart any future French threat. His conclusions were radically different from those propounded by Jomini, Lloyd, von Bülow, and the other writers of the Military Enlightenment. Clausewitz thought no discoverable set of rules determined the successful conduct of war, no predictable action-reaction dynamic that could be repeated like an experiment in a laboratory. War was instead a clash of human wills unique to its participants, and success would come to those who pursued it to its ends with both vigor and creativity. His was, in a word, the "genius" theory of military leadership. To Clausewitz, maneuvers were useless unless they ultimately confronted the enemy, and no battle was worth engaging unless it furthered the final object—the ultimate *political* object, that is—of the war. He is best remembered and most often quoted for his pithy phrase "War is the continuation of politics by other means," but he would have been even clearer if he had written that war is *only* war *when* it pursues politics by other means, that anything else, as he writes elsewhere, is a "senseless thing without an object." To Clausewitz, war was no chess game. War was war.

While Lincoln did not read Clausewitz, a few biographers have jumped to the conclusion that he did, and Gore Vidal, in his novel *Lincoln*, even imagines a conversation between the president and Seward (it is *fiction*, after all) at around the time of the sacking of McClellan ("'I have been studying the art of war,' said the President, dreamily, eyes half shut. 'Almost every day I send John [Hay] down to the Library of Congress to take out books that I see referred to in my reading. You know, there are actually times when I think that I may have the knack, since war is not all that different from politics. . . . ' '"An extension of politics by other means,"' Seward quoted, or paraphrased. He was never certain what the line was. . . . Lincoln nodded. 'Clausewitz,' he said, drawing out each syllable deliberately and correctly.") But, as with the early war and the influence of Jomini, it is not so important whether Lincoln read Clausewitz as that his leadership of the war now demonstrated the principles that Clausewitz espoused and indeed, evidence suggests that a few of those around Lincoln *had* read Clausewitz, notably a close confidant of Halleck's, the Prussian immigrant Francis Lieber, whose importance began to emerge in the fall of 1862.

Lieber's story is yet another marvel of pan-historical experience, his array of talents astonishing for a man so little known beyond his own times. Born in Germany in 1798, he, like Clausewitz, had powerful memories of Napoléon's aggression. Too young to enlist, he watched his older brothers go off to war, vowing that he would one day murder Napoléon, "that son of crime and sin." While he would never get that close, Lieber was eventually part of a regiment that, after Waterloo, pushed Napoléon's army back toward Paris. He was wounded twice in the engagement—taking a bullet in the neck and another in the chest—and nearly died.

Branded a subversive by the reactionary Prussian government, he went to university and earned a doctorate in the non-subversive field of mathematics. Then he left. Possessed of a "youthful ardor to assist the oppressed and struggling," Lieber joined the fight for Greek independence in 1821. Short periods in Rome and London followed before he fled for the United States, where he entered the publishing business, founding *Encyclopedia Americana* (which, by the 1850s, had made its way into the personal library of Abraham Lincoln). Lieber eventually settled in South Carolina, where he taught political economy at South Carolina College (the forerunner of the University of South Carolina). There, he would often lecture on war, arguing that death through war was the most noble sacrifice a citizen could make, justice being more valuable than human life. Quitting South Carolina, where he had come under attack for an *Encyclopedia Americana* entry condemning slavery as "inconsistent with the moral nature of man" (though he himself owned slaves while living there, arguing that "it is no injustice to have slaves where slavery exists and emancipation does not happen"), Lieber moved to New York City, where he became a professor of political science at Columbia College (today's Columbia University). He was in New York when the Civil War broke out, and it pained him that the opening shots were heard in his old home state of South Carolina. As the fighting continued, he lectured on secession, arguing, as Lincoln had, that it was unconstitutional. "Why, my dear doctor . . . ," Lieber quoted Lincoln as saying to him. "Here I find in your admirable lectures two passages which I have almost verbatim in my message; and people will say I copied from you, but I didn't, I assure [you] I didn't."

The war took a toll on Lieber's family. Two of his sons, Hamilton and Guido, fought for the Union. His third son, Oscar, stayed behind in South Carolina and joined the Confederate Army. Hamilton was critically injured fighting at Fort Donelson in February 1862, leading Lieber to reflect that while he knew war as a soldier, as a suffering victim, and as a citizen, he had "yet to learn it in the phase of a father searching for his wounded son, walking through the hospitals, peering in the ambulances." An even more painful experience awaited. Three months after Hamilton was wounded, Oscar was killed at the Battle of Eltham's Landing, Virginia.

While searching for Hamilton at Fort Donelson, Lieber met Henry Halleck, who was familiar with Lieber's lectures, and they struck up a friendship. Lieber soon developed correspondence with Stanton and Attorney General Bates as well. In July of 1862, Lieber met Lincoln at the White House. Columbia University was conferring an honorary degree on the president, and Lieber took the occasion to sit down with Lincoln and set out his ideas to him. Lieber found the president reluctant, unready for the aggression that Lieber wished the Union to undertake. "Well, Mr. President, won't you give us a little fight?" he asked. Lincoln demurred. "I'll see," he responded, sounding like a father not wanting to say "no" to a child. Lieber saw Lincoln as a "peculiarly truthful simple hearted man." He disappointed the professor, who had already made it known that he believed in a more forceful policy toward the rebels, something more than what he called Lincoln's "scattered pelting." In lectures published in the *New York Times* the previous winter, Lieber disdained what he called the "Happiness Period" of history when the highest human intellects were directed toward reducing the scourge of war. "The people seemed to think it was a dreadful thing for men to turn the ingenuity God had given them towards mutual

destruction; they thought there was no redeeming quality in it."
Lieber disagreed.

In August, Halleck asked Lieber to tackle the delicate and
complicated subject of the treatment of the many guerrilla fight-
ers in the South, marauding bands of irregulars, organized outside of the authorized Confederate Army, but who nonetheless
carried on "raids, extortion, destruction, and massacre." Were
they entitled to the protections offered to lawful combatants like
the uniformed soldiers fighting for the Confederate Army? Jomini had never addressed this because war to him was a gentleman's sport fought exclusively by armies. In a sixteen-page
treatise on the subject, Lieber concluded that guerrillas were not
to be afforded lawful status, and his pamphlet became the guide
for officers in the field, who thereafter commonly authorized
summary executions for those caught fighting without any con-
nection to an organized command source.

For Lieber, this was only the start. He wrote Halleck about
the need now for a new code of war, laying out what should
be deemed lawful in a different era. Halleck initially deflected
the offer, but it had in fact arrived at precisely the right time.
Frustrated by McClellan's failures, Old Brains had lost some
faith in his own textbook for "chivalric warfare" and was ready to
look upon war with fresh eyes. Responding to news that rebels
in Kentucky were being treated with "milk and water," Halleck
scolded the officer in charge, writing, "Domestic traitors, who
seek the overthrow of our Government, are not entitled to its
protection and should be made to feel its power. . . . Make them
suffer in their persons and property for their crimes. . . . Let the
guilty feel that you have an iron hand. . . . Don't be influenced by
those old political grannies, who are only half way Union men,

and who are ever ready to shield and apologize for traitors." Days later, Halleck gave Lieber the go-ahead on his plan.

Lieber began to draft a set of regulations that emphasized his personal beliefs about war. In roughly ten thousand words divided into 157 crisply articulated articles, he provided the license for a robust assault of the enemy. "The more vigorously wars are pursued," he explained, "the better it is for humanity. Sharp wars are brief."

In the Lieber Code (as it would come to be known) virtually anything was acceptable, including the destruction of property, of the instruments and pathways of travel, and of all methods and tools of communication. Soldiers were free to starve the enemy and to appropriate whatever was necessary for their own army's subsistence and safety. Civilian noncombatants were to be spared, but only "as much as the exigencies of war will permit." Men did not stop being moral creatures, he advised. They remained "responsible to one another and to God." But this only meant that they were not to engage in gratuitous violence and that they were to provide civilized conditions for prisoners of war (including "plain and wholesome food"), for instance, that they were to respect hospital zones and the sacredness of domestic relations. Lieber included a prohibition on perfidy (one side could not raise a flag of surrender and then engage in an assault as the other side emerged to accept it) and on revenge for the sake of revenge (though revenge that served some military purpose was okay). War is not its own end, he wrote, but the *means to obtain* the ends delineated by the state. Each article of his code described the limitations on conduct in light of this test.

There was no doubt that emancipation was consistent with these new Lieber rules of warfare. McClellan was right—emancipation did not fit with the form of war he had been trained to conduct. What did slavery have to do with the maneuvering of armies and the capture of territory? But in Lieber's vision of warfare, emancipation only had to meet the "military necessity" standard, which it did. Slavery was central to the Southern economy, and slave labor was being utilized directly by the South in the war effort. Therefore, the destruction of the practice would hasten the end of the war. Still, in his landmark code, the professor dedicated two articles to a special discussion of the subject, quoting the Romans to declare slavery an affront to natural law and asserting that a person made free by an act of war would thereafter receive "the shield of the law of nations," preventing him from ever being enslaved again.

As far as we know, Lincoln did not confer with Lieber while the professor was drafting the code. Lincoln made no edits and no suggestions. He left that process to Halleck and Stanton. Lincoln may not even have read it before it arrived on his desk on April 24, 1863, under the title of General Order 100, "Instructions for the Government of Armies of the United States in the Field." There, it awaited the judgment and signature of the man Lieber once described as "kind hearted"—too much, he feared—to make war as war should be made.

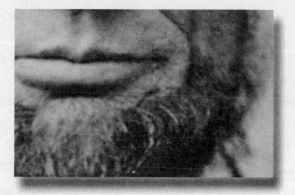

XI.

WEAKENED

I T WOULD BE HARD to reconcile any of the many stalwart por-
trayals of Abraham Lincoln, anything from the pen of Carl
Sandburg, say, or from the big-screen representations of Ray-
mond Massey or Henry Fonda, from one of the many children's
books over the years, or from the big bold-print and worship-
ful images on posters taped to the walls of social studies classes
across Kansas and Minnesota and Indiana, or, frankly, 90 percent
of the biographies, especially those written in the seventy-five
years or so after his death, but even many of the triumphant ones
written today—it would be hard to reconcile *any* of these with
the Abraham Lincoln who greeted December 1862.

Sure, Lincoln had issued the "preliminary" Emancipation Proclamation, and that had been met with something close to awe by all who had been waiting in earnest for the essential justice of this act, but besides the many legitimate critiques that inevitably followed from the reading of the document's fine print, there was also, increasingly, the genuine worry that the proclamation—even this *flawed* proclamation—would never come to pass, that maybe Lincoln never intended it to come to pass, that he was posturing with the lives of 4 million, that he would yet find some way to deny them this revolutionary act, that he would deflect it, postpone it, amend and alter it, that he would knead the language that formed it until it no longer even resembled an act of emancipation. He was, after all, still caught between two seemingly incompatible constituencies, sitting at once on "two stools," as one nineteenth-century historian described it, not so much balanced as poised to sprawl between them, and on which stool did he feel, in his heart, that he belonged?

The answer remained an enigma. Edward Stanly, the military governor of North Carolina (protecting Union-occupied territory along the coast), asked Lincoln to explain why he had defied his pledge, the one he made to Stanly, that he would only seek to restore the Union, not fight to end slavery now, a pledge that had convinced Stanly to stand up for Lincoln in an antagonistic Confederate state, and Lincoln reportedly responded by saying it had become "a civil necessity"—not a military necessity, but a *civil* necessity—to do so, for he had to "prevent the Radicals from openly embarrassing the government in the conduct of the war." Lincoln anticipated that unless he issued a proclamation of freedom, the Republican Congress would use the power of the purse to stay his hand, to stop the war, "leaving the whole land in anarchy." He had "prayed to the Almighty to save him from this necessity," the president told Stanly. "If it be possible, let this cup pass from me," he had said, quoting from the book of Matthew. But his prayer had gone unfulfilled.

If Stanly is to be believed (and this was reported not from his lips but by a journalist who met with Stanly and recorded it in his diary), then it was political blackmail, not the quest for military supremacy, and certainly not moral pluck, that had prompted Lincoln to issue the Preliminary Proclamation. Perhaps he had to speak this way to a politician from North Carolina who, as a Unionist, was putting his reputation on the line for the president, but was Lincoln now just saying whatever he thought his listener might want to hear, turning like a top to be all things to all people? If so, it would come at the price of respect. Zachariah Chandler had already pronounced Lincoln as "unstable as water" and spoken of the need for someone to "control and hold him." One has the sense of an impressionable leader whose closest advisers feared that he must be locked away lest he spontaneously follow the ideas of the next person who was able to work his way into his imagination.

If Lincoln was not trusted, he was also not popular. The midterm elections in November had produced mixed results. Republicans lost the governorships of New Jersey and New York and the legislatures of New Jersey, Indiana, and Illinois. They retained a majority in the Senate. (Until the ratification of the Seventeenth Amendment to the Constitution, in 1913, senators were not popularly chosen; they were elected by state legislatures.) In New England, the proclamation had earned back Republican voters who were thrilled that Lincoln had made emancipation a mission of this war—however limited that emancipation might be—but elsewhere the Preliminary Proclamation had not been greeted with enthusiasm. Lincoln's suspension of habeas corpus had given the Democrats another issue to run on. The *Ottawa* [Illinois] *Free Trader* described Lincoln and Seward and other Republican moderates as having come under the influence of abolitionist "fanatics," and that could only lead, it predicted, to "scenes as bloody and dark as any which appalled the world during the despotism of Cromwell or"—here came that favorite image again—"the 'Reign of Terror' in the French Revolution." In New York, the Democratic Party candidate for governor, Horatio Seymour, eschewed state issues to focus solely on Lincoln's abuse of civil liberties—and won. He asserted that Lincoln could not do a selective reading of the Constitution. If the Constitution was powerless to stop him from instituting emergency measures such as the suspension of habeas corpus or the Emancipation Proclamation, then it was also powerless to keep the South within the Union. We either live within constitutional limits, Seymour asserted, or we do not.

In Lincoln's home district of Springfield, Illinois, his onetime law partner John Todd Stuart (cousin of Mary Todd Lincoln) campaigned for Congress as a Democrat, promising, essentially, to "reform" Lincoln by urging him to limit himself to "the ample powers conferred upon him by the Constitution," instead of acts that approached a "military despotism." The goal, he urged voters, should be a "peace which will degrade no section of the Union," which, translated, meant no forced emancipation. Lincoln's old friend Leonard Swett was the Republican candidate running against Stuart. He stood firmly by the proclamation and lost. Swett had to contend not only with generalized opposition to emancipation but also with worries about an impending rush of free blacks into the state. "Shall Illinois be Africanized?" read one pamphlet attacking him. This was the Northern counterpart to the South's fantasy of a "slave rebellion," that blacks would come in droves over the fences to take away white laborers' jobs. Vallandigham had preyed on such anxiety in Ohio, but this dark, threatening vision wasn't isolated to the river towns there. Slaves seized as contraband under the Confiscation Acts were sent north to Illinois, too, where the levees, complained a writer in the *Cairo Gazette,* were "so dark with negroes" that white pedestrians would need "lanterns" to move about. What would happen once emancipation was proclaimed?

Meanwhile, Lincoln had fired McClellan, and that, most agreed, had been long overdue, but this act alone could not resolve his troubles on the battlefront. Many, particularly the Radical Republicans, worried that McClellan's replacement, Burnside, was too weak, that they needed a hard-shell commander such as General Joseph Hooker, who had distinguished himself at Antietam. In addition to such strategic questions, morale among the troops was a growing issue. Many soldiers resented McClellan's firing. Others disputed the expansion of the mission to include emancipation. Some were just tired of war, their initial rush of enthusiasm for the fight having long passed. Desertions were rampant, in the tens of thousands, some of them encouraged or even arranged by people on the home front who wanted their boys home to handle the harvest on the farm. By January, an accounting would show a full quarter of the Army of the Potomac absent.

Disliked; distrusted; failing in a deadly struggle that he did not fully understand; not yet a year out from the death of his beloved Willie; his wife, Mary, still reeling from the effects of that death and busy attending to spirits (indeed, she had advanced to where she could induce her own visions, without the help of a medium), Lincoln was spent. Watching from the gallery as the president arrived at a November 30 service at Dr. Gurley's church, the journalist Noah Brooks found him wasted, his hair "grizzled, his gait more stooping, his countenance sallow." There was "a sunken, deathly look about the large, cavernous eyes" that Brooks, who admired Lincoln, found saddening. However blemished it had been upon his arrival in office, his face was now well plowed by the scars of worry. A few months after Brooks first saw him, the president would deflect the recommendation that he take a rest by saying, "I suppose it is good for the body, but the tired part of me is inside and out of reach."

What a wonderfully elliptical and yet revealing expression. He could not rest the part of him that was exhausted *because that part of him was no longer within his grasp*. He had no control over it; it was a settled fact of his life, like an injury that would never heal. Lincoln used other similar images at around the same time, referring to a "tired spot, which can't be got at" and, on another occasion, to how "nothing could reach the tired spot within" him. This elusive fatigue was not a physical exhaustion—"I suppose [rest] is good for the body," he had said—but likely not simply mental exhaustion either. He seemed almost to be referring to that same battle weariness of soldiers, captured as they are by experiences that deplete them, that tire with their very permanence, that respond to no palliative. This was Abraham Lincoln in December 1862.

On the first of the month, he delivered his Annual Message to Congress, the constitutionally required address on the "state of the union." In Lincoln's day, the address was not given as a speech by the president in person. Thomas Jefferson had found that tradition redolent of monarchy, so Jefferson provided only a written text to be read by a clerk. That set the pattern until Woodrow Wilson resumed the tradition of an appearance before Congress in 1913. In 1862, it was not Lincoln, then, but the secretary of the Senate, John W. Forney, a Philadelphia journalist who was Lincoln's intimate friend and political ally, who delivered all 8,443 words of Lincoln's Annual Message.

For Lincoln, there may be no more peculiar piece of writing, none in his gifted history as a man of words, than this strange, disjointed, sometimes contradictory address. It is often cited, deservedly so, for its stirring conclusion—more on that later—but the great bulk of the speech was divided between routine administrative business rendered clumsily (a report from the Treasury that was likely written by Chase; a treaty established with the sultan of Turkey that fit in a section on foreign affairs likely written by Seward; a recognition of the renewed efficiency of the postal service); and a discussion of the ongoing rebellion.

Offering that he could not improve on the spirited language he had used in his first Annual Message, one year earlier, Lincoln reiterated his belief that the only difference between North and South was that "one section of our country believes slavery is right and ought to be extended, while the other believes it is wrong and ought not to be extended." This, he wrote, was not sufficient reason to rend the country, and anyway, such a split would lack the prospect of longevity. Since the geography itself could not change nor could an impassable wall be built between North and South, the earth would always unite the people of Indiana with the people of Kentucky and the people of Kentucky with the people of Tennessee. Why, one could walk across the border, wade across it where it was formed by a river. If anything, the contiguous nature of the states would continue to force them together, "however much of blood and treasure the separation might have cost."

Where the natural world was eternal, the strife between its peoples was merely temporal, and it "could be hushed forever" if there was but the will to do that now, with this generation. Therefore, Lincoln proposed three constitutional amendments. One would make "forever free" those slaves who "enjoyed actual freedom by the chances of war." This referred not to those who would be freed by the Emancipation Proclamation—his address, it was becoming clear, was an attempt to avoid the necessity for making the Preliminary Proclamation real—but, instead, those who had been seized according to the Confiscation Acts or who had on their own effort or through some other series of accidents or actions otherwise made it to freedom. That amendment, then, just gave legal status to an existing state of affairs, though it did include compensation to masters who lost slaves but had not themselves been disloyal. By contrast, the next two amendments were confounding in their nature, scope, and detail. Lincoln proposed compensation in the form of federal bonds to states that opted for a gradual emancipation *by the year 1900*, and should any state reintroduce slavery—after all, nothing here made slavery illegal; it just regulated the practice—it would have to repay the federal government with interest. Finally, he proposed federal funding for that persistent idea of colonizing "free colored persons" someplace outside the United States, though only with their consent. He acknowledged that Haiti and Liberia were willing to accept "such persons" as full and equal citizens, yet most American blacks, regretfully, did not seem inclined to move to those countries despite its being "in their interest" to do so. He worried that, for African-Americans, sudden and complete emancipation could only lead to lives of "vagrant destitution." Therefore, his plan of gradual emancipation and colonization would give them a better chance at success in freedom. If accepted, Lincoln's post–Civil War world would have looked like this: an end to the fighting now, slavery legal but on the path to a gradual disappearance over the next *forty years*, slaveholders compensated for forgoing the practice, freed slaves encouraged to leave the country, and all that at a cost, so far, of 419,979 casualties (230,196 of those on the Union side alone). This, in December 1862, was the plan of the man who would one day be known as the Great Emancipator.

To be fair, some sort of accommodation for the slaveholding states had been promised in the Preliminary Proclamation text as an inducement for the rebels to cease their rebellion. He owed them this chance. But few expected anything as broad and tolerant and generous toward the enemy as this, not this late in the game. In what surely put his argument for emancipation in dangerous constitutional territory, Lincoln acknowledged that the destruction of slavery was indeed the destruction of property. He also, remarkably, put the onus for slavery on both the South and the North, declaring that "when it is remembered how unhesitatingly we all use cotton and sugar and share the profits of dealing in them, it may not be quite safe to say that the South has been more responsible than the North for [slavery's] continuance." One has to wonder how that was received in the homes of the dead soldiers of the Twenty-Eighth Massachusetts or the Seventy-Ninth New York.

All of this rhetoric formed a dissonance with the event that everyone was anticipating, the looming proclamation, which Lincoln never directly mentioned, but he had something he still wanted to argue here, in what was becoming a frightful eleventh hour, and that argument went this way: Yes, emancipation is good, but is immediate emancipation, with all its potential for social disruption, is *that* good? Is it better than a slow and deliberate emancipation, one that takes into account the interests of the slaveholders and the relatively meager chances for racial harmony in a society with a history so long polluted by a system of systemized cruelty and injustice? If there is to be immediate emancipation, what motivation would the Southern white population have to end its rebellion? It could only lose. And if there is no colonization, what future does a united nation have with a population—the former slaves—that had to be ready to release a long-suppressed rage? Lincoln believed the fears of white slaveholders on the likelihood of some, perhaps repeated, and deadly expressions of black anger, even going so far as to include in the Preliminary Proclamation a plea to the newly emancipated to "abstain from all violence, except in self-defence." As for the fears in the North about competition for jobs, colonization would solve that, too. The work the former slaves abandoned on the plantation would still need to be done, and if enough blacks took advantage of his offer to facilitate their departure from the country, there would actually be a shortage of workers, leading to higher wages. The message was unsettling. While he referred to voluntary migration of the free Americans of African descent, he also referred to "deportation" four times in the address, an ominous sign since that word could only connote forced expulsion.

In this patchwork Annual Message, Lincoln's proposals and

parts of his concluding paragraphs also clashed. Lincoln being Lincoln, he did not miss this chance to awaken his listeners— or readers—with words of poetry, and the close of the address contains some of the more rousing phrases that Lincoln ever penned: "The dogmas of the quiet past are inadequate to the stormy present. . . . As our case is new, so we must think anew and act anew. We must disenthrall ourselves, and then we shall save our country."

The words are inspiring—they are often quoted even today— but they likely confused their listeners in the moment. Several key phrases had to have lingered in the ear for their awkward juxtaposition with his new plans. While Lincoln derided the "dogmas of the past," he had just proposed their slow and steady continuation, and if he wished old ideas to be discarded for new, then why in this very speech had he returned to, even expanded upon, proposals—colonization; gradual, compensated emancipation— that he had made before and that had failed before?

His request that Americans "disenthrall" themselves had interesting overtones. The word means "to set free," which is what the North was seeking to do—to free the slave, either now or, as Lincoln had just proposed, well down the road—but Lincoln was not speaking here about freeing the slave population; rather, he was speaking about disenthralling *ourselves*—*freeing* ourselves. In one sense, this is a repeat of his notion that in freeing the slave, we ensure freedom for all others, an idea that he had intoned before and repeated in this address. But his use of the word *disenthrall* makes this also a much larger and more interesting idea. He was asking his listeners, both North and South, to disengage themselves from what had become an almost unnatural attachment to the subject of slavery. He had rightly detected that the walk up to this war had included an increasingly shrill public dialogue, one that went beyond the attack and defense of slavery. In the South, slavery was wrapped up with tradition and folkways, with regional identity, with the protection of private property, and, more subtly, the protection of the virtue of Southern women. To many Southerners, it was also, remember, that notion that through the argument over the future of slavery, the nation was replaying the dynamics of the American Revolution, with Lincoln serving as King George and the North as the distant empire utilizing brute force to impose its will on ungrateful subjects. The North, too, had its perverse preoccupations, which could be discovered in the heated religiosity and moral self-righteousness of some abolitionists. *Enthrall* is a romantic word, a word of passion. To be enthralled is to be attached beyond the arguments of reason, and so to *disenthrall* oneself is to remove the ardor, the lust for victory, and take a sober look at the facts. Slavery was done, he was saying. History had already marked it for extinction. The only question was how it was to be made extinct, and here Lincoln was saying that the how could either be more acts of war or it could be the "plain, peaceful, generous, just" proposals he had just put before the country, "a way which, if followed, the world will forever applaud, and God must forever bless."

Chase thought Lincoln was in some kind of trance. There was no way this Congress would pass such amendments, and even if it did, it would take years for the states to consider ratification, much less grant it. Illinois senator Orville Browning (who had been appointed to take Stephen Douglas's Senate seat after Douglas died in 1861) described Lincoln's proposals as representing a man in the grip of a "hallucination." For Browning, who had lost in the November elections and was about to be replaced by a Democrat, Lincoln's speech seemed to betray a "singular reticence with regard to the war." Without any reason other than his own cockeyed optimism, Lincoln had come to believe that he was on the verge of an agreement with the Border States to accept remunerative emancipation, that at least two Confederate states were ready to return to the Union on the same terms, and that the army with its new leadership was poised to take a commanding position over the rebels in Virginia. He could hardly have been more wrong.

On December 11, the Army of the Potomac, now under the leadership of General Ambrose Burnside, began an assault on the Army of Northern Virginia at positions near the Rappahannock River at Fredericksburg, Virginia. Burnside hoped to cross the river, push Lee back, and then move quickly on to Richmond. Though the plan once again valued the capture of territory over the defeat of the enemy army, Lincoln reluctantly approved it. (He may have been thinking like a Clausewitzian, but he was not acting like one, not yet.) When the details of the operation then became confused in conversations between Halleck and Burnside, a true disaster was in the making. Burnside stopped outside of town, awaiting the delivery of pontoons for bridging the river, but the pontoons did not come. Halleck thought the general would cross where the river was shallow and could be traversed by foot. By the time the pontoons were delivered, it was late, too late. In the delay, Burnside lost all the advantage of surprise, and Lee was able to carefully position his forces in the hills just west of the Rappahannock, primed and protected for the assault. Union forces finally made their crossing, in frigid temperatures and a blinding snow, but the conditions, especially the terrain, were against them. The high ground on the south bank of the river was formidable and controlled by Confederate forces. As the Union soldiers advanced, nothing protected them from the direct aim of rebel fire. By the end of the battle, more than 13,353 Union men were killed, wounded, or missing, compared to 4,567 for the Confederates.

The Tenth Massachusetts, Oliver Wendell Holmes Jr.'s regiment, was there for the fight, but Holmes himself was in a nearby hospital, recovering from a bout of dysentery. Upon hearing the gunfire, he left his bed and climbed to a small hill to gaze upon the action. It is a "terrible sight," he wrote his mother, "when your regiment is in it but you are safe." The Tenth Massachusetts alone lost forty-eight men. They had been led in "obedience to superior command" to what amounted, wrote Holmes, to nothing more than "certain and useless death."

The Fifty-First New York Volunteers were there, too, including among them Captain George Washington Whitman, one of the most storied of Civil War veterans, who had already served at Cedar Mountain, Second Bull Run, Chantilly, and Antietam. When news that Whitman had been wounded at Fredericksburg reached his brother, the celebrated poet Walt Whitman, it brought the author of *Leaves of Grass* to Washington in search of him. Upon his arrival at the hospital where his brother was recovering, Whitman encountered a pile of discarded limbs and other body parts lying outside the entrance. George Whitman had suffered only a grazing to his cheek from an exploded shell— but he had been lucky. Of the fifteen hundred members of the Volunteers, only two hundred survived the battle. Walt Whitman was shaken by the suffering he encountered there, and the Civil War he'd read about back home in Brooklyn became very real for him. He spent the rest of the war in Washington, moving through the area hospitals, where he assisted the wounded.

Burnside's incompetence at Fredericksburg had been stunning, for he chose the most disadvantageous path in a disadvantageous situation, advancing on the enemy at the steepest part of the well-fortified hillside. Afterward, he nobly took the blame for the defeat—more than that, he seemed emotionally crippled by the losses that had been endured under his leadership—but even his subordinates agreed that he was not fit for the job, with two of them later taking the extraordinary step of visiting Lincoln to report their lack of confidence. Though they insisted that their purpose was not to undermine their superior officer's authority (which could have resulted in serious disciplinary consequences), this was precisely what they intended. They wanted Burnside out.

Lincoln's response was tone-deaf. He liked Burnside and wanted to stick with him, which he did, for the time being. Then, on December 22, Lincoln issued a hollow, almost disingenuous letter to the troops, beginning, "I have just read your Commanding General's preliminary report of the Battle of Fredericksburg. Although you were not successful, the attempt was not an error, nor the failure other than accident." Lincoln knew that the attempt had indeed been an error and its failure was the result of a series of colossal leadership blunders. Yet he continued, sounding cold, almost cruel, "The courage with which you, in an open field, maintained the contest against an entrenched foe, and the consummate skill and success with which you crossed and re-crossed the river, in face of the enemy, show that you possess all the qualities of a great army, which will yet give victory to the cause of the country and of popular government." This was "congratulations" to the troops, then, for following a plan that did little more than sacrifice wave upon wave of them to enemy target practice in a flat, open field.

Perhaps, however, Lincoln meant something more than mere cheerleading in this last line, and if so, it was another hint that his strategic approach to the war was changing. If Lincoln's assistant secretary William Stoddard is to be believed, the president's private analysis of the failure at Fredericksburg was that there needed to be more bloodshed, not less. Stoddard, whose 1890 memoir, *Inside the White House in War Times*, carries a novelist's tone (his post-Washington career was as a children's book author), describes the author overhearing Lincoln wishing for a decisive battle that would have put the vast supply of Union soldiers up against the smaller Confederate numbers until Lee was down to his last man, the Confederacy was defeated, and the war was over. That, he argued, would have been so much more productive than fighting these many smaller battles, which dragged the war on and on in want of a resolution. The one-decisive-battle approach would also be more humane, as a single engagement fought to the end would likely mean fewer casualties than multiple skirmishes fought over years, and of course the longer the war continued, the more deaths there would be from disease. He was coming to believe what Francis Lieber believed, that short, brutal wars are kinder and more effective than long, protracted wars. War was all arithmetic, simple arithmetic. He had just not yet found a general who could add as he did.

After Fredericksburg, Lincoln looked feeble, insubstantial, confused, his administration absent of strong leadership. Around Washington, there was a palpable "thirst for a victim," someone to be made to pay for the months of mistakes that had riddled the war effort. Republicans considered whether they should ask the president to shake up his cabinet or even to resign his office. The strongest criticism, however, first fell upon those around Lincoln who were suspected of wielding undue influence on the president. In particular, Radical Republicans aimed their attack at Seward for his moderating influence. "He is Lincoln's evil genius," wrote Joseph Medill of the *Chicago Tribune*, summing up the attitude of many. "He has been President de facto, and has kept a sponge saturated with chloroform to Uncle Abe's nose."

Seward had plenty of enemies among Senate Republicans, and they caucused on the afternoon of the sixteenth, plotting his removal. Trumbull of Illinois spoke bitterly of him. Morton Wilkinson of Minnesota blamed Seward for Lincoln's not taking a more aggressive stance in the war. The senators found Seward wanting on the issue of slavery. Seward, after all, had urged Lincoln to postpone the proclamation back in July. Was this really for strategic reasons or because he didn't want emancipation itself? William Fessenden of Maine said he heard that there was a "back stairs influence" on the president, overruling the rest of the cabinet, and that this maligner was Seward. Why, a member of the cabinet had told him as much.

That cabinet member was Chase. For nearly two years, Lincoln had successfully managed the rivalry between Seward and the nation's treasury secretary, the two men having observed a "cold courtesy" (Welles's phrase) throughout, but under the pressure from the administration's failures and the loss of respect for Lincoln himself, that delicate balance had been lost. Chase, who had long complained privately about Seward, still harbored hopes for his own run at the presidency, and in the present crisis he saw an opportunity to push Seward from the same path.

Others in the cabinet also objected to Seward. Welles continued to resent the former New York governor, whom he described as running to the president two or three times a day to manipulate him to dispose of measures that others had convinced him to adopt. But it was the tactless Chase who whispered strategy and argument in the ears of the disgruntled Senate Republicans; it was Chase who reinforced a picture of a wayward presidency in need of an overhaul.

At the suggestion of Senator James Grimes of Iowa, the caucus considered a vote of no confidence in the secretary of state, but in the end, the senators opted to first send a committee of their own to visit the president and speak of their grave concerns. Lincoln received them on the evening of December 18. He listened while Ben Wade of Ohio castigated him for entrusting the conduct of the war to officers who were "bitter and malignant Democrats." Fessenden added to the charge by saying that the army was being run by "largely pro-slavery men" who "sympathized strongly with the Southern feeling." The cabinet did not act like a cabinet. Why, it was their understanding that the president barely consulted them. Then the senators addressed their main theme, that Lincoln had placed too much trust in Secretary Seward.

Earlier in the day, hours before the meeting with the senators, Lincoln had received a letter of resignation from Seward. The secretary had heard word of the senators' plot against him and decided that he should resign lest the president be put in the awkward position of defending him. Lincoln responded by visiting Seward at his home, where he asked him to reconsider. Seward demurred, protesting that it would be a relief for him to be free of official concerns and return to his family in New

York. "Ah, yes, Governor, that will do very well for you," said Lincoln, "but I am like the starling in [Laurence] Sterne's story, 'I can't get out.'" The reference was to the eighteenth-century English novelist's *A Sentimental Journey Through France and Italy*, in which the narrator, while visiting Paris, comes upon a bird in a cage pleading for its freedom, prompting him to reflect on "the miseries of confinement." Lincoln understood that the senators' real target was not Seward, nor the leaders of the army, nor any other member of his cabinet. Their target was Lincoln himself.

What followed was an ingenious political move, especially for a weakened president. At the specially called cabinet meeting on December 19, Lincoln told the members about his "earnest and sad session" with the senators and how it had resulted in the resignation of the secretary of state, who was, at the moment, packing boxes for his move back to New York. He said the senators had come to him with no malicious intent. Nonetheless, they seemed convinced that Seward was responsible for "a lukewarmness" in the conduct of the war, and that he was "the real cause of our failures." Using what Edward Bates, in his diary, described as "quaint language," Lincoln said the senators believed that any good purposes that the president might have, "Mr. Seward contrived to suck them out of him unperceived." Lincoln then invited them to return that evening for a night of "free talk" about their delicate situation.

Unbeknownst to the cabinet secretaries, Lincoln also invited the Senate Republican caucus for the evening talk. The discussion went on for four hours. The senators did not hold back, openly criticizing Seward and the administration. In response, Lincoln acknowledged that his communication with the cabinet may not always have been regular, but he did feel that on issues of grave importance he had always sought their advice. He then turned to the cabinet members in front of him to ask "whether there had been any want of unity or of sufficient consultation." Several cabinet members agreed that there had not been. But all eyes were on Chase. He was the reason they were all there. The question put him in an awkward position, for if he repeated what he had said to the senators, then he would be revealed as having been disloyal to Lincoln, and if he denied any disappointment about consultation, he would be betraying the caucus and undermining the case against Seward. At first, Chase protested the nature of the forum. He had not, he said, come there to be "arraigned." Then, begrudgingly, he admitted that, no, at least on important issues the cabinet had not had a lack of unity. Shamed, he submitted his own resignation the next morning.

Lincoln accepted neither Seward's nor Chase's nor Stanton's resignations (the secretary of war, responding to criticism, had added his name to the list of those who should be seen suddenly departing), and soon all three were back at their jobs. For the president, however, this was but a minor triumph. He had averted a crisis of command with a nimble handling of egos, yet it was an essentially benign event, restoring things as they were, not changing them for the better. In fact, the "national ailment," as Welles described the state of things, seemed only to be worsening. Lincoln was still distrusted, the war was still against him, and none of his proposals aimed at averting the need for an Emancipation Proclamation had stirred Congress to action.

"They wish to get rid of me," he told Orville Browning (one imagines an emphasis here on the word *me*), "and I am sometimes half disposed to gratify them." Browning pitied the president. "Some of them do wish to get rid of you," he replied, "but the fortunes of the country are bound up with your fortunes, and you stand firmly at your post and hold the helm with a steady hand. To relinquish it now would bring upon us certain and inevitable ruin." Browning's words, while sympathetic, were hardly comforting. "We are now on the brink of destruction," Lincoln responded. "It appears to me the Almighty is against us, and I can hardly see a ray of hope."

None of the proposals that Lincoln made in his Annual Message, none of the constitutional amendments aimed at bringing a "plain, peaceful, generous," and "just" end to both the war and to the persistent sectional dispute over slavery, none of the talk about colonization and compensated emancipation went anywhere. It was all essentially forgotten; that is, if it was even heard in the first place. With his insistence on old policies already rejected, with a split in his own party growing with each day, with a cabinet crisis—however cleverly he may have resolved it—demonstrating the fissures in his administration, and with some of his closest aides already jockeying to succeed him, Lincoln was becoming increasingly irrelevant. It appeared as though Congress had simply grown tired of the delays, the obfuscations, the reticence, and was ready to let January 1 arrive and see if the president would really do what he had said he would, proclaim freedom. Days from his deadline, Lincoln still had everyone guessing.

XII.

A BIRTHING:
JANUARY 1, 1863

SOMETIME IN THE WEEK of December 28, 1862, Zenas C. Robbins, a patent attorney and friend of Lincoln's, visited the president to urge him to stay the course. The chaplain of the Senate, the Reverend Byron Sunderland, whose faith in Lincoln's commitment to the proclamation had also been waning, accompanied Robbins. On the Sunday before, Sunderland had preached to his congregation at Washington's First Presbyterian Church on the subject. Ushered into the White House, they found Lincoln standing at the end of a long table in the cabinet room. With only one gaslight illuminating the scene, the president was shrouded in darkness. Robbins greeted Lincoln from the doorway and introduced Sunderland, who announced rather abruptly that he was there to address the president on the "serious condition of the country."

"Go ahead, Doctor," Lincoln replied, adding, in what Sunderland took as a wry comment on his lack of height, "every little bit helps." (Wry it may have been, but that was more likely because Lincoln had grown tired of unsolicited advice.) Sunderland then confronted the president, saying that he had heard that Lincoln would not keep his promise, that he would miss his date with history and withdraw the proclamation. The president responded elliptically, "Peter denied his master," a reference to the gospel story of the Apostle Peter, who, as Jesus foretold at the Last Supper, would betray him three times "before the rooster crows." The comment was clearly tailored for a man of the clergy. "He thought he wouldn't," Lincoln said, "but he did."

Sunderland retorted that Peter did not deny Jesus until after his master had rebuked him. "You have a master, too, Mr. Lincoln, the American people. Don't deny your master until he has rebuked you before all the world." The exchange apparently impressed Lincoln, and he became more attentive to their conversation. He suggested they sit.

In an awkward spell of silence, Lincoln's gnarled hands were clasped at his forehead. Then he launched into a soliloquy in which he restated many of the perplexing questions that had left him paralyzed these last six months. "If it had been left to you and me, there would have been no cause for this war," he told the pastor, "but it was not left to us. God has allowed men to make

slaves of their fellows. He permits this war." Prefiguring a theme
of his second inaugural speech, he talked of how both sides pray
to the same God and how both sides believe they are right and
yet both cannot be right. He had examined this same idea in his
"Meditation on the Divine Will." Sounding full of despair, the
president then asked, what will come from this struggle? What
will be the effect of it all on the whites and on the Negroes?

Lincoln remembered a fable of Aesop's from a book he had
read in his youth. Next to the story were woodcuts showing
"four white men scrubbing a negro in a potash kettle filled with
cold water." The men thought that if they scrubbed him hard,
they could make him white, and so they scrubbed and scrubbed
and "just about the time when they thought they were succeeding, he took cold and died." Sunderland and Robbins laughed,
though likely an awkward laugh given the pathetic nature of the
scene just described to them, before Lincoln interrupted to re-
late the story's relevance: "Now, I am afraid that by the time we
get through this war the negro will catch cold and die."

Lincoln's summation may have demonstrated concern that
the interest of the Negro race was being overlooked in the clash
between North and South, or he may even have been obliquely
referring to colonization, as if to say that the Negro, ill suited
for success in a post–Civil War America, could only "catch cold
and die" without some plan to correct the error of his having
been brought here in the first place; that is, unless he was to be
returned to the place where he naturally belonged. But his use
of the fable remains mysterious. The story, which only appears
in a few editions of Aesop's, where it is titled "The Blackamoor"
or "Washing the Ethiopian White," would seem to support multiple interpretations. The most innocuous would be a lesson in

expectations, that you simply can't change some things, and that if you try to change them, you could sacrifice what you have (not exactly a good omen for the impending proclamation). But the tale clearly carried appalling racist allusions, too, chief among them that equality is an unreasonable ideal, that nature never intended for the races to be treated alike, and if you try to change that, you will fail. Given the times, it would be too much to expect something other than the assumption that there is no inherent beauty or goodness to being black, that the prime goal of being black should be to be white. But the fable and its progeny (many subsequent stories have borrowed from this theme) go beyond that to degrade the black race.

While here Lincoln recalled the story as rendered by Aesop, he had to have been aware of its usage by two of his other favorite authors. The nineteenth-century English humorist Thomas Hood had a similar idea in his poem "The Black Job." It, too, tells the story of a "charitable" effort to "wash the black off." In this case the experiment is being carried out on slaves to bring them to freedom, "to see each Crow, or Jim, or John / Go in a raven and come out a swan." The story was also told in John Bunyan's *Pilgrim's Progress*, in which two characters, Fool and Want-wit, try to wash an "Ethiopian," with the intention of making him white, only to find that their efforts fail. The shepherds tell them, "Thus shall it be with the vile person: all means used to get such an one a good name, shall, in the end tend but to make him more abominable."

For half an hour after his telling of the fable, Lincoln held forth with his visitors. He described the range of arguments for and against emancipation, sounding in his wisdom and in his appreciation for all sides like "an old prophet." The men listened intently,

then departed "comforted and uplifted," related Sunderland, and
with a strong belief in Abraham Lincoln, yet no more certain of
his intentions regarding the Emancipation Proclamation.

The cabinet members received a clearer signal of Lincoln's
plans when, on December 29, three days before New Year's, Lincoln brought them a draft of what would be the final Emancipation Proclamation text and read it aloud. It had come a long way,
this still-modest and inelegant piece of writing, a long way since
Lincoln had first spoken of the idea when riding with Welles
and Seward en route to the Stanton baby's funeral, a long way
since Lincoln had sat in the telegraph office working out its dry,
inflexible language while the spiders wriggled their way through
a web just outside the window. From there, he had tinkered with
it until it reached the preliminary form that he wanted, but looking for the best timing in which to deliver it, he had tinkered
with it some more before he issued it publicly on September 22.
There, breathed into the national conversation, it had languished
through inconclusive elections and the political battles succeeding the elections, through the firing of McClellan, through the
news of the near massacre of Union troops at Fredericksburg
under the command of McClellan's replacement, and through
the cabinet crisis as well, a hundred-day warning period leading to the trigger day, New Year's, 1863, which was now finally
upon him and the nation.

This draft differed slightly from what had been promised before. It still freed the slaves in the states in rebellion, justified
emancipation as a war measure, and pledged the full force of the
federal government, including the efforts of the army and navy,
to "recognize and maintain" that freedom. But in this newest
version, Lincoln tried to soften fears that Union forces would

encourage the dreaded "servile insurrection." The notion that slaves would eventually rise up "like so many wild beasts" ready to "devastate and devour" their former masters was shared in the North and the South. Ironically, this fear had even been used as an argument *for* emancipation. Without emancipation, insurrection was "inevitable," said Charles Sumner, and "destined to be wild and lawless." With emancipation, the Union Army might be able to protect the South from the "spirit of revenge." Of course, all that assumed that the slaves would be the only aggressors. But the army could also protect the population of former slaves. Many worried that a slave rebellion could only result in a genocidal massacre of the black race.

Thus, while Lincoln's newest draft still prevented Union soldiers from interfering with the continuing efforts of slaves to initiate their own freedom by, say, running to the Union lines, the president now included the modifier *suitable* before the word *effort*, an odd decision since it is hard to imagine a run for freedom being judged for its appropriateness and then refused on that judgment. He also added an "appeal" to the former slaves to "abstain from all disorder, tumult, and violence, unless in necessary self defence" and, in the event that their freedom was agreed to, to "labor faithfully for reasonable wages." The cabinet didn't take fully to either edit. Chase, Seward, and Bates all urged Lincoln not to insert the word *suitable* and instead leave the language about self-emancipating exactly as it had been in the preliminary document, the vagaries there perhaps working as an asset. Lincoln finally agreed. As to the additional language discouraging violence, Montgomery Blair wanted Lincoln to toughen that by cautioning the newly freed slaves that a restraint from violence would show them to be "worthy of freedom." Seward suggested that instead of "appealing" to the newly freed, Lincoln should "enjoin" them to resist violence, *enjoin* being a much stronger word. Lincoln took Seward's suggestion, but he rejected Blair's idea of making the slaves show that they deserved their liberty.

Chase objected strongest to what may have been the most significant modification in this version. Lincoln had added that the freed slaves would be welcomed into the armed services of the United States. That had not appeared in any earlier draft (though section 11 of the second Confiscation Act had opened the door to the subject when it authorized the president to employ "as many persons of African descent as he may deem necessary and proper for the suppression of this rebellion"), and since this meant not just black laborers but black soldiers, it was a sharp break with tradition. Of course, if ever there was an image ripe for those fearful of servile insurrection, it had to be this one: freed slaves in crisp blue Union uniforms returning to the states where they once lived in captivity, armed for blood.

Chase didn't object to former slaves serving in the Union Army. Indeed, he had been an advocate of coupling emancipation with the recruitment of the freemen all at once. But Chase worried that by proclaiming this plan, Lincoln risked drawing attention to it rather than "leaving it to the natural course of things already begun." This was consistent with Chase's overall feeling about emancipation itself, which he still believed would be better achieved "quietly," by Union Army regiments on the ground, rather than as a bold proclamation issued from the White House.

If the language had to be there, Chase suggested turning the fear of insurrection on its head by stressing that the former slaves who joined the army would be operating under a strict authority. "In order to secure the suppression of rebellion without servile insurrection or licentious marauding," read his suggested edit, "such numbers of the population declared free, as may be found convenient, will be employed in the military and naval service of the United States." Lincoln stayed with his original text.

Two other passages demanded the president's attention. Chase suggested that Lincoln acknowledge that this was no ordinary military order, that it was more than battlefield strategy. It was righteousness. Shouldn't the document say that somewhere? He proposed that Lincoln close with "and upon this act, sincerely believed to be an act of justice, warranted by the Constitution, and an act of duty demanded by the circumstances of the country, I invoke the considerate judgment of mankind and the gracious favor of Almighty God." Lincoln took Chase's counsel and adopted the line, but he struck "an act of duty warranted by the circumstances of the country" and replaced it with "upon military necessity." Throughout the fall, the argument over the constitutionality of the Emancipation Proclamation had continued, with former Supreme Court justice Benjamin Curtis attacking Lincoln for assuming extraordinary powers. Lincoln felt the need to reinforce the proclamation's fragile constitutional moorings.

The last issue to be addressed regarded the permanence of the act and could well have been inspired by former justice Curtis when he charged that "if the President, as commander-in-chief of the army and navy in time of war, may, by an executive decree, exercise this power to abolish slavery in the States, what other power, reserved to the States or to the people, may not be exercised by the President, for the same reason, that he is of opinion he may thus best subdue the enemy?" Lincoln needed an answer for this, and he needed it quickly.

The first point of any considered reply to such a question

would have been that the powers the president was assuming had to have some legitimate military utility. The second would have been to establish that by definition these same powers would expire when the military need was over. The third would have been to point out that "emancipation" is not "abolition." Emancipation does not end slavery and does not therefore assume a power reserved to the states. All of these arguments had flaws, but for Lincoln's purposes they also raised the specter of a seriously dangerous consequence.

Throughout his drafts of the proclamation, Lincoln had written that the slaves are "then, thenceforward, *and forever* free." Perhaps because of his concern over the inherent clash between the limited nature of military necessity and the word *forever*, Lincoln had, in this final draft, substituted the more ambiguous term *henceforward*, as in "all persons held as slaves within said designated States, and parts of States, are, and *henceforward* shall be free." But this still invited a critical challenge. If emancipation is not abolition, and if the powers to emancipate for military necessity are inherently temporary, then why couldn't those freed by the Emancipation Proclamation simply be re-enslaved once the war was over? To Lincoln and all others who wanted an end to slavery, that would be nothing less than a travesty.

Chase had worried about this distinction as well, so much so that in September, shortly after the release of the Preliminary Proclamation, he had asked Attorney General Bates to issue an opinion as to whether native-born, free "colored men" are citizens of the United States. It was related to, but not the same issue, that the Supreme Court had been asked to decide in *Dred Scott*. There, as Chief Justice Taney expressed in the majority opinion, the Court had determined that Scott, a slave, was not a citizen and could not therefore bring a case for his freedom in federal court. The Court's analysis should have stopped with that, because once jurisdiction had been denied, the justices had nothing to decide. But Taney continued on, asserting that no colored person could ever be a citizen of the United States and that slavery could not be barred from the territories.

Bates delivered his opinion to Chase on November 29. He referred to *Dred Scott* as decided on issues distinct to that case and said that Taney's extension of his opinion to declare that no colored person could ever be a citizen of the United States was *dictum*; that is, unnecessary to the ruling, and therefore not binding as law. Working from a "natural rights" argument he borrowed from Francis Lieber, Bates then asserted that all native-born freemen are citizens, irrespective of their race or color.

Bates's opinion had holes in it, too. While his logic may have been sound for those born free on American soil, applying it to those born to slavery and emancipated only by the proclamation took an extra step of reasoning. The logic went this way: since the freed slaves at the moment of emancipation would be both free and native born, they would have citizenship in the United States, and having citizenship, they would be entitled to the protection afforded all citizens, including a prohibition upon being involuntarily held without due process of law. While relying upon Bates's reading for the moment, Lincoln could only hope that the proclamation would so disrupt the institution of slavery that, like a broken egg, it could never be put together again, and that in the tranquillity of a postwar environment there would finally be a constitutional amendment making slavery illegal (There would be, of course, when the Thirteenth Amendment was adopted in December 1865).

Along with making the final edits on the proclamation, Lincoln spent New Year's Eve Day occupied with other executive business, and there was plenty. He signed a bill admitting forty-eight counties of western Virginia into the Union as "West Virginia," but as part of the agreement the new state had to adopt a plan for gradual emancipation. The act had its own constitutional issues. If the president agreed that the Unionist region of western Virginia, which had far fewer slaves than those supporting the tobacco plantations of the eastern part of the state, could secede from Virginia and gain statehood, then how could he maintain that Virginia itself and the rest of the rebel states in the Confederacy did not have the same right to secede from the nation as a whole? In an opinion he attached to the bill, Lincoln distinguished between "secession against the Constitution, and secession in favor of the Constitution," but he knew this argument was weak. Indeed, his own attorney general, Bates, counseled him to veto the bill as unconstitutional.

Lincoln prepared to meet with his top general, Ambrose Burnside, knowing that he would have to tell him that he had lost confidence in him, that junior officers from Burnside's staff had come to complain about him, and that he was ready to request that Halleck personally review all of Burnside's future plans, a humiliating situation for any general, but especially one who had just been shamed in battle. Lincoln came to an agreement with entrepreneur Bernard Kock for the resettlement of five thousand former slaves on the coast of Haiti (no matter what he would do by morning, Lincoln had not given up on colonization). He also met "with a piteous old lady of genteel appearance" (Lincoln's own description) who had been evicted from her home by the War Department and had no place to go.

Lincoln dashed off a note to Stanton asking him to look into the matter. Then, as night fell on the streets of Washington, Lincoln went to his study and paced.

Robert Lincoln told a friend decades later that his father stayed up this entire night. Why the younger Lincoln waited so long to reveal that tantalizing fact is unknown. But, if true, what a cinematic scene it suggests, especially from the vantage point of 150 years of history. There is Lincoln, our mythic Lincoln— whoever that Lincoln may really be—alone in his cold, dark study in what was likely the first time in a long time when he could permit himself the luxury of concentration. While we do not know for certain about this particular night, Tad usually fell asleep in his father's study, and eventually Lincoln would pick up the boy and carry him to bed. But once Lincoln was alone and settled into the enveloping silence, what went through his mind? Robert Lincoln said his mother, before she retired, repeated her opposition to the proclamation. But even then, Lincoln, in reply, had not revealed his intentions. He simply paced, pausing once in a while to read a few favorite verses from the Bible and to gaze through the White House window at the night sky.

The six months preceding this had been transformative for him. He had built a career on reason and argument, on the powers of human agency to effect change. His entire life was an example of that Enlightenment creed; he was a self-educated backwoodsman of questionable birth whose literary, oratorical, and political labors brought him to the greatest of heights. Yet the awful war and the exasperating task of ending slavery had reawakened in him a humbling respect for the unreasonable, for what he did not know and for what he could not know. It was uncanny. The same sort of personal epiphany had occurred around all the challenges in his life. He had trusted the war to men who plotted the movements of troops and artillery with slide rules and diagrams, yet they had failed, and now in light of their failure he leaned toward a more muscular, less cerebral war, one that permitted any act deemed to be of "military necessity," *any* act that furthered the intended ends of the war. He had believed in a gradual, peaceful, and compensated path to the extinction of slavery, one that took into account the interests of both slaveholders and slaves, that rejected the riskiness of sudden emancipation with its harsh rebuke and potential for violence, yet here he was hours from freeing the slaves not by the construction of some deliberate and measured plan vetted by the legislative process, but by presidential fiat announced from the barrel of a gun.

An attorney, he had believed firmly in the law as the governing force of a just society, yet he had stretched the boundaries of the Constitution, first in suspending civil liberties and, now, in the document that awaited his signature, the seizing of private property without statutory authority. Yes, it was an act of war, and, yes, this property was different in that it breathed the air and walked the earth, that it was property in people, not things, and Francis Lieber was hard at work on articulating that distinction for his code. But there remained the question whether Lincoln was interpreting the law to serve the outcome he wanted rather than for what the law said. Only eleven months later, in the most eloquent 272 words written by any president, Lincoln would tell a gathering at the federal cemetery at Gettysburg that the "honored dead" buried there gave their "last full measure of devotion" so that "government of the people, by the people, for the people, shall not perish from the earth." Yet in this, a government of laws, not men, Lincoln had assumed nothing less than "transcendent executive power" (Justice Curtis's words) to do as he, and he alone, willed.

Ironically for someone accused of such a bold-faced grab for power, Lincoln had privately moved increasingly toward a submission to the will of something greater than himself. The idea was by no means new for him. Indeed, it recalled his 1848 profession of youthful interest in the doctrine of necessity, which asserted that there was no free will, that one's actions were directed by some exterior force in the fulfillment of an eternal, yet essentially unknowable, design. Lincoln may have described this force as the "Almighty God," and indeed his references to "Providence" and the "Divine Being" increased as the conditions in the war and his presidency got worse, but it was the same God he had contemplated in his September "Meditation on the Divine Will," God as a force of inevitability, of cause and effect, of the working out of a process only He could understand. In this design, man was nothing more than an instrument in a process, "compelled to feel, think, will, and to act . . . by this vast world machine, working in grooves and moving in deep-cut channels forever and forever." Lincoln's philosophy, wrote his law partner William Herndon, was the source of his legendary grace and humility. For if men are "mere tools in the hands of fate . . . made as they are made, by conditions," then "to praise them or blame them was pure folly." It was a philosophy that stressed equality. Ironically, the president upon whom so many "great man" theories of American history depends saw himself as no different from anyone else. No one was less or more responsible for the conditions of the world than the next person because all were helpless to change events as they were directed from above. When Mary and Robert arrived in Lincoln's study in the morning, asking what he had decided, the president looked up at them, "a great light illuming his face," and answered, "I am a man under orders. I cannot do otherwise."

New Year's was a special day at the White House. The tradition was a reception at the Executive Mansion, beginning at eleven and running until two. Lincoln had hoped to sign the proclamation before opening the doors to the throngs of well-wishers. He had sent his handwritten draft to the State Department to be formalized, the section from the Preliminary Proclamation cut and pasted "to save writing." But when Secretary Seward arrived with the official copy ready for the president's pen, Lincoln noticed an error. The State Department copyist had used the wrong formal text at the end of the document. The copy presented to Lincoln said, "In testimony whereof I have hereunto set my name and caused the seal of the United States to be affixed." That was the traditional language used for treaties. Lincoln wanted the language used for proclamations, which read, "In witness whereof *I have hereunto set my hand* . . . " While the document was being recopied into the correct form, Lincoln went to the Blue Room to meet his guests.

As was customary, the first hour of the reception was reserved for dignitaries: the foreign diplomatic corps arrayed in "gold lace, feathers, and other trappings"; the officers of the army and the navy, including Halleck and Burnside in their dress blues; the cabinet members, including Seward and Chase and Welles and Bates; and the justices of the Supreme Court, including the chief justice, Roger Taney. At noon, the doors opened for the general public, thousands of people moving through in a tumultuous rush, greeting Lincoln and then departing on a temporary bridge constructed of a piece of wood extending through a long window to the outside. Ward Hill Lamon stood to Lincoln's right. He would inform Lincoln of the name and home state of each guest, and Lincoln would then work his "blessed old pump handle" (Noah Brooks's phrase) while looking the man in the eyes and, depending on where the man was from, saying something about the great state of California or the faithful men supporting the army from the loyal state of New York.

After three hours of greeting guests, a fatigued Lincoln retreated upstairs. Secretary Seward and his son, Frederick, who served as an assistant secretary under him, arrived from the State Department and found the president alone. They put the proclamation on the cabinet table in front of him. "Mr. Lincoln dipped his pen in the ink," wrote Frederick Seward later, "and then, holding it a moment above the paper, seemed to hesitate. Looking around, he said, 'I never, in my life, felt more certain that I was doing right, than I do in signing this paper. But I have been receiving calls, and shaking hands since . . . [early] this morning, till my arm is stiff and numb. Now, this signature is one that will be closely examined, and if they find my hand trembled, they will say he had some compunctions. But, any way, it is going to be done.'" This was disingenuous. Lincoln *did* have compunctions and was *very* uncertain. He had wanted to end slavery, but not this way, and even now, perhaps *especially* now, he feared the consequences of this act, that it might extend the war, not hasten its end; that it could permanently divide North from South; that it would lose him the Border States; that it would lead to a massacre of the slaves or their masters; that a society incorporating black and white could only result in a future of racial antagonism and violence. What is now heralded as one of the greatest acts in the advancement of human liberty, an act that christened Lincoln the Great Emancipator, that brought men and women to their knees in his presence as if he were divinely touched, was, in the mind of its author, a roll of the dice.

The pause completed, Lincoln looked back at the document in front of him. Then, on the afternoon of January 1, 1863, using a steel pen with a wood shaft that he had nervously chewed, Abraham Lincoln, the sixteenth president of the United States, signed the Emancipation Proclamation. The president punctuated the moment with a laugh, which Frederick Seward believed to be directed at Lincoln's own nervousness over the quality of his signature. Then Secretary Seward signed his name as well. The great seal of the United States was affixed, and the act was done. "We are like whalers who have been long on a chase," Lincoln said not long afterward, reflecting, with trepidation, about what lay ahead. "We have at last got the harpoon into the monster, but we must now look how we steer, or with one 'flop' of his tail he will yet send us all into eternity."

Around the country, crowds had been waiting for this moment, and when the proclamation was not issued in the morning as planned, anxiety built. In Boston, three thousand had arrived early at the Baptist worship center known as the Tremont Temple, waiting for "the first flash of the electric wires," as Frederick Douglass, who was among them, put it. Douglass was not confident. "Mr. Lincoln was known to be a man of tender heart, and boundless patience [and] no man could tell to what length he might go, or might refrain from going, in the direction of peace and reconciliation. Hitherto, he had not shown himself a man of heroic measures, and, properly enough, this step belonged to that class."

The gathering at the temple was organized by the Union Progressive Association, a "Negro abolitionist group," and was overwhelmingly African-American. Its celebration was to be a daylong affair, but the tenor of the event could only be restrained until the proclamation's signing had been confirmed. The people still did not know if they could count on Lincoln. A "line of messengers" had been formed, stretching from the nearest telegraph office to the platform of the temple, so that as soon as word of the signing had been received, it could quickly be passed voice to voice through the streets of Boston until it was finally heard in the crowd. Then, in the early afternoon, just when despair was setting in, a man arrived shouting from the rear of the hall. "It is coming . . . ," he bellowed. "It is on the wires." With that, the place erupted in a joyous commotion topped off with cries of "Glory to God!" The news was, in fact, wrong. Someone had leaked the original flawed copy of the document to the *Washington Evening Star*, and the *Star* had published it as real, generating word across the country, to celebrations in New York and Philadelphia and Boston. But the error was of little consequence. The news of the actual, official signing was a mere formality now, for there was no stopping the revelry that had already begun. Soon, impromptu, the crowd at the Tremont began singing a rousing hymn in unison. "Sound the loud timbrel o'er Egypt's dark sea, Jehovah hath triumphed, his people are free."

Later in the afternoon, a more formal gathering occurred at the Boston Music Hall, near the Tremont Temple, including an appearance by the Boston Philharmonic, which played Beethoven's "Egmont Overture," a stirring piece of music based on Goethe's story of resistance to oppression, as well as Mendelssohn's reverent *Hymn of Praise* symphony. Ralph Waldo Emerson, Harriet Beecher Stowe, Henry Wadsworth Longfellow, and Oliver Wendell Holmes Sr. offered recitations. Holmes had composed two new stanzas to his popular "Army Hymn," which he read aloud to the gathering: "We lift the starry flag on high / That fills with light our stormy sky. / No more its flaming emblems wave / To bar from hope the trembling slave; / No more its radiant glories shine / To blast with woe a child of Thine."

By evening, a crowd had assembled at the White House, too, a mixed-race audience. Lincoln appeared at the window to greet them, and they asked him to speak, but, likely still uncomfortable at claiming authorship of an act about which he had been so ambivalent, he demurred. Instead, he simply bowed to them and they shouted back that they wanted to "hug him to death."

The limited nature of the proclamation—that it only freed some slaves and only freed them as a war measure, and that it would not have the force of law at the end of hostilities, that it wasn't even certain that it had the force of law *during* the hostilities—none of that seemed to matter to these crowds of supporters. They may have understood something that the lawyers and the politicians and Lincoln himself did not quite comprehend; that the details of this emancipation decree were less significant than the mere fact that there *was* an emancipation decree, and that while the proclamation read like a dull legal brief, filled with qualifying clauses and exceptions, it was not language that made this, finally, a moral document. It was its existence, its title, its arrival into this world, its challenge to the accepted order, and from that there was no turning back. In this sense it was a revolutionary statement, like the Declaration itself, and nearly as significant.

The reaction of the Confederate leadership to the news of

the proclamation's signing was, predictably, outrage. Jefferson Davis feigned dismay. The slaves, while "of an inferior race," are "peaceful and contented laborers in their sphere." So why, he demanded to know, would the president of the United States encourage them to "a general assassination of their masters"? One Southern newspaper editorialist took a sarcastic tone. "The Pope's bull against the comet has been issued," declared the *Charleston Courier*, recalling Lincoln's earlier comment about the futility of an emancipation proclamation, ". . . and I suppose Mr. Lincoln now breathes more freely. The wonderful man by a dash of his wonderful pen has set free (on paper) all the slaves of the South, and henceforth this is to be in all its length and breadth the land of liberty!"

Word of the signing spread to the Southern slaves through whispers on the "grapevine telegraph," which was nothing more, of course, than one slave's telling another slave, and that slave, having been sent on a mission, say, to retrieve the mail from the local post office, spreading word while he was there to a slave from up the road. Perhaps because the message traveled through an oral medium, as fleeting as the breath, the permanent record of the slave response to the proclamation is scant. Even after the fact, few slaves were literate enough to put down on paper what they saw, heard, and felt. That work was left for later generations, to the Federal Writers' Project of the Works Progress Administration, for instance, whose researchers interviewed thousands of elderly ex-slaves in the 1930s for an oral-history archive that was the first of its kind. Among those whose memories were recorded then was George Washington Albright, who recalled that, at the age of fifteen, he had been recruited by a group called Lincoln's Legal Loyal League to spread the word of the signing to slaves near his home in Mississippi. "I traveled about the plantations within a certain range, and got together small meetings in the cabins to tell the slaves the great news. Some of these slaves would in turn find their way to still other plantations—and so the story spread." Albright had to work in "dead secret," utilizing clandestine passwords and codes. It was, he said, his "first job in the fight for the rights of my people."

Once emancipation had been proclaimed, the war took on a new character. In one stroke, Lincoln had turned the Union Army into an army of liberation. Wherever it went, it freed slaves, and wherever Union control had been established, special agents commissioned by the newly established Bureau of Colored Troops fanned out through the occupied zones, spreading the news of emancipation and recruiting able-bodied men to serve as soldiers in the Union Army. "The usual method of proceeding was upon reaching a designated point, to occupy the most desirable public building," wrote the historian of the army's Seventh Regiment, "and with this as a rendezvous, small parties were sent into the surrounding country, visiting each plantation within a radius of twenty or thirty miles. . . . Recruits were taken wherever found, and as their earthly possessions usually consisted of but what they wore upon their backs, they required no time to settle their affairs. The laborer in the field would throw down his hoe or quit his plow and march away with the guard, leaving his late owner looking after him in speechless amazement." In the remaining years of the war, the Northern free states would supply 37,723 "colored troops" and the Border States deliver 41,719 more, but the bulk of African-Americans who joined the Union Army were former slaves: 93,542 recruits came from the Confederate states alone.

The influx of black soldiers energized the Union Army. While the most famous regiment remains the Fifty-Fourth Massachusetts Volunteers (the subject of the 1989 film *Glory*), the many others included Louisiana's Native Guards, at Port Hudson in May 1863, and the Ninth Louisiana Volunteers of African Descent, at Milliken's Bend in June 1863, which suffered losses of 67 percent in that battle alone. The abolitionist Harriet Tubman was among those who cared for the wounded at Fort Wagner, where the Fifty-Fourth Massachusetts was defeated in a heroic clash. "And then we saw the lightning, and that was the guns," she later wrote, "and then we heard the thunder, and that was the big guns; and then we heard the rain falling, and that was the drops of blood falling; and then we came to get in the crops, it was dead men that we reaped."

Even as black soldiers were distinguishing themselves on the battlefront, there were voices in the North that continued to doubt the wisdom of their freedom. Lincoln would have none of it. "You say you will not fight to free negroes," he wrote in a rebuke to his friend James Conkling, who had asked that he retract the proclamation and reassert his mission as one of restoring the Union alone. "Some of them seem willing to fight for you; but, no matter. Fight you, then, exclusively to save the Union. I issued the proclamation on purpose to aid you in saving the Union. Whenever you shall have conquered all resistance to the Union, if I shall urge you to continue fighting, it will be an apt time, then, for you to declare you will not fight to free negroes."

Lincoln no longer restricted his rhetoric. He now embraced the end of slavery as a worthy war mission in itself, one not necessarily predicated on military necessity. "Why should they do any thing for us, if we will do nothing for them?" he asked

Conkling, referring to the black soldiers. "If they stake their lives for us, they must be prompted by the strongest motive—even the promise of freedom. And the promise being made, must be kept." But ironically, it *was*, in the end, a military necessity to free the slaves, if only because the freed slaves not only sapped the Confederacy's labor supply but, as soldiers, served as replacements for the weary and increasingly demoralized white Union soldiers. The African-American fighting men were fresh to the struggle, and they had something very American to fight for: their freedom.

Both emancipation and the subsequent recruitment of black soldiers helped to turn this from a war of armies into a war of societies, for that was how a civil war, or at least *this* civil war, had to be fought. This was the hard lesson that Lincoln and his generals had needed to learn. At issue was not simply the control of territory or of political institutions, which is the goal of most foreign wars. To win, the North needed to gain that and more; it needed to squash every resource, free every slave, and, as Sherman finally showed, terrorize the population into submission. This new kind of war, a "total war," as historians have long described it, erased all of the West Point intellectual theory that so many officers on both sides carried into battle and replaced it with a brute simplicity. Even that once-dedicated Jominian Henry Halleck admitted that things were different. "The character of the war has very much changed within the last year," he said in early 1863. ". . . We must conquer the rebels or be conquered by them. Every slave withdrawn from the enemy is the equivalent of a white man put *hors de combat.*"

Southern leaders objected that the North was acting contrary to the rules of "civilized nations," but soon the South, too, in retaliation, threw dignity to the winds, treating captured black soldiers not as prisoners of war, but as fugitives whose crimes were punishable by death. The North's need for "total war," for a war against Southern society, was predicated on the increasing feeling that without it the rebellion would simmer and, simmering, rekindle. Without targeting Southern society, it is unlikely that the Union could have achieved a sustainable victory; even with targeting it, regional identity remained strong, bitterness raged, and retaliation on the former slaves became a blood sport for succeeding decades.

The assassination of Abraham Lincoln in 1865 sealed his image as Father Abraham, and with that the legend of Lincoln as emancipator began to gain speed. He had not anticipated a spectacular death that would come to be seen as the sacrifice for a nation reborn, nor had he asked to become the object of a myth of grandeur that would forever cast him as America's Moses. But both happened. The act that he had so ambivalently approached and then retreated from, that was the target of critics on both sides before and after he signed it, was larger than one man, even a man of the stature of Abraham Lincoln. The Emancipation Proclamation brought conclusion to a war that Lincoln had never wanted and to a vile human institution he despised but that he had expected would survive his presidency and beyond. It led to the establishment of "equality"—a notion that Lincoln had resisted, at least in its full-blown form—as an American value on a par with "liberty" and made America officially a biracial (and, ultimately, a multiracial) country, which he had seen as an unrealistic and unsustainable dream. Yet Lincoln had played the protagonist in the drama that led to all of this and more.

Acknowledgments

The historian Fred Siegel long ago cautioned me about the regrettable trend toward "plumb-line" histories—threads dropped into the well of the past and adjusted so that they attach only to those pieces of evidence that prove the writer's point while ignoring everything else. Trusting that insight, I have attempted here to give a picture that embraces contradiction and defies the facile understanding. I hope I have succeeded. I am indebted to Fred as well for his reading of parts of the original manuscript and to the historians Brandon Gauthier and Brigadier General (Ret.) Lance Betros for their careful reading of all or part of this book in its early stages. I am deeply indebted to my brother, Christopher Brewster, who read the manuscript and gave detailed and valuable advice, and my wife, Sylvia Steinert, who did the same. Charles Pieterse, Kayce Freed Jennings, Tom Yellin, Albert Brok, and Commander (Ret.) Scott Granger all offered their suggestions upon reading the proposal or listening to me wrestle with the idea. I am indebted to University of Texas law professor Sanford Levinson, author Walter Stahr, and Princeton professor James McPherson, who answered my queries promptly and even shared their work. The Yale law professor and friend Akhil Amar, with whom I lectured on the "the perfect president," helped crystallize my thinking on Lincoln as combining the two parallel lines of presidential leadership—warrior and lawyer—into one executive. Tony Thomas offered insight into the folk music of the period. Paul Mercer, senior librarian for Manuscripts and Special Collections at the New York State Library, provided assistance. My editor, Colin Harrison, was a blessing. From the start, we saw the book the same way—part narrative history, part literary essay—and he worked tirelessly to help me find the balance. I believe his edits, especially where he urged me to remember the ticking clock during these six months of Lincoln's life, improved the book immensely. My trusted lemon beagle, Bagel, offered the kind of unconditional love that a writer needs as he ventures off into the loneliness of an all-consuming text. I sometimes deluded myself into thinking that her satisfied sighs were in reaction to my muttering prose lines out loud. On those occasions, I would pat her and say, "Good dog" (and I really, really meant it). George Greenfield brought me the kernel of an idea on the Emancipation Proclamation a few years back. He had a different book in mind, I know, one that someone may someday write, but having represented many writers diligently and faithfully, he understood how ideas change and assume new shapes, often satisfyingly so. I hope he feels that about the shape of this one. I am grateful for the assistance of the Ridgefield (CT) Public Library and the Abraham Lincoln Presidential Library and Museum in Springfield, Illinois. Finally, there are no words to convey my gratitude for the support and love of my wife, Sylvia, and my children, Jack and Ben, who endured my distraction with this work on the assumption that it would be a temporary departure and did not complain when, like so many books to so many authors, it proved to distract longer than anticipated. To them I can say that I have returned now, at least until the next subject pulls me away. I promise not to let that happen too soon.

Todd Brewster
Ridgefield, Connecticut

APPENDIX

T HE THREE VERSIONS of the Emancipation Proclamation are
gathered here, beginning with the draft that Lincoln read to his
cabinet on July 22, 1862. The original of this document, which is in
the archives of the Library of Congress among the Robert Todd Lincoln Family Papers, is reproduced along with a transcript of that draft.
The September 22, 1862, version, or the Preliminary Emancipation
Proclamation, follows, and it too is reproduced in its original handwritten form and again in its first printed form. The document is in
the possession of the New York State Library in Albany, having arrived there through an interesting path. In 1864, it was auctioned off
at a fund-raiser for the Albany Army Relief Association, one of many
groups organized under the United States Sanitary Commission and
dedicated to bringing badly needed supplies—including clothing and
food as well as medical necessities—to the soldiers fighting the war.
Five thousand one-dollar tickets were to be sold. Though he was on
the committee overseeing the sale, abolitionist Gerrit Smith bought
one thousand for himself and, to no one's surprise, won. "I have
never been proud of owning houses and lands," he later wrote, "but I
confess that I am somewhat elated by being the owner of this glorious
Proclamation of Freedom, in the very form in which it came from
our President's strong and honest hand." Still, Smith announced

his intentions to offer the document up for resale with the intention that the next round of proceeds also go to the relief of the soldiers, this time directly to the US Sanitary Commission. In April 1865, as Lincoln's funeral train made its way through Albany, the New York State Legislature voted to purchase the Preliminary Proclamation for $1,000 and keep it in Albany where it has resided until this day. The original draft of the final Emancipation Proclamation, which is also reproduced here, met a darker fate. Like the Preliminary Proclamation, it was provided to a Sanitary Fair—in this instance, the Northwestern Soldiers Fair in Chicago—only it was Lincoln himself who made the donation. He wrote that he had "some desire to retain the paper; but if it shall contribute to the relief or comfort of the soldiers that will be better." Offered for auction a few months before the Albany event, it went for less money than the preliminary document, three thousand dollars. Photocopies were made, and that is what is reproduced here along with a transcript of the final proclamation, but the original of Lincoln's draft perished in the Chicago fire of 1871.

[July. 22, 1862]

In pursuance of the sixth section of the act of congress entitled "An act to suppress insurrection and to punish treason and rebellion, to seize and confiscate property of rebels, and for other purposes" Approved July 17. 1862, and which act, and the Joint Resolution explanatory thereof, are herewith published, I, Abraham Lincoln, President of the United States, do hereby proclaim to, and warn all persons within the contemplation of said sixth section to cease participating in, aiding, countenancing, or abetting the existing rebellion, or any rebellion against the government of the United States, and to return to their proper allegiance to the United States, on pain of the forfeitures and seizures, as within and by said sixth section provided—

And I hereby make known that it is my purpose, upon the next meeting of congress, to again recommend the adoption of a practical measure for tendering pecuniary aid to the free choice or rejection, of any and all States which may then be recognizing and practically sustaining the authority of the United States, and which may then have voluntarily adopted, or thereafter may voluntarily adopt, gradual abolishment ~~adoption~~ of slavery, within such State or States— that the object is to practically restore, thenceforward to be maintain, the constitutional relation between the general government, and each, and all the States, wherein that relation

17232

is now suspended, or disturbed; and that, for this object, the war, as it has been, will be, prosecuted. And, as a fit and necessary military measure for effecting this object, I, as Commander-in-Chief of the Army and Navy of the United States, do order and declare that on the first day of January, in the year of our Lord one thousand, eight hundred and sixtythree, all persons held as slaves within any State or states, wherein the Constitutional authority of the United States shall not then be practically recognized, submitted to, and maintained, shall then, thenceforward and forever, be free,

First Draft of the Emancipation Proclamation
July 22, 1862

In pursuance of the sixth section of the act of congress entitled "An act to suppress insurrection and to punish treason and rebellion, to seize and confiscate property of rebels, and for other purposes" Approved July 17, 1862, and which act, and the Joint Resolution explanatory thereof, are herewith published, I, ABRAHAM LINCOLN, President of the United States, do hereby proclaim to, and warn all persons within the contemplation of said sixth section to cease participating in, aiding, countenancing, or abetting the existing rebellion, or any rebellion against the government of the United States, and to return to their proper allegiance to the United States, on pain of the forfeitures and seizures, as within and by said sixth section provided.

And I hereby make known that it is my purpose, upon the next meeting of congress, to again recommend the adoption of a practical measure for tendering pecuniary aid to the free choice or rejection, of any and all States which may then be recognizing and practically sustaining the authority of the United States, and which may then have voluntarily adopted, or thereafter may voluntarily adopt, gradual abolishment of slavery within such State or States—that the object is to practically restore, thenceforward to be maintained, the constitutional relation between the general government, and each, and all the states, wherein that relation is now suspended, or disturbed; and that, for this object, the war, as it has been, will be, prosecuted. And, as a fit and necessary military measure for effecting this object, I, as Commander-in-Chief of the Army and Navy of the United States, do order and declare that on the first day of January in the year of

Our Lord one thousand, eight hundred and sixty-three, all persons held as slaves within any state or states, wherein the constitutional authority of the United States shall not then be practically recognized, submitted to, and maintained, shall then, thenceforward, and forever, be free.

By the President of the
United States of America
A Proclamation.

I, Abraham Lincoln, President of the United
States of America, and Commander-in-Chief
of the Army and Navy thereof, do hereby proclaim and declare that hereafter, as heretofore, the war will be prosecuted for the object of practically restoring the constitutional relation between the United States, and each
of the states, and the people thereof, in which
states, that relation is, or may be, suspended, or
disturbed.

That it is my purpose, upon the next meeting
of Congress to again recommend the adoption of
a practical measure tendering pecuniary aid to
the free acceptance or rejection of all slave-
states, so called, the people whereof may not then
be in rebellion against the United States, and
which states, may then have voluntarily adopted, or thereafter may voluntarily adopt, immediate, or gradual abolishment of slavery within their respective limits; and that the effort
to colonize persons of African descent upon this
continent, or elsewhere, will be continued.

2

That on the first day of January in the year of
our Lord, one thousand eight hundred and sixty-
three, all persons held as slaves within any
state, or designated part of a state, the people
whereof shall then be in rebellion against the
United States shall be then, thenceforward,
and forever free; and the executive govern-
ment of the United States, *including the military and naval authority thereof,* will, ~~during the con-~~
~~tinuance in office of the present incumbents,~~ re-
cognize, *and maintain the freedom of* such persons, ~~and being free,~~ and will
do no act or acts to repress such persons, or any
of them, in any efforts they may make for their
actual freedom.

That the executive will, on the first day of January aforesaid, by proclamation, designate the
States, and parts of states, if any, in which the
people thereof respectively, shall then be in rebellion against the United States; and the fact
that any state, or the people thereof shall, on
that day be, in good faith represented in the
Congress of the United States, by members chosen
thereto, at elections wherein a majority of the

qualified voters of such state shall have participated, shall, in the absence of strong countervailing
testimony, be deemed conclusive evidence that
such state and the people thereof, are not then
in rebellion against the United States.

That attention is hereby called to an Act of Congress entitled "An Act to make an Additional
Article of War" approved March 13. 1862, and
which Act is in the words and figures following:

> *Be it enacted by the Senate and House of Representatives of the United States of America in Congress assembled,* That hereafter the following shall be promulgated as an additional article of war for the government of the army of the United States, and shall be obeyed and observed as such:
>
> Article ——. All officers or persons in the military or naval service of the United States are prohibited from employing any of the forces under their respective commands for the purpose of returning fugitives from service or labor, who may have escaped from any persons to whom such service or labor is claimed to be due, and any officer who shall be found guilty by a court-martial of violating this article shall be dismissed from the service.
>
> Sec. 2. *And be it further enacted,* That this act shall take effect from and after its passage.

Also to the ninth and tenth sections of an
Act entitled "An Act to suppress Insurrection,
to punish Treason and Rebellion, to seize and confiscate property of rebels, and for other purposes,"
approved July 17. 1862, and which sections are
in the words and figures following:

> Sec. 9. *And be it further enacted,* That all slaves of persons who shall hereafter be engaged in rebellion against the government of the United States, or who shall in any way give aid or comfort thereto, escaping from such persons and taking refuge within the lines of the army; and all slaves captured from such persons or deserted by them and coming under the control of the government of the United States; and all slaves of such persons found on [or] being within any place occupied by rebel forces and afterwards occupied by the forces of the United States, shall be deemed captives of war, and shall be forever free of their servitude, and not again held as slaves.
>
> Sec. 10. *And be it further enacted,* That no slave escaping into any State, Territory, or the District of Columbia, from any other State, shall be delivered up, or in any way impeded or hindered of his liberty, except for crime, or some offence against the laws, unless the person claiming said fugitive shall first make oath that the person to whom the labor or service of such fugitive is alleged to be due is his lawful owner, and has not borne arms against the United States in the present rebellion, nor in any way given aid and comfort thereto; and no person engaged in the military or naval service of the United States shall, under any pretence whatever, assume to decide on the validity of the claim of any person to the service or labor of any other person, or surrender up any such person to the claimant, on pain of being dismissed from the service.

And I do hereby enjoin upon and order all
persons engaged in the military and naval
service of the United States to observe, obey,
and enforce, within their respective spheres of
service, the act, and sections above recited.
In due time ~~it he will enjoin upon them~~
And the executive will recommend that
all citizens of the United States, who shall have
remained loyal thereto throughout the rebellion shall (upon the restoration of the constitutional relation between the United States, and
their respective states, and people, if that relation
shall have been suspended or disturbed) be
compensated for all losses by acts of the United
States, including the loss of slaves.

In witness whereof, I have
L. S.   hereunto set my hand, and caused
the seal of the United States to be
affixed.
Done at the City of Washington,
this twenty second day of September,
in the year of our Lord, one thousand eight
hundred and sixty two, and sixty two,
and of the Independence of the United
States, the eighty seventh.
Abraham Lincoln

By the President
William H. Seward,
Secretary of State

Notice of issuance of Proclamation emancipating slaves in States in rebellion on January 1, 1865. (SIC)

BY THE PRESIDENT OF THE UNITED STATES OF AMERICA:

A PROCLAMATION.

I, ABRAHAM LINCOLN, President of the United States of America, and Commander-in-chief of the Army and Navy thereof, do hereby proclaim and declare that hereafter, as heretofore, the war will be prosecuted for the object of practically restoring the constitutional relation between the United States and each of the States, and the people thereof, in which States that relation is or may be suspended or disturbed.

That it is my purpose, upon the next meeting of Congress, to again recommend the adoption of a practical measure tendering pecuniary aid to the free acceptance or rejection of all Slave States, so called, the people whereof may not then be in rebellion against the United States, and which States may then have voluntarily adopted, or thereafter may voluntarily adopt, immediate or gradual abolishment of slavery within their respective limits; and that the effort to colonize persons of African descent, with their consent, upon this continent or elsewhere, with the previously obtained consent of the governments existing there, will be continued.

That on the first day of January, in the year of our Lord one thousand eight hundred and sixty-three, all persons held as slaves within any State or designated part of a State, the people whereof shall then be in rebellion against the United States, shall be then, thenceforward, and forever free; and the Executive Government of the United States, including the military and naval authority thereof, will recognise and maintain the freedom of such persons, and will do no act or acts to repress such persons, or any of them, in any efforts they may make for their actual freedom.

That the Executive will, on the first day of January aforesaid, by Proclamation, designate the States, and parts of States, if any, in which the people thereof respectively shall then be in rebellion against the United States; and the fact that any State, or the people thereof, shall on that day be in good faith represented in the Congress of the United States, by members chosen thereto at elections wherein a majority of the qualified voters of such State shall have participated, shall, in the absence of strong countervailing testimony, be deemed conclusive evidence that such State, and

2

the people thereof, are not then in rebellion against the United States.

That attention is hereby called to an act of Congress, entitled "An act to make an additional Article of War," approved March 13, 1862, and which act is in the words and figure following:

" Be it enacted by the Senate and House of Representatives of the United States of America in Congress assembled, That hereafter the following shall be promulgated as an additional article of war for the government of the Army of the United States, and shall be obeyed and observed as such :

"ARTICLE —. All officers or persons in the military or naval service of the United States are prohibited from employing any of the forces under their respective commands for the purpose of returning fugitives from service or labor who may have escaped from any persons to whom such service or labor is claimed to be due; and any officer who shall be found guilty by a court-martial of violating this article, shall be dismissed from the service."

"SEC. 2. *And be it further enacted,* That this act shall take effect from and after its passage."

Also, to the ninth and tenth sections of an act entitled "An act to suppress insurrection, to punish treason and rebellion, to seize and confiscate the property of rebels, and for other purposes," approved July 17, 1862, and which sections are in the words and figures following:

"SEC. 9. *And be it further enacted,* That all slaves of persons who shall hereafter be engaged in rebellion against the government of the United States, or who shall in any way give aid or comfort thereto, escaping from such persons and taking refuge within the lines of the army; and all slaves captured from such persons, or deserted by them and coming under the control of the government of the United States; and all slaves of such persons found *on* [or] being within any place occupied by rebel forces and afterwards occupied by the forces of the United States, shall be deemed captives of war, and shall be forever free of their servitude, and not again held as slaves.

"SEC. 10. *And be it further enacted,* That no slave escaping into any State, Territory, or the District of Columbia, from any other State, shall be delivered up, or in any way impeded or hindered of his liberty, except for crime, or some offence against the laws, unless the person claiming said fugitive shall first make oath that the person to whom the labor or service of such fugitive is alleged to be due is his lawful owner, and has not borne arms against the United States in the present rebellion, nor in any way given aid and comfort thereto; and no person engaged in the military or naval service of the United States shall, under any pretence whatever, assume to decide on the validity of the claim of any person to the service or labor of any other person, or surrender up any such person to the claimant, on pain of being dismissed from the service."

And I do hereby enjoin upon and order all persons engaged in the military and naval service of the United States to observe,

2013.A
4 M. 59

3

obey, and enforce, within their respective spheres of service, the act and sections above recited.

And the Executive will in due time recommend that all citizens of the United States who shall have remained loyal thereto throughout the rebellion shall (upon the restoration of the constitutional relation between the United States and their respective States and people, if that relation shall have been suspended or disturbed) be compensated for all losses by acts of the United States, including the loss of slaves.

In witness whereof, I have hereunto set my hand and caused the seal of the United States to be affixed.

Done at the City of Washington, this twenty-second day of September, in the year of our Lord one thousand eight hundred and sixty-two, and of the independence of the United States the eighty-seventh.

[L. S.]

ABRAHAM LINCOLN.

By the President:

WILLIAM H. SEWARD,
    Secretary of State.

By the President of the United States of America:
A Proclamation.

Whereas, on the twentysecond day of September, in the
year of our Lord one thousand eight hundred and
sixtytwo, a proclamation was issued by the President
of the United States, containing, among other things, the
following, towit:

> "That on the first day of January, in the year of our Lord one thousand eight hundred and sixty-three,
> all persons held as slaves within any State or designated part of a State, the people whereof shall then be in
> rebellion against the United States, shall be then, thenceforward, and forever free; and the Executive Govern-
> ment of the United States, including the military and naval authority thereof, will recognize and maintain
> the freedom of such persons, and will do no act or acts to repress such persons, or any of them, in any efforts
> they may make for their actual freedom,
>
> "That the Executive will, on the first day of January aforesaid, by proclamation, designate the States
> and parts of States, if any, in which the people thereof, respectively, shall then be in rebellion against the
> United States; and the fact that any State, or the people thereof, shall on that day be, in good faith, repre-
> sented in the Congress of the United States by members chosen thereto at elections wherein a majority of
> the qualified voters of such State shall have participated, shall, in the absence of strong countervailing testi-
> mony, be deemed conclusive evidence that such State, and the people thereof, are not then in rebellion
> against the United States."

Now, therefore I, Abraham Lincoln, President of the
United States, by virtue of the power in me vested as
Commander-in-Chief, of the Army and Navy of the
United States in time of actual armed rebellion against authority and government of the United States,
and as a fit and necessary war measure for suppressing said rebellion, do, on this first day of January, in the year of our Lord one thousand eight hundred and sixtythree, and in accordance with
                                     publicly
my purpose so to do, proclaimed for the full period
of one hundred days, from the day first above mentioned, order and designate

20820

as the States and parts of States wherein the people thereof respectively, are this day in rebellion against the United States, the following, towit:

Arkansas, Texas, Louisiana, (except the Parishes of
St. Bernard, Plaquemines, Jefferson, St. Johns, St. Charles, St. James
Ascension, Assumption, Terrebonne, Lafourche, St. Mary, St. Martins,
and Orleans, including the City of New Orleans) Mississippi,
Alabama, Florida, Georgia, South-Carolina, North-Carolina,
and Virginia, (except the fortyeight counties designated
as West Virginia, and also the counties of Berkly, Accomac, Northampton, Elizabeth-City, York, Princess Ann,
and Norfolk, including the Cities of Norfolk, & Portsmouth; and which excepted parts are, for the present, left precisely as if this proclamation were not issued.

And by virtue of the power, and for the purpose aforesaid, I do order and declare that all persons held
as slaves within said designated States, and parts of
States, are, and henceforward shall be free; and that
the Executive government of the United States, including the military and naval authorities thereof, will
recognize and maintain the freedom of said persons.

And I hereby enjoin upon the people so declared
to be free to abstain from all violence, unless in neces=
sary self-defence; and I recommend to them that,
in all cases when allowed, they labor faithfully
for reasonable wages.

And I further declare and make known,
that such persons of suitable condition, will be
received into the armed service of the United
States to garrison forts, positions, stations, and other
places, and to man vessels of all sorts in said ser=
vice.

And upon this act, sincerely believed to be
an act of justice, warranted by the Constitution, up=
on military necessity, I invoke the considerate judg=
ment of mankind, and the gracious favor of Al=
mighty God.

In witness whereof, I have hereunto set my
hand and caused the seal of the United States
to be affixed.

Done at the city of Washington, this first day of
January, in the year of our Lord one thousand
eight hundred and sixty three, and of the

L. S. Independence of the United States
of America the eighty=seventh.

Abraham Lincoln

By the President;
William H. Seward
Secretary of State.

20823

The Emancipation Proclamation
January 1, 1863

By the President of the United States of America:

A Proclamation.

Whereas, on the twenty-second day of September, in the year of our Lord one thousand eight hundred and sixty-two, a proclamation was issued by the President of the United States, containing, among other things, the following, to wit:

"That on the first day of January, in the year of our Lord one thousand eight hundred and sixty-three, all persons held as slaves within any State or designated part of a State, the people whereof shall then be in rebellion against the United States, shall be then, thenceforward, and forever free; and the Executive Government of the United States, including the military and naval authority thereof, will recognize and maintain the freedom of such persons, and will do no act or acts to repress such persons, or any of them, in any efforts they may make for their actual freedom.

"That the Executive will, on the first day of January aforesaid, by proclamation, designate the States and parts of States, if any, in which the people thereof, respectively, shall then be in rebellion against the United States; and the fact that any State, or the people thereof, shall on that day be, in good faith, represented in the Congress of the United States by members chosen thereto at elections wherein a majority of the qualified voters of such State shall have participated, shall, in the absence of strong countervailing testimony, be deemed conclusive evidence that such State, and the people thereof, are not then in rebellion against the United States."

Now, therefore I, Abraham Lincoln, President of the United States, by virtue of the power in me vested as Commander-in-Chief, of the Army and Navy of the United States in time of actual armed rebellion against the authority and government of the United States, and as a fit and necessary war measure for suppressing said rebellion, do, on this first day of January, in the year of our Lord one thousand eight hundred and sixty-three, and in accordance with my purpose so to do publicly proclaimed for the full period of one hundred days, from the day first above mentioned, order and designate as the States and parts of States wherein the people thereof respectively, are this day in rebellion against the United States, the following, to wit:

Arkansas, Texas, Louisiana, (except the Parishes of St. Bernard, Plaquemines, Jefferson, St. John, St. Charles, St. James Ascension, Assumption, Terrebonne, Lafourche, St. Mary, St. Martin, and Orleans, including the City of New Orleans) Mississippi, Alabama, Florida, Georgia, South Carolina, North Carolina, and Virginia, (except the forty-eight counties designated as West Virginia, and also the counties of Berkley, Accomac, Northampton, Elizabeth City, York, Princess Ann, and Norfolk, including the cities of Norfolk and Portsmouth[)], and which excepted parts, are for the present, left precisely as if this proclamation were not issued.

And by virtue of the power, and for the purpose aforesaid, I do order and declare that all persons held as slaves within said designated States, and parts of States, are, and henceforward shall be free; and that the Executive government of the United States, including the military and naval authorities thereof, will recognize and maintain the freedom of said persons.

And I hereby enjoin upon the people so declared to be free to abstain from all violence, unless in necessary self-defence; and I recommend to them that, in all cases when allowed, they labor faithfully for reasonable wages.

And I further declare and make known, that such persons of suitable condition, will be received into the armed service of the United States to garrison forts, positions, stations, and other places, and to man vessels of all sorts in said service.

And upon this act, sincerely believed to be an act of justice, warranted by the Constitution, upon military necessity, I invoke the considerate judgment of mankind, and the gracious favor of Almighty God.

In witness whereof, I have hereunto set my hand and caused the seal of the United States to be affixed.

Done at the City of Washington, this first day of January, in the year of our Lord one thousand eight hundred and sixty three, and of the Independence of the United States of America the eighty-seventh.

By the President: ABRAHAM LINCOLN

WILLIAM H. SEWARD, Secretary of State

Lincoln's Letter to Hodges

MORE THAN A YEAR after he had signed the Emancipation Proclamation, Lincoln entertained a group of visitors from the state of Kentucky that included Governor Thomas Bramlette, former senator Archibald Dixon, and the journalist Albert G. Hodges. The purpose of their visit was one of complaint. They had been disturbed by the policy of emancipation, particularly by the enlistment of former slaves as soldiers. Lincoln used their time together to expound on the reasoning that he had adopted during the six months that led up to the proclamation's issuance, and when he did so with remarkable clarity, Hodges, the journalist, asked him if he could have a copy of his words. There was no such written copy, Lincoln told him, but he offered to write Hodges a letter re-creating what he had said. That letter, dated April 4, 1864, is reproduced here.

Executive Mansion,

Washington, April 4, 1864.

A. G. Hodges, Esq,
Frankfort, Ky.
My dear Sir:

You ask me to put in writing the substance of what I verbally said the other day, in your presence, to Governor Bramlette and Senator Dixon. It was about as follows:

"I am naturally anti-slavery. If slavery is not wrong, nothing is wrong. I can not remember when I did not so think, and feel. And yet I have never understood that the Presidency conferred upon me an unrestricted right to act officially upon this judgment and feeling. It was in the oath I took that I would, to the best of my ability, preserve, protect, and defend the Constitution of the United States. I could not take the office without taking the oath. Nor was it my view that I might take an oath to get power, and break the oath in using the power. I understood, too, that in ordinary civil administration this oath even forbade me to practically indulge my primary abstract judgment on the moral question of slavery. I had publicly declared this many times, and in many ways. And I aver that, to this day, I have done no official act in mere deference to my abstract judgment and feeling on slavery. I did understand however, that my oath to preserve the Constitution to the best of my ability, imposed upon me the duty of preserving, by every indispensable means, that government—that nation—of which that Constitution was the organic law. Was it possible to lose the nation, and yet, preserve the Constitution?

By general law life and limb must be protected; yet often a limb must be amputated to save a life; but a life is never wisely given to save a limb. I felt that measures, otherwise unconstitutional, might become lawful, by becoming indispensable to the preservation of the Constitution, through the preservation of the nation. Right or wrong, I assumed this ground, and now avow it. I could not feel that, to the best of my ability, I had even tried to preserve the Constitution, if, to save slavery, or any minor matter, I should permit the wreck of government, country, and Constitution all together. When, early in the war, Gen. Fremont attempted military emancipation, I forbade it, because I did not then think it an indispensable necessity. When a little later, Gen. Cameron, then Secretary of War, suggested the arming of the blacks, I objected, because I did not yet think it an indispensable necessity. When, still later, Gen. Hunter attempted military emancipation, I again forbade it, because I did not yet think the indispensable necessity had come. When, in March, and May, and July 1862 I made earnest, and, successive appeals to the border states to favor compensated emancipation, I believed the indispensable necessity for military emancipation, and arming the blacks would come, unless averted by that measure, They declined the proposition; and I was, in my best judgment, driven to the alternative of either surrendering the Union, and with it, the Constitution, or of laying strong hand upon the colored element. I chose the latter. In choosing it, I hoped for greater gain than loss; but of this, I was not entirely confident. More than a year of trial now shows no loss by it in our foreign relations, none in our home popular sentiment, none in our white military force,—no loss by it any how, or any where. On the contrary, it shows a gain of quite a hundred and thirty thousand soldiers, seamen, and laborers. These are palpable facts, about which, as facts, there can be no cavilling. We have the men; and we could not have had them without the measure.

And now let any Union man who complains of the measure, test himself by writing down in one line that he is for subduing the rebellion by force of arms; and in the next, that he is for taking these hundred and thirty thousand men from the Union side, and placing them where they would be but for the measure he condemns. If he can not face his case so stated, it is only because he can not face the truth.

I add a word which was not in the verbal conversation. In telling this tale I attempt no compliment to my own sagacity. I claim not to have controlled events, but confess plainly that events have controlled me. Now, at the end of three years struggle the nation's condition is not what either party, or any man devised, or expected. God alone can claim it. Whither it is tending seems plain. If God now wills the removal of a great wrong, and wills also that we of the North as well as you of the South, shall pay fairly for our complicity in that wrong, impartial history will find therein new cause to attest and revere the justice and goodness of God.

Yours truly

A. Lincoln

32078

A. G. Hodges, Esq
   Executive Mansion,
      Frankfort, Ky.

My dear Sir:

You ask me to put in writing the substance of what I verbally said the other day, in your presence, to Governor Bramlette and Senator Dixon. It was about as follows:

"I am naturally anti-slavery. If slavery is not wrong, nothing is wrong. I can not remember when I did not so think, and feel. And yet I have never understood that the Presidency conferred upon me an unrestricted right to act officially upon this judgment and feeling. It was in the oath I took that I would, to the best of my ability, preserve, protect, and defend the Constitution of the United States. I could not take the office without taking the oath. Nor was it my view that I might take an oath to get power, and break the oath in using the power. I understood, too, that in ordinary civil administration this oath even forbade me to practically indulge my primary abstract judgment on the moral question of slavery. I had publicly declared this many times, and in many ways. And I aver that, to this day, I have done no official act in mere deference to my abstract judgment and feeling on slavery. I did understand however, that my oath to preserve the constitution to the best of my ability, imposed upon me the duty of preserving, by every indispensable means, that government—that nation—of which that constitution was the organic law. Was it possible to lose the nation, and yet preserve the constitution? By general law life and limb must be protected; yet often a limb must be amputated to save a life; but a life is never wisely given to save a limb. I felt that measures, otherwise unconstitutional, might become lawful, by becoming indispensable to the preservation of the constitution, through the preservation of the nation. Right or wrong, I assumed this ground, and now avow it. I could not feel that, to the best of my ability, I had even tried to preserve the Constitution, if, to save slavery, or any minor matter, I should permit the wreck of government, country, and Constitution all together. When, early in the war, Gen. Fremont attempted military emancipation, I forbade it, because I did not then think it an indispensable necessity. When a little later, Gen. Cameron, then Secretary of War, suggested the arming of the blacks, I objected, because I did not yet think it an indispensable necessity. When, still later, Gen. Hunter attempted military emancipation, I again forbade it, because I did not yet think the indispensable necessity had come. When, in March, and May, and July 1862 I made earnest, and successive appeals to the border states to favor compensated emancipation, I believed the indispensable necessity for military emancipation, and arming the blacks would come, unless averted by that measure. They declined the proposition; and I was, in my best judgment, driven to the alternative of either surrendering the Union, and with it, the Constitution, or of laying strong hand upon the colored element. I chose the latter. In choosing it, I hoped for greater gain than loss; but of this, I was not entirely confident. More than a year of trial now shows no loss by it in our foreign relations, none in our home popular sentiment, none in our white military force,—no loss by it any how or any where. On the contrary, it shows a gain of quite a hundred and thirty thousand soldiers, seamen, and laborers. These are palpable facts, about which, as facts, there can be no cavilling. We have the men; and we could not have had them without the measure.

["]And now let any Union man who complains of the measure, test himself by writing down in one line that he is for subduing the rebellion by force of arms; and in the next, that he is for taking these hundred and thirty thousand men from the Union side, and placing them where they would be but for the measure he condemns. If he can not face his case so stated, it is only because he can not face the truth.["]

I add a word which was not in the verbal conversation. In telling this tale I attempt no compliment to my own sagacity. I claim not to have controlled events, but confess plainly that events have controlled me. Now, at the end of three years struggle the nation's condition is not what either party, or any man devised, or expected. God alone can claim it. Whither it is tending seems plain. If God now wills the removal of a great wrong, and wills also that we of the North as well as you of the South, shall pay fairly for our complicity in that wrong, impartial history will find therein new cause to attest and revere the justice and goodness of God.

Yours truly,

A. Lincoln

NOTES

A Note on Sources

MORE THAN FIFTY years ago, Roy Basler and the Rutgers University Press published *The Collected Works of Abraham Lincoln* in association with the Abraham Lincoln Association. The association has made the *Collected Works* available on the Internet, as well as "The Lincoln Log," a day-by-day of Lincoln's life. There you can learn the precise dates of Lincoln's historic activities as president, along with plenty of personal minutiae. (On April 28, 1855, Lincoln had $7 worth of repairs done on his buggy at Lewis' Carriage Shop and on February 5, 1860, he deposited $100 in the Springfield Marine Bank and withdrew $10.)

For research, the Internet has a trove of original source material. So, for instance, not only can you read the classic biography *Herndon's Lincoln* there as an ebook, you can also read an ebook version of *Lincoln's Herndon* by David Herbert Donald, which is essentially a biography of the biographer, and when you are done with that, you can tackle *Herndon's Informants*, Douglas Wilson's compilation of the "letters, interviews, and statements" that Herndon used to write his biography of Lincoln. There, you can check to see if Herndon used the material faithfully, and if you want to find the notes of a particular interview, you can log on to the University of Illinois site for *Herndon's Informants*, which allows you to search the material electronically.

All of that allows you to check up on Herndon and those who spoke to Herndon about Lincoln. When you want to discover what

Lincoln *himself* said, you have both the Basler *Collected Works* and another worthy companion, Donald Fehrenbacher's *Recollected Words of Abraham Lincoln*. Here, Fehrenbacher introduces just about anything that Lincoln is purported to have said and passes judgment on the trustworthiness of the source, leaving many famous lines in the dust heap. When asked how much attributed to him was true, Lincoln is said to have responded, "About half." Of course, the source of that anecdote is Homer Bates, whom Fehrenbacher describes as reliable in only about half of what *he* wrote.

Armed with these resources during the writing of this book, I avoided anything that had the distinct odor of falsity to it. On material that seemed plausible but had been questioned as to its truthfulness, I tried to indicate this either in the text or in the notes that follow here. Ultimately, however, we are all dependent on the goodwill and competence of those who attempted this task before us, and when it comes to Lincoln, much of the accepted wisdom hangs on very little.

Where possible, for ease of research, I worked from ebooks, mostly Kindle editions but also Google Books. Because ebooks can be altered in type size for the convenience of the reader, page numbers vary and should therefore not be referenced. In all cases where I used an electronic edition of a source, I tried to reference the chapter number, and of course any reader of an ebook can do a quick search by word. Readers of old-fashioned print books, which many of us still prefer, will, sorry to say, have to work a bit harder.

Finally, as to abbreviations in the notes below, most are self-evident when examined with the bibliography. Two which are not are Basler's *Collected Works*, which goes by the initials *CW*, and *The War of the Rebellion: A Compilation of the Official Records of the Union and Confederate Armies*, which goes by the initials *OR*.

Introduction: A Man, Imperfect

1 **"He liked smutty stories and was a politician":** W. E. B. Du Bois, "Opinion of W. E. B. Du Bois," *Crisis*, July 1922.

3 **"from a stagnant, putrid pool":** Herndon and Weik, *Herndon's Lincoln*, Preface. Herndon was coy about this paternity story, never exactly declaring it to be true, but repeating it nonetheless and seeming to enjoy himself as he did. "The evidence is not conclusive," he observed in an 1870 letter to Ward Hill Lamon, "but men have been hung on less evidence." In an 1886 letter to Jesse Weik—the collaborator who actually wrote *Herndon's Lincoln*, working from notes and letters provided by Herndon—Herndon repeated a story he had heard that Thomas Lincoln was impotent and that Enloe and Thomas Lincoln once had a fight in which Lincoln "bit off Enloe's nose." These letters can be found in Hertz's *Hidden Lincoln*.

3 **with the unfortunate subtitle *An Essay on the Chastity*:** Barton, *Paternity*.

4 **"events have controlled me":** Lincoln's letter to A. G. Hodges, April 4, 1864, *CW*, 8:282.

4 **"because we have watered him":** Hofstadter, *Political Tradition*, chap. 5.

4 **"by age forty, a man is responsible":** No credible Lincoln scholar has confirmed that Lincoln authored this popular adage. Few have even addressed it. But if you do a Google search on it, you will find it attributed regularly to Lincoln. You will also find that the adage changes from citation to citation. Sometimes it is altered to read "by age *fifty*, a man is responsible for his own face" (probably by people over forty), and other times as "at a *certain age*, a man is" (probably by people over fifty). So you may wonder why I include it here. In popular culture, an adage such as this gets attached to someone who may not have said it simply because it seems like something *the person might well have said.* That tells us something about how people viewed Abraham Lincoln: as believing that our actions in life mold our character over time. I include it also because the subject of free will plagued Lincoln throughout these six months and is therefore key material for this book. He may well have believed that "a man is responsible for his own face," but he was just as likely to say that fate is immovable, and whatever Lincoln was really thinking, it seems as though we want him to have been thinking that free will can overpower fate, which is why we like to hear him say things like "by age forty a man is responsible for his own face."

4 **"live through all time or die by suicide":** Lincoln's "Address Before the Young Men's Lyceum of Springfield, Illinois," January 27, 1838, *CW*, 1:109.

5   **an effort to wring meaning from their suffering:** See Drew Gilpin
     Faust's excellent book *This Republic of Suffering* for a thorough discussion
     of this.
5   **Congress to pass legislation creating the first national resting
     places:** Holt, *Cemeteries*, 1.
6   **Lincoln was not simply to be saluted:** As one small piece of evidence
     of this, take note of the description of an 1868 address by Edwin Stan-
     ton, Lincoln's secretary of war. Delivering a presidential campaign speech
     for Ulysses S. Grant, Stanton uses the memory of Lincoln as a way of
     inspiring his audience to vote for Grant. Here is how the scene, worthy
     of Jimmy Swaggart, was portrayed in Flower's *Edwin McMasters Stanton*:
     "His address occupied only about thirty-five minutes, but his earnestness
     was irresistible. Several times during the delivery, paroxysms of asthma
     so choked him that he was compelled to support himself from falling by
     a small table standing near; yet, to the astonishment of the great audi-
     ence, he took no notice of these attacks, but was lost in the effort to con-
     vince his hearers that it was the solemn duty of every citizen to vote for
     Grant. Stopping to rest a moment, he requested the presiding officer to
     read Lincoln's Gettysburg speech. At its conclusion he sprang forward and
     exclaimed: 'That is the voice of God speaking through the lips of Abraham
     Lincoln! . . . You hear the voice of Father Abraham here tonight. Did he
     die in vain? Shall we not dedicate ourselves to the work he left unfinished?
     Let us here, every one, with uplifted hand, declare before Almighty God
     that the precious gift of this great heritage, consecrated in the blood of our
     soldiers, shall never perish from the earth!'"
6   **More than twenty-two counties and thirty-five cities:** Peterson,
     Memory, chap. 4.
6   **"The grip that swung the ax in Illinois":** Ibid., chap. 5.
7   **glance through the entire list:** These titles can all be found in the bib-
     liography.
7   **According to WorldCat . . . 23,274 books:** The number of Lincoln
     books differs according to what criteria one uses. Does it only include
     books written specifically about Lincoln and not, for instance, the Civil
     War or the Republican Party in the nineteenth century or books that have
     essays on Lincoln as well as on other subjects? Does it include pamphlets
     along with books or compilations of his speeches? Does it include books
     where Lincoln's name is in the title but he is not the exclusive subject
     of the book (such as *America in the Age of Lincoln* or *Presidential Power from
     Jackson to Lincoln*)? Does it count only books in the English language? In
     2010, the museum at Ford's Theater in Washington unveiled a tower of
     Lincoln books as a kind of "sculpture" representing the amount of ink
     that had been dedicated to the study of the sixteenth president. While the

sculpture only included a representative amount, the museum reported that there were fifteen thousand books on Lincoln. That seems to be a popular number among those who have tried to characterize the historical Lincoln bibliography. Still, if you go to the Library of Congress, which is relatively speaking more selective in its holdings, they have about half of that. The most impressive number of all, and the one that I use here, is the WorldCat number. It only includes books with Lincoln in the title, and while it includes new editions of existing books (meaning that the number of *actual titles* is likely closer to the fifteen thousand number used by Ford's Theater), those new editions of, say, Sandburg's *Lincoln* or Nicolay and Hay's *Lincoln* should probably be in the count as they further illustrate the continuing demand of new generations to know more about Lincoln. The number here also includes books in all languages, not just English. Thus, the Chinese- and French-language editions of Doris Kearns Goodwin's *Team of Rivals* are counted with the American edition as three separate books. The popularity of Lincoln in other languages is another staggering thought to behold. There are Lincoln books in French, Spanish, and German, of course, but also Kannada, Telugu, Xhosa, Sinhalese, Marathi, Assamese, Ewe, Dakota, Oriya, Amharic, Sindhi, and Swahili.

I. A Funeral: July 13, 1862

11   **"dript from him as he walked":** Herndon and Weik, *Herndon's Lincoln*, chap. 20. The passage continues, "His apparent gloom impressed his friends and created sympathy for him—one means of his great success. He was gloomy, abstracted, and joyous—rather humorous by turns; but I do not think he knew what real joy was for many years." One has to give enormous credit to Herndon for the detail of his recollection. Consider, for instance, his description of Lincoln's gait: "When he walked he moved cautiously but firmly; his long arms and giant hands swung down by his side. He walked with even tread, the inner sides of his feet being parallel. He put the whole foot flat down on the ground at once, not landing on the heel; he likewise lifted his foot all at once, not rising from the toe, and hence he had no spring to his walk. His walk was undulatory—catching and pocketing tire, weariness, and pain, all up and down his person, and thus preventing them from locating. The first impression of a stranger, or a man who did not observe closely, was that his walk implied shrewdness and cunning—that he was a tricky man; but, in reality, it was the walk of caution and firmness."

12   **"God has called him home":** Keckley, *Behind the Scenes*, chap. 6. Keckley goes on to describe a picture of Lincoln in grief: "He buried his head in his hands, and his tall frame was convulsed with emotion. I stood at the foot

of the bed, my eyes full of tears, looking at the man in silent, awe-stricken wonder. His grief unnerved him, and made him a weak, passive child. I did not dream that his rugged nature could be so moved. I shall never forget those solemn moments—genius and greatness weeping over love's idol lost. There is a grandeur as well as a simplicity about the picture that will never fade."

13 **"like the wild, faint sobbing of far off spirits":** Ibid.

15 **the casualty toll approaching 150,000 on each side:** For running casualty figures, see Darroch Greer's "Counting Civil War Casualties Week by Week for the Abraham Lincoln Presidential Library and Museum," which can be found on the Internet.

16 **"he is not Caliban":** *Hartford Evening Press*, March 6, 1860. A full account of the meeting is in Niven, *Welles*, 289. The reference is to the subhuman beast Caliban in Shakespeare's *The Tempest*.

16 **Lincoln once joked that he himself:** Brooks, *Abraham Lincoln*, 426.

17 **thinking themselves "cavaliers, imbued with chivalry":** Welles, *Diary*, 2:276, entry for April 7, 1865. Here is an extended quote: "This Rebellion which has convulsed the nation for four years, threatened the Union, and caused such sacrifice of blood and treasure may be traced in a great degree to the diseased imagination of certain South Carolina gentlemen, who some thirty and forty years since studied Scott's novels, and fancied themselves cavaliers, imbued with chivalry, a superior class, not born to labor but to command, brave beyond mankind generally, more intellectual, more generous, more hospitable, more liberal than others. Such of their countrymen as did not own slaves, and who labored with their own hands, who depended on their own exertions for a livelihood, who were mechanics, traders, and tillers of the soil, were, in their estimate, inferiors who would not fight, were religious and would not gamble, moral and would not countenance dueling, were serious and minded their own business, economical and thrifty, which was denounced as mean and miserly. Hence the chivalrous Carolinian affected to, and actually did finally, hold the Yankee in contempt. The women caught the infection. They were to be patriotic, Revolutionary matrons and maidens. They admired the bold, dashing, swaggering, licentious, boasting, chivalrous slave-master who told them he wanted to fight the Yankee but could not kick and insult him into a quarrel. And they disdained and despised the pious, peddling, plodding, persevering Yankee who would not drink, and swear, and fight duels."

17 **"Only a war could wipe out this arrogance and folly":** Ibid., 2:277, entry for April 7, 1865.

17 **A short, thin reed of a man:** Depending on the source, Seward was somewhere between five feet four and five feet eight. Glyndon Van Deusen's biography says five feet six.

17   **"wise macaw"**: Adams, *Education of Henry Adams*, chap. 10. *Collected Works*. "A slouching, slender figure; a head like a wise macaw; a beaked nose; shaggy eyebrows; unorderly hair and clothes; hoarse voice; offhand manner; free talk, and perpetual cigar."

17   **"how much was nature and how much was mask"**: Ibid. "At table, among friends, Mr. Seward threw off restraint, or seemed to throw it off, in reality, while in the world he threw it off, like a politician, for effect. In both cases he chose to appear as a free talker, who loathed pomposity and enjoyed a joke; but how much was nature and how much was mask, he was himself too simple a nature to know."

17   **"We cannot . . . be either true Christians or real freemen"**: Baker, *Works*, 1:67.

18   **which compared Buchanan and the justices**: Collusion was suspected because Buchanan had secretly encouraged the vote of Justice Robert Cooper Grier. Grier's vote gave Buchanan political cover on an issue where he had maintained a studied public neutrality, though most Northerners, including Seward, suspected him a "doughface," Northern in roots but Southern in sympathies. Seward, *Seward at Washington*, 337; Simon, *Lincoln and Taney*, chap. 5; Stahr, *Seward*, 172.

18   **"an irrepressible conflict"**: Baker, *Works*, 4:293.

19   **"sovereign on the subject of slavery"**: Stahr, *Seward*, 183.

19   **preferring that Lincoln select only former Whigs**: Niven, *Welles*, 304–6.

20   **"he was to be the *de facto* president"**: Welles, *Lincoln and Seward*, 39. For a thorough exposition on the *Powhatan* affair, see Stahr, *Seward*, chap. 10.

21   **But it was Seward who pushed Lincoln toward it**: Donald, *Lincoln*, chap. 10; Stahr, *Seward*, 247.

23   **"a prejudice for my own race"**: Sears, *McClellan*, 119.

23   **a pique brought on by "ultras"**: Ibid., 65.

24   **"I cannot take my vittles regular"**: Donald, *Lincoln*, 358. Lincoln is reported to have said this to Dr. Henry Bellows in April 1862. In July, he was confronted by Senator Orville Browning, who was concerned about Lincoln's health. Browning's diary entry for July 15, 1862, includes the following: "I shook hands with him and asked how he was. He said 'tolerably well.' I remarked that I felt concerned about him—regretted that troubles crowded so heavily upon him, and feared his health was suffering. He held me by the hand, pressed it, and said in a very tender and touching tone, 'Browning, I must die sometime.'"

24   **and one of ten prewar presidents who had owned slaves**: The ten are George Washington, Thomas Jefferson, James Madison, James Monroe, Andrew Jackson, Martin Van Buren, William Henry Harrison, John Tyler, James Polk, and Zachary Taylor. The charge that Harrison fathered

children with one of his slaves is derived from the story of Walter White, who was head of the NAACP in the 1930s and who claimed to be descended from a slave named Dilsia, who served on the Harrison plantation when William Henry was a young man. See Janken, *White*, 3.

25   **Lincoln, six feet four inches before:** We know this from Lincoln himself, who, in a December 20, 1859, letter, provided a short character sketch to be included in the *Chester County* [Illinois] *Times*. "If any personal description of me is thought desirable, it may be said, I am, in height, six feet, four inches, nearly; lean in flesh, weighing, on an average, one hundred and eighty pounds; dark complexion, with coarse black hair, and grey eyes—no other marks or brands recollected." *CW*, 3:512.

25   **"like a pair of tongs on a chair back":** Wiley, "Billy Yank," 108.

25   **whose self-esteem was once described:** Thayer, "Lincoln and Some Union Generals," 93.

25   **"strong frank letter":** McClellan, July 8, 1862, letter to Mary Ellen McClellan, Sears, *McClellan Papers*.

25   **"highest principles known to Christian Civilization":** McClellan, July 7, 1862, letter to Lincoln, ibid.

26   **They had suffered mightily, with 1,734 dead:** Sears, *Richmond*, 344.

26   **"torn almost to shreds by the balls of the enemy":** *New York Times*, July 12, 1862.

II. "In Regard to Your Slaves . . ."

30   **"that under the war power the right had come":** Donald, *Sumner*, 323.

30   **Some Union commanders even allowed slave owners:** Ibid., 343.

30   **the "suppression of rebellion," the "preservation of the Union":** These phrases, used in a letter Senator Orville Browning wrote to Lincoln on April 18, 1861, are taken from resolutions adopted by a meeting in Illinois attended, Browning wrote, by "almost the entire mass of both parties." Hubbard, *Illinois's War*, 62.

32   **"I never should have had votes enough":** Lester, *Sumner*, 359. Lincoln's comments to Lester date to 1861. The context was the president's response to the news that Major General Frémont, commander of the Western Department, had proclaimed emancipation of the slaves of Confederate agitators in Missouri.

33   **The word takes its origins:** Davis, *Inhuman Bondage*, chap. 3.

33   **the forced migration of African peoples:** Ibid., chap. 4.

33   **greatest concentration of African slave labor:** African slaves made up at least 90 percent of the population of the Caribbean. Ibid.

34   **"color-coded" racism:** Fredrickson, *Racism*, chap. 1.

34   **an "otherness" that "made it psychologically easier":** Ibid.

35   **a robust Cotton Kingdom arose:** Davis, *Inhuman Bondage*, chap. 6.

35   **There were seven hundred thousand slaves in 1790:** US census figures, as summarized in Dattel, *Cotton and Race*, 52.

35   **"my obligations under the Constitution":** Lincoln's August 24, 1855, letter to Joshua Speed. *CW*, 2:321.

36   **"more akin to his feeling for tortured animals":** Hofstadter, *Political Tradition*.

37   **"the real knell of the Union?":** Lincoln, "Speech on the Kansas-Nebraska Act at Peoria, Illinois," October 16, 1854, *CW*, 2:248.

37   **"the harlot, slavery":** Donald, *Sumner*, 239. Here is more of Sumner's speech: "The senator from South Carolina has read many books of chivalry, and believes himself a chivalrous knight, with sentiments of honor and courage. Of course he has chosen a mistress to whom he has made his vows, and who, though ugly to others, is always lovely to him; though polluted in the sight of the world, is chaste in his sight; I mean the harlot slavery. For her his tongue is always profuse with words. Let her be impeached in character, or any proposition made to shut her out from the extension of her wantonness, and no extravagance of manner or hardihood of assertion is then too great for this senator. The frenzy of Don Quixote in behalf of his wench Dulcinea del Toboso is all surpassed."

37   **"I did not intend to kill him":** Ibid., 247.

38   **"half slave and half free":** *CW*, 2:461. This comes from Lincoln's "House Divided" speech (the image comes from the Gospels), delivered June 16, 1858, upon his acceptance of the nomination of the Republican Party for US senator from Illinois: "We are now far into the fifth year, since a policy was initiated, with the avowed object, and confident promise, of putting an end to slavery agitation. Under the operation of that policy, that agitation has not only, not ceased, but has constantly augmented. In my opinion, it will not cease, until a crisis shall have been reached, and passed. 'A house divided against itself cannot stand.' I believe this government cannot endure, permanently half slave and half free. I do not expect the Union to be dissolved—I do not expect the house to fall—but I do expect it will cease to be divided. It will become all one thing, or all the other. Either the opponents of slavery, will arrest the further spread of it, and place it where the public mind shall rest in the belief that it is in course of ultimate extinction; or its advocates will push it forward, till it shall become alike lawful in all the States, old as well as new—North as well as South."

38   **"abolitionize":** Lincoln's first debate with Stephen Douglas, Ottawa, Illinois, August 21, 1858, *CW*, 3:2.

38   **"In repose, I must confess"**: *New York Evening Post*, August 27, 1858, 1.

39   **That could well mean that "ultimate extinction"**: Lincoln returned
      to this idea twice during his debates with Douglas. Here he sounds the
      theme in the first debate at Ottawa, Illinois, on August 21, 1858: "Now, I
      believe if we could arrest the spread, and place it where Washington, and
      Jefferson, and Madison placed it, it would be in the course of ultimate
      extinction. . . . The crisis would be past and the institution might be let
      alone for a hundred years, if it should live so long, in the States where it
      exists, yet it would be going out of existence in the way best for both the
      black and the white races." *CW*, 3:2. Lincoln makes the same claim in
      Charleston, Illinois, on September 18, 1858: "I do not mean that when it
      takes a turn towards ultimate extinction it will be in a day, nor in a year,
      nor in two years. I do not suppose that in the most peaceful way ultimate
      extinction would occur in less than a hundred years at the least; but that it
      will occur in the best way for both races in God's own good time, I have no
      doubt. [Applause.] But, my friends, I have used up more of my time than
      I intended on this point." *CW*, 3:182.

40   **"You work and toil and earn bread, and I'll eat it"**: Lincoln addresses
      this in the last debate with Douglas, at Alton, Illinois, on October 15, 1858:
      "That is the real issue. That is the issue that will continue in this country
      when these poor tongues of Judge Douglas and myself shall be silent. It
      is the eternal struggle between these two principles—right and wrong—
      throughout the world. They are the two principles that have stood face to
      face from the beginning of time; and will ever continue to struggle. The
      one is the common right of humanity and the other the divine right of
      kings." *CW*, 3:284.

40   **"we never hear of the man who wishes"**: This fragment, to which Lin-
      coln's secretaries Nicolay and Hay assigned the date of April 1854, was
      probably part of a draft for a speech never finished. *CW*, 2:222.

41   **the Constitution set a date allowing**: The text of the Constitution is
      as follows: "The Migration or Importation of such Persons as any of the
      States now existing shall think proper to admit, shall not be prohibited by
      the Congress prior to the Year one thousand eight hundred and eight, but
      a tax or duty may be imposed on such Importation, not exceeding ten dol-
      lars for each Person." Note that the word *slave* is never used here. Note,
      also, that the provision allowed for the regulation of slave trade but it did
      not require it. Finally, this was one of only two clauses in the Constitu-
      tion (clause four of Article I, section 9, prohibiting direct taxation, being
      the other) that were immune from amendment, at least temporarily. In
      Article V, which lays out the process for amending the Constitution, it
      exempts these two clauses until 1808. The fear among the Southern states,
      which pushed for this provision, was that a coalition of antislavery states

could immediately amend the Constitution to end the slave trade earlier than initially agreed. See Amar, *America's Constitution.*

42   **Fletcher Webster . . . would succumb to a bullet:** *New York Times,* September 2, 1862.

43   **with the picture (think *frame* here):** Lincoln speech at Peoria, Illinois, October 16, 1854, *CW,* 2:248.

43   **"Did he intend to say in that Declaration":** Douglas, in fifth debate with Lincoln, at Galesburg, Illinois, October 7, 1858, *CW,* 3:208.

43   **It cared not for "the negro, the savage Indians":** Douglas, in third debate with Lincoln, at Jonesboro, Illinois, September 15, 1858, *CW,* 3:103.

44   **"slavery would have been fastened by a constitutional provision":** Douglas, in first debate with Lincoln, at Ottawa, Illinois, August 21, 1858, *CW,* 3:2.

44   **that the earth belongs "in usufruct":** Thomas Jefferson, letter to James Madison, September 6, 1789. Kurland and Lerner, *Founders' Constitution,* chap. 2, document 2.

44   **"I am not, nor have I ever been":** Lincoln, in fourth debate with Douglas, at Charleston, Illinois, September 18, 1858, *CW,* 2:146. He uses the same language in the fifth and sixth debates.

45   **"little Abolition orators":** Douglas, in first debate with Lincoln at Ottawa, Illinois, August 21, 1858, *CW,* 3:2.

45   **"a covenant with death":** Paludan, *Covenant,* chap. 1. "Then he reached for a copy of the Constitution, held it in his hand and declared that it was 'the parent of all other atrocities.' 'A covenant with death,' he called it."

45   **"Free them, and make them politically":** Lincoln, speech at Peoria, Illinois, October 16, 1854, *CW,* 2:248.

III. Nerve Center

49   **"His tall, homely form":** Bates, *Lincoln in the Telegraph Office,* 7.

50   **"If they kill me":** Brooks, *Lincoln Observed,* 204–5.

50   **"I come here to escape my persecutors":** Tarbell, *Life,* 2:105.

50   **"What hath God wrought!":** Silverman, *Lightning Man,* chap. 10; Mabee, *American Leonardo.*

52   **which he regarded as benefiting both slave and slave master:** Silverman, *Lightning Man,* chap. 17. See also Morse, *Argument on the Ethical Position of Slavery.*

52   **"freedom-shriekers, Bible-spurners":** Extracts from a letter of Professor S. B. F. Morse, as found in the *Portsmouth* [Ohio] *Times,* April 18, 1863, 4. Here is a fuller quote: "Look at that dark conclave of conspira-

tors, freedom-shriekers, Bible-spurners—fierce, implacable, headstrong, denunciatory, Constitution and Union haters, noisy factions, breathing forth threatenings and slaughter against all who venture a difference of opinion from them, murderous, passionate advocates of imprisonments and hangings, bloodthirsty—and if there is any other epithet of atrocity found in the vocabulary of wickedness, do they not every one fitly designate some phase of abolitionism?"

52 **"demons in human shape"**: Silverman, *Lightning Man*, chap. 11.

53 **he once referred to him as an "imbecile"**: Ibid., chap. 17.

53 **man "dig[s] out his destiny"**: Lincoln, First Lecture on Discoveries and Inventions, April 6, 1858, *CW*, 2:438.

53 **was invention with purpose—a *democratic* purpose**: Gilmore, *Aesthetic Materialism*, 40.

54 **As late as May 1862, Lincoln was sending**: Wheeler, *Mr. Lincoln's T-mails.*

54 **"Well, boys, I am down to the raisins"**: Bates, *Lincoln in the Telegraph Office*, 41.

55 **asked "for some paper, as he wanted to write"**: Ibid., 138.

55 **from a reading of an 1865 biography authored by Lincoln's friend Joseph Hartwell Barrett**: Barrett, *Life*, 414. In a later book on Lincoln, *Abraham Lincoln and His Presidency*, Barrett is more expansive on this subject. There, he reports that Lincoln "completed his rough draft" of the proclamation on the way back from Harrison's Landing. He also indicates that Hamlin saw the draft after Lincoln returned to Washington. But these are reflections published in 1904, more than forty years after the fact, and one wonders why he was not more explicit in his 1865 book.

56 **"As soon as we had started he withdrew"**: "Senator Hamlin, of Maine," *New York Times*, September 8, 1879.

56 **after opening up about it to Welles and Seward**: Welles, "History of Emancipation," 851. Welles's thinking was that Lincoln waited for his proposal for compensated emancipation to the Border States to be rejected, and when it was, on July 12, 1862, he opened up to Seward and Welles about his decision to issue the proclamation. Only then, writes Welles, did Lincoln begin writing it, for to have started earlier would have been "disingenuous." How could he be bargaining with the Border States for a gradual emancipation when he was writing a proclamation of emancipation as a military necessity? Welles found the two policies incompatible.

57 **Eckert is himself interesting**: Eckert's greatest notoriety comes from a tale popular among conspiracy theorists who have been tantalized that on the night of April 14, 1865, Lincoln asked Eckert to accompany him as his

bodyguard during the president's fateful visit to Ford's Theater, and that Eckert, under orders from Stanton, turned him down, claiming that he had work to do in the telegraph office. When he was later notified of Lincoln's killing, Eckert was at home, not at work, and this, along with a few other inconvenient facts (Stanton had also encouraged Ulysses Grant not to join Lincoln at the show, even though he, too, had been invited by the president), has led some, especially Otto Eisenschiml—in a widely read 1937 book, *Why Was Lincoln Murdered?*—to accuse Stanton of complicity in a plot to kill Lincoln, a theory that is now largely discounted.

58 **"I procured some foolscap":** Bates, *Lincoln in the Telegraph Office*, 138. The entire story here about Lincoln and the first draft of the proclamation comes largely from Bates, chapter 10.

61 **To Lincoln, then, the rebel states were:** This was one reason why it was so important that the European states, especially Great Britain, not recognize the Confederacy, for foreign recognition would give the South a greater claim to independence from Washington.

61 **for civil wars "may be prosecuted on the same footing":** From the opinion of the Court: "War has been well defined to be, 'That state in which a nation prosecutes its right by force.' The parties belligerent in a public war are independent nations. But it is not necessary, to constitute war, that both parties should be acknowledged as independent nations or sovereign States. A war may exist where one of the belligerents claims sovereign rights as against the other. . . . As a civil war is never publicly proclaimed, *eo nomine* [by that name], against insurgents, its actual existence is a fact in our domestic history which the Court is bound to notice and to know. The true test of its existence, as found in the writings of the sages of the common law, may be thus summarily stated: When the regular course of justice is interrupted by revolt, rebellion, or insurrection, so that the Courts of Justice cannot be kept open, civil war exists, and hostilities may be prosecuted on the same footing as if those opposing the Government were foreign enemies invading the land."

64 **There, whites, outnumbered by slaves ten to one:** Garrigus, *Before Haiti*, 7.

65 **"And it would be perfectly right for anyone to interfere":** From "Verbatim Report of the Questioning of Old Brown by Senator Mason, Congressman Vallandigham and Others," *New York Herald*, October 21, 1859, in Lande, *Dispatches from the Front*, 99.

65 **he, as the "arch agitator":** Stahr, *Seward*, 180–83.

65 **nothing more than "an enthusiast":** Lincoln, Address at Cooper Institute, February 27, 1860, *CW*, 3:523.

66 **Militia Act:** McDonald, *Select Statutes*, 54.

66   **In the second act:** Ibid., 52.

66   **"not brains enough":** Henry Winter Davis to Samuel Francis Du Pont, July 1862, S. F. Du Pont Papers, Hagley Museum, Wilmington, DE, in Burlingame, *Lincoln*, vol. 2.

66   **"feel that we are at war":** Frank E. Foster to John Sherman, Columbus, May 10, 1862, ibid.

66   **"bound hand and foot":** Harlow, *Smith*, 431–32.

67   **"contending factions":** W. M. Dickson to Friedrich Hassaurek, Cincinnati, June 9, 1862, in Burlingame, *Lincoln*, vol. 2.

67   **"storm of enthusiasm within the Border States":** Pease and Randall, *Browning Diary*, 558.

IV. First Reading

70   **"Do you think, Mr. Carpenter, that":** Carpenter, *Six Months*, 19.

70   **"which would have been out of place":** Ibid., 81.

71   **"then I shall at least have":** Ibid., 25.

72   **"timid, vacillating, and inefficient":** Chandler in a letter to his wife, Washington, October 27, 1861, in Burlingame, *Lincoln*, vol. 2.

73   **"not at liberty to substitute my convictions for theirs":** Chase, *Chase Papers*, 36.

76   **compulsory deportation of the freed slaves to Africa:** Welles, "History of Emancipation," 845.

76   **"the family relation, shrouded in artificial darkness":** Ibid.

78   **"God protect us from such contact":** Agassiz's December 2, 1846, letter to Rose Agassiz, in Stanton, *Leopard's Spots*, 103; Marcou, *Life*, 293. The original, which is in French, can be found in the Louis Agassiz Correspondence and Other Papers at Harvard's Houghton Library. Both Louis Menand, in *The Metaphysical Club*, and Stephen Jay Gould, in *The Mismeasure of Man*, include long passages on Agassiz and his theories.

78   **"that of the imperfect brain of a seven-month's infant":** Stanton, *Leopard's Spots*, 100.

79   **"They rested upon the assumption of the equality of races":** Cleveland, *Alexander Stephens*, 721. The speech was actually delivered extemporaneously, so there is no known official text. The accepted text is one written out by a reporter from the *Savannah Republican*.

79   **"The defenders of slavery forget":** Agassiz's December 2, 1846, letter to Rose Agassiz, in Menand, *Metaphysical*.

80   **"philanthropists":** Ibid.

80   **a field of study called niggerology:** Graves, *Emperor's Clothes*, 48; Nott and Gliddon, *Types of Mankind*.

80   **Welles says Bates's views on race and intermarriage:** Welles, "History of Emancipation," 845.

81   **"I need not have her for either":** Lincoln, speech at Springfield, Illinois, June 26, 1857, *CW*, 2:399.

82   **"Won't you give me a little lesson":** Brooks, *Lincoln Observed*, 203.

82   **Union generals "organize and arm the slaves":** Chase, *Diary*, 47–49.

83   **That move—by an inexperienced and incompetent officer":** For a character study of Frémont, see Williams, *Lincoln and His Generals*. Lincoln's September 2 and 11, 1861, letters to Frémont requesting that he reverse his order for the confiscation of property and the liberating of slaves can be found in *CW*, vol. 4.

83   **But Lincoln forced him to rescind this order as well:** *CW*, 5:223.

83   **The freed slaves, he told the group:** Carpenter, *Six Months*, 21.

84   **"a social revolution, with all its horrors":** Stahr, *Seward*, chap. 12.

84   **"the former [for] making the most desperate attempts":** Seward to Adams, July 5, 1862, in *Papers Relating to Foreign Affairs, 1862* (Washington, DC: United States Department of State, Government Printing Office), 124.

84   **He approved of the emancipation move:** This is the accepted version of Seward's reactions. However, Stahr, in *Seward*, is skeptical that the secretary was approving of the measure itself. He cites Stanton's notes, which describe Seward as "against it," and speculates that other accounts that have Seward approving, but for the timing—Carpenter's and that of Whitelaw Reid, a journalist—were authored after the fact and perhaps with the intention of reconstructing Seward's reputation on this subject.

84   **"until you can give it to the country":** Carpenter, *Six Months*, 22.

85   **"victories are yet delayed and seem indeed further off":** *New York Times*, July 22, 1862.

V. Send Them Away

87   *Louisville Daily Democrat* **had come out for "disunion":** Chase, *Diary*, 53.

88   **"the loyal whites remaining, if they would not":** Ibid., 54.

88   **"turn fifty thousand bayonets from loyal Border States":** Lincoln, "Remarks to Deputation of Western Gentlemen," August 4, 1862, *CW*, 5:357.

88   **Rafael Repeater:** Two days later, Lincoln wrote a note to Secretary of War Stanton: "I have examined and seen tried the 'Rafael Repeater' and consider it a decided improvement upon what was called the 'Coffee Mill Gun' in these particulars that it dispenses with the great cost and liability

to loss of the Steel cartridges and that it is better arranged to prevent the escape of gas." *CW*, 5:366.

88 **"Feeling a lively interest in all that":** *CW*, 5:364.

88 **thanking him for the gift of the senator's:** *CW*, 5:365.

88 **sat down with a delegation of "colored men":** "Address on Colonization to a Deputation of Negroes," *CW*, 5:371.

90 **had founded the American Colonization Society:** Davis, *Inhuman Bondage*, chap. 13. See also Staudenraus, *African Colonization Movement*, and Sherwood, "American Colonization Society."

91 **"promoters of mischief":** "Early History of the American Colonization Society," 54. Here is the extended quote from Randolph: "It was a notorious fact, he said, that the existence of this mixed and intermediate population of free negroes was viewed by every slaveholder as one of the greatest sources of the insecurity, and also unprofitableness, of slave property; that they serve to excite in their fellow beings a feeling of discontent, of repining at their situation, and that they act as channels of communication not only between different slaves, but between the slaves of different districts; that they are the depositaries of stolen goods, and the promoters of mischief."

92 **Governor Tim Kaine pardoned Prosser:** *New York Times*, October 30, 2002.

92 **for every slave in Baltimore in the 1830s:** Moser, "Pioneers."

93 **opposition from abolitionists at home:** Sherwood, "American Colonization Society."

93 **Prince Hal:** Heidler and Heidler, *Clay*, 45.

94 **"every one of us, to restore peace:** Colton, *Works of Clay*, 3:304.

95 **"most corrupt, depraved, and abandoned":** Heidler and Heidler, *Clay*, 132.

95 **"however ardent can secure their admission":** Alexander, *History of Colonization*, 322.

95 **"the power nor the will to affect":** Colton, *Works of Clay*, 4:339.

96 **"depopulated the fields and forests of the West":** Peterson, *Triumvirate*, 167.

96 **prized member of a "second generation":** Ibid., 486.

96 **"beau ideal of a statesman":** Lincoln's first debate with Douglas at Ottawa, Illinois, August 21, 1858, *CW*, 3:30. Here is the extended quote: "Henry Clay, my beau ideal of a statesman, the man for whom I fought all my humble life—Henry Clay once said of a class of men who would repress all tendencies to liberty and ultimate emancipation, that they must, if they would do this, go back to the era of our Independence, and muzzle the cannon which thunders its annual joyous return; they must blow out the moral lights around us; they must penetrate the human soul, and

eradicate there the love of liberty; and then and not till then, could they perpetuate slavery in this country!"

97   **"the world's estimate of him"**: Lincoln, "Eulogy on Henry Clay," July 6, 1852, *CW*, 2:122.

97   **saw his love of reading as "lazy"**: McPherson, *Lincoln*.

97   **"it is doubtful whether it would not be"**: Lincoln, letter to his step-brother, John D. Johnston, January 12, 1851, *CW*, 2:97.

97   **However, as the author of an article in H. L. Mencken's:** de Roul-hac Hamilton, "Many-Sired Lincoln." Here is an extended quote: "Seven cities claimed Homer dead, but seven sires are all too few for Lincoln. We are asked to believe that he was the son of Thomas Lincoln of Kentucky, who was, at least, his putative father; of Abraham Enlow, of Hardin county, Kentucky; of Abraham Enloe, of Swain county, North Carolina; of Abraham Inlow, of Bourbon county, Kentucky; of George Brownfield, of Kentucky; of Martin D. Hardin, of Kentucky; of Samuel Davis, of Kentucky; of Patrick Henry, of Virginia, of Henry Clay, of Kentucky; of John C. Calhoun, of South Carolina; of Adam Springs, of North Carolina; of one Andrew, an adopted son of Chief Justice Marshall; and, presumably, of any and every male person of his time who ever came—or did not come—within hailing distance of any locality where any person named Nancy Hanks ever lived."

100 **black American leaders with the purpose:** Mitchell, *Report*, 5.

100 **"inexpedient, inauspicious, and impolitic"**: Quarles, *Negro*, 149.

101 **"able-bodied men, with a mixture of women and children"**: Lincoln, "Address on Colonization to a Deputation of Negroes," August 14, 1862, *CW*, 5:371.

102 **"a wise effort to give freemen homes in America!"**: Chase, *Diary*, 59, August 15, 1862.

102 **"colored car"**: Stauffer, *Giants*, 39.

103 **"We should not be surprised if both"**: *Douglass' Monthly*, August 1862, 6.

103 **reference to "playing the lawyer"**: Kendrick and Kendrick, *Douglass and Lincoln*, 75.

103 **"his contempt for Negroes and his canting hypocrisy"**: *Douglass' Monthly*, September 1862, 1.

103 **"by means of theft, robbery, and rebellion"**: Ibid.

104 **"Are you a patriot? So are we"**: Foner, *Trial*, chap. 7.

104 **"magnanimity or principle of justice and humanity"**: *Douglass' Monthly*, September 1862, 1.

105 **"As to the policy I 'seem to be pursuing'"**: Lincoln, letter to Horace Greeley, August 22, 1862, *CW*, 5:389.

VI. God Knows

111 **"clear conscience in regard to my action on this momentous question":** Carpenter, *Six Months*, 77.

111 **growing "irritable" and "overstrung":** Nicolay and Hay, *Lincoln*, 6:154. Here is an extended quote: "Individuals and delegations came to him to urge one side or the other of a decision, which, though already made in his own mind, forced upon him a reexamination of its justness and its possibilities for good or evil. Imperceptibly these mental processes became a species of self-torment, and well-meaning inquirers or advisers affected his overstrung nerves like so many persecuting inquisitors. A phlegmatic nature would have turned them away in sullen silence, or at most with an evasive commonplace. But Lincoln felt himself under compulsion, which he could not resist, to state somewhat precisely the difficulties and perplexities under which he was acting, or, rather, apparently refusing to act; and in such statements his public argument, upon hypothesis assumed for illustration, was liable to outrun his private conclusion upon facts which had controlled his judgment."

111 **"probably much harm":** Letter from James Speed to Abraham Lincoln, July 28, 1862, Abraham Lincoln Papers, Library of Congress.

112 **"as a witness of the President's mental operations":** Tarbell, *Life*, 2:113. It is important to note that this story comes not from Swett to the author, but from Swett's friend and law partner, Peter Stenger Grosscup, a judge on the Seventh Circuit Court of Appeals, whom Tarbell interviewed. But the story also appears elsewhere.

113 **"cautious, dilatory, reticent":** Greeley, *Conflict*, 2:251.

114 **"leave Pope to get out of his scrape":** McClellan telegram to Lincoln, August 29, 1862, 2:45 p.m., in Sears, *War Papers*.

114 **"render your retreat safe":** McClellan telegram to Fitz John Porter, September 1, 1862, 5:30 p.m., ibid.

114 **"desponding feeling than I have ever witnessed":** Welles, *Diary*, 1:105, entry for September 1, 1862.

114 **"He is a good engineer":** Ibid.

114 **"ready to hang himself":** See annotation on Bates's notes, *CW*, 5:404.

115 **"Yet the contest proceeds":** Ibid. The dating of this officially undated passage (known as "Meditation on the Divine Will") has long been a task of guesswork, and guesswork it remains. Working from the sense that the passage displays a sense of profound despair, appropriate to the war at its lowest point, Hay chose to put it in the despair-filled month of September 1862. Later, working from some faulty assumptions, he and Nicolay attached the actual date of September 30. The editors of Lincoln's *Collected Works* chose instead the date of September 2, reflecting on Bates's

reference to Lincoln saying that he was ready to hang himself, and most recently scholars point to considerable evidence that the passage may not have been penned in 1862 at all, but as late as 1864. Douglas Wilson offers the most complete examination of this mystery in *Lincoln's Sword* and makes the compelling point that the meditation is written on stationery that has an image of the domed US Capitol embossed on it. Images of the design of the Capitol were available before its 1863 completion, but Wilson has not been able to recover an example of stationery with the domed Capitol any earlier than April 1863.

117 **"I have not in any respect injured your feelings"**: Lincoln, "Reply to Emancipation Memorial Presented by Chicago Christians of All Denominations," September 13, 1862, *CW*, 5:420.

118 **Lincoln was a devout, though private, Christian:** Holland, *Life*. Holland closes his book with the image of Lincoln and Christ blended into one: "Thus sad and weary, working early and late, full of the consciousness that God was working through him for the accomplishment of great ends, praying daily for strength and guidance, with a heart full of warm charity toward his foes, and open with sympathy toward the poor and the suffering, this Christian President sat humbly in his high seat, and did his duty. It is with genuine pain that the writer is compelled to leave behind, unrecorded, save in the floating literature of the day, multiplied instances which illustrate his tender-heartedness, his pity, his overruling sense of justice, his patience under insult, his loveliness of spirit, his devotion to humanity, his regard for the poor and the despised, his truthfulness, his simplicity, and the long list of manly virtues which distinguished his character and his career. They would of them selves fill a volume. Mr. Lincoln's character was one which will grow. It will become the basis of an ideal man. It was so pure, and so unselfish, and so rich in its materials, that fine imaginations will spring from it, to blossom and bear fruit through all the centuries. This element was found in Washington, whose human weaknesses seem to have faded entirely from memory, leaving him a demi-god; and it will be found in Mr. Lincoln in a still more remarkable degree. The black race have already crowned him. With the black man, and particularly the black freed man, Mr. Lincoln's name is the saintliest which he pronounces, and the noblest he can conceive. To the emancipated, he is more than man—a being scarcely second to the Lord Jesus Christ himself. That old, white-headed negro who undertook to tell what 'Massa Linkum' was to his dark-minded brethren, imbodied the vague conceptions of his race, in the words 'Massa Linkum, he ebery whar; he know ebery ting; he walk de earf like de Lord.'"

119 **in New Salem, Illinois, among a group of liberal thinkers:** Herndon and Weik, *Herndon's Lincoln*, chap. 14.

120 **Yet Lincoln's favorite poet . . . the satirist Robert Burns:** Letter from N. W. Branson to W. H. Herndon, in Wilson and Davis, *Herndon's Informants*. Here is an extended quote: "He used to read a great deal, improving every opportunity, by day and by night. . . . History and poetry & the newspapers constituted the most of his reading. Burns seemed to be his favorite. . . . He read aloud very often; and frequently assumed a lounging position when reading. He read very thoroughly, and had a most wonderful memory. Would distinctly remember almost every thing he read. Used to sit up late of nights reading, & would recommence in the morning when he got up."

120 **"he found in Burns a like thinker and feeler":** Herndon, interview with James H. Matheny, March 2, 1870, ibid.

120 **"we might become infidels on that subject":** Herndon and Weik, *Herndon's Lincoln*, chap. 14.

121 **to one observer he even "bordered on atheism":** Ibid.

121 **"I have never spoken with intentional disrespect":** *CW*, 1:382.

122 **"in the Christian sense of the term":** David Davis, interview with Herndon, in Herndon and Weik, *Herndon's Lincoln*, chap. 14.

122 **"dying man who puts his trust in him":** Lincoln, letter to his stepbrother, John D. Johnston, January 12, 1851, *CW*, 2:97.

123 **"they have not read their Bibles aright":** Holland, *Life*, 237.

123 **"in Springfield, to which Mrs. Lincoln belongs":** Scripps, *Life*, 72.

123 **"greater than that which rested upon Washington":** Lincoln, "Farewell Address at Springfield, Illinois," February 11, 1861, *CW*, 4:190.

124 **"best way all our present difficulty":** Lincoln, First Inaugural Address, March 4, 1861, *CW*, 4:263.

124 **"a more devout man than I am":** *CW*, 6:535. It seems clear that Gurley had some reservations about Lincoln. A few weeks after Lincoln was assassinated, he preached a sermon that raised moral objections to the president's love of theater: "Had he been murdered in his bed, or in his office, or on the streets, or on the steps of the Capitol, the tidings of his death would not have struck the Christian heart of the country quite so painfully; for the feeling of that heart is that the theater is one of the last places to which a good man should go and among the very last in which his friends should wish him to die."

125 **"it required a surgical operation to get a joke into his head":** Brooks, "Recollections," 222.

126 **"He was not a technical Christian":** Herndon's interview with Mary Todd Lincoln, September 1866, in Wilson and Davis, *Herndon's Informants*. Here is the extended quote from Herndon's notes: "Mr Linc[oln] had a Kind of Poetry in his Nature: he was [a terribly] firm man when he set

his foot down—none of us—no man nor woman Could rule him after he had made up his mind. I told him about Sewards intention to rule him—: he said—'I shall rule myself—shall obey my own Conscience and follow God in it['] Mr Lincoln had no hope & no faith in the usual acceptation of those words: he never joined a Church: he was a religious man always, as I think: he first thought—to say think—about this subject was when Willie died—never before. he felt religious More than Ever about the time he went to Gettysburg: he was not a technical Christian: he read the bible a good deal about 1864."

126 **"ill will into friendship":** Ibid. Here is the extended quote from Herndon's notes: "When we first went to Washington Many thought that Mr Lincoln was weak, but he rose grandly with the Circumstances [and] Men soon learned that he was above [them all.] I never saw a man's mind develope so finely: his manners got quite polished. [He] used to say to me when I talked to him about Chase and those who did him Evil—'Do good to those who hate you and turn their ill will to friendship' Sometimes in Washington [being] worn down he spoke crabbedly to men—[Harshly so—] yet it seemed that the People underst[ood the] Conditions around him and forgave."

127 **Brooks claimed, in a dubious account, that Lincoln regularly prayed:** Brooks never published this reference to Lincoln's praying regularly, but two weeks after Lincoln's assassination, he wrote a letter to the Reverend Mr. Langworthy where he proffered the following: "For myself, I am glad to say that I have a firm belief in Mr. Lincoln's saving knowledge of Christ; he talked always of Christ, his cross, his atonement; he prayed regularly, cast all his cares on God and felt inexpressible relief thereby." Yet this seems wholly out of character with Lincoln, and since it was intended not for a public audience, but for the eyes of the Christian minister, it may have been written to please its recipient. In the same letter, Brooks tells Langworthy that, freed by Lincoln's death from "the natural delicacy at speaking of his religious exercises," he intends to publish an article in *Harper's Monthly* on the president's character. The article appeared in July of 1865, but made no mention of Lincoln's "firm belief in Christ," of praying, or of any other religious practice. For an interesting discussion of Brooks as a source, see Gabor Borritt's *Gettysburg Gospel.*

127 **"no *prayers* of ours can reverse the decree":** Herndon and Weik, *Herndon's Lincoln*, chap. 14.

128 **"'There's a divinity that shapes our ends'":** Ibid.

VII. One Day: September 17, 1862

129   **when nearly twenty-three thousand casualties were counted:** The
      National Park Service lists 22,720 casualties at Antietam, with the Union
      forces suffering 12,400 and the Confederates 10,320. Among these, 3,650
      died. The Congressional Research Service report for Congress shows
      1,733 battle deaths in the Mexican War.

131   **"Certainly the joy of conflict was not":** Sears, *Civil War*.

131   **"conveys . . . the dignity of age":** Goethe, *Colors*, 315.

131   **"already far advanced in putrefaction":** Strother, "Recollections of
      the War," 285. The captain here is David Hunter Strother, a Virginia loy-
      alist who was in McClellan's army. In his civilian life he had been a sketch
      artist, trained by Samuel F. B. Morse. Strother's art regularly appeared in
      Harper's. The extended version of the quote is as follows: "One lay with his
      musket grasped firmly in one hand, and his ramrod in the other raised in
      the air, as if in act of loading. Another, with staring eyes and hands clasped
      together extended toward heaven, as if in prayer. A third hung across the
      remnant of a fence, doubtless killed as he was getting over. These were all
      bodies of the rebels, already far advanced in putrefaction, hideously swol-
      len, and many of them black as soot, reminding me of certain representa-
      tions of the charnel-houses of Florence during the great plague to be seen
      in the wax museum of that city. Many were so covered with dust, torn,
      crushed, and trampled that they resembled clods of earth, and you were
      obliged to look twice before recognizing them as human remains. Beyond
      this mass, which even in death seemed convulsed with the passion, terror,
      and agony of violent conflict, lay a well-defined line in close double ranks
      of those who died in line-of-battle, with calmer faces and more natural
      attitudes than those who fell in the onset or in flight."

132   **"about a quart of dark-looking maggots working away":** Diary of
      Otho Nesbitt, in McPherson, *Crossroads*, introduction.

132   **"unburied and uncared for":** Greiner, Coryell, and Smithers, *Surgeon's
      War*, 28.

132   **"they were climbing when the fatal shot struck them":** Richardson,
      Secret Service, 289.

132   **"one vast hospital":** *Hagerstown Herald*, September 24, 1862, in McPher-
      son, *Crossroads*, introduction.

132   **"wounded men hollering, 'Oh, Lord, Oh, Lord'":** Ward, *Slaves' War*,
      97.

133   **"The men are loading and firing with demoniacal fury":** Dawes,
      Service, 91.

133   **One Texas regiment lost 82 percent of its men:** Keegan, *American
      Civil War*.

133 **"precisely as they had stood in their ranks"**: Herbert, *Hooker*, 142.

134 **nicknamed for its practice of dunking**: Falkenstein, *German Influence*.

134 **recalled hearing the sounds of cannon fire**: National Park Service, Antietam National Battlefield.

135 **"maimed pilgrims"**: Holmes, *Soundings*, 46. Here is an extended quote: "It was a pitiable sight, truly pitiable, yet so vast, so far beyond the possibility of relief, that many single sorrows of small dimensions have wrought upon my feelings more than the sight of this great caravan of maimed pilgrims. The companionship of so many seemed to make a joint-stock of their suffering; it was next to impossible to individualize it, and so bring it home as one can do with a single broken limb or aching wound. . . . Yet among them were figures which arrested our attention and sympathy. Delicate boys, with more spirit than strength, flushed with fever or pale with exhaustion or haggard with suffering, dragged their weary limbs along as if each step would exhaust their slender store of strength. At the roadside sat or lay others, quite spent with their journey. Here and there was a house at which the wayfarers would stop, in the hope, I fear often vain, of getting refreshment, and in one place was a clear, cool spring, where the little bands of the long procession halted for a few moments, as the trains that traverse the desert rest by its fountains."

135 **"central seam of coat and waistcoat collar"**: Letter from Oliver Wendell Holmes Jr. to his parents, September 18, 1862, in Howe, *Holmes Letters*, 64.

135 **had equipped him with a bottle of laudanum**: White, *Holmes*, 25.

136 **"the stains upon them are my blood"**: Letter from John Flannery to Mark de Wolfe Howe, May 13, 1942, Oliver Wendell Holmes Collection, Harvard Law School Library. Here is an extended quote: "After his death, when we opened his private safety box, we found therein only three articles—the miniature of a beautiful young woman, which we assumed to be the picture of his mother; the two gold medallions given him by Harvard and the American Bar Association, and a little paper parcel, the size of one finger, which, when opened, was found to contain two old musket balls and on the paper was written in his handwriting, 'These were taken from my body in the Civil War.' In the closet in his bedroom we found two old Civil War uniforms (those of a Captain and Major, I believe) and to them was pinned a piece of paper, on which he had written, 'These uniforms were worn by me in the Civil War and the stains upon them are my blood.'"

137 **1850s, most importantly Roger Fenton**: It is hard to treat the Crimean War without something more than a passing glance. For the world as a whole, it was the most important war of the nineteenth century, involving many of the elements of modern warfare: artillery, trench warfare,

and true war reporting. In the middle of that war, then US secretary of
war Jefferson Davis commissioned three officers to witness the siege of
Sebastopol and return with insights valuable for the training and development of the American army. One of those officers was George B. Mc-
Clellan, and a close read of his part of the report on the Crimean War
reveals insight into how McClellan would conduct himself in the Civil
War. There, he recommends political separation from the conduct of the
war and, impossible to overlook given his later conduct, declares the Russian *retreat* to be "the finest operation of the war: so admirably was it carried
out that not a straggler remained behind; a few men so severely wounded
as to be unfit for rough and hurried transportation were the sole ghastly
human trophies that remained to the allies." As for Fenton, he has become
the subject of a great deal of speculation and disparagement, not so much
because he shielded the public from the true story of war—that much we
knew—but because he is said to have altered the scene in one of his most
famous photographs, a shot he titled *The Valley of the Shadow of Death*, by
moving cannonballs strewn across a barren road to increase the feeling of
immediacy. In 2007, the filmmaker Errol Morris set out to dissect Fenton's pictures (another shot, taken from precisely the same position, had
no cannonballs on the road) in a series of articles for the *New York Times*
and a book, *Believing Is Seeing: Observations on the Mysteries of Photography*.
Morris's search takes him to the scene of the battle itself and includes the
insights of historians, curators, and even a self-described "shadow expert."

137 **"Organized murder"**: Spiller, *Instinct*, 215.
137 **a journalist, represents a remarkable act of reportorial bravery:**
Bravery, yes, and because he was *not* a journalist, we can also forgive some
of the mistakes that Gardner made, most notably, that at Gettysburg he
apparently moved bodies into new positions for his photographs and
added props, such as rifles at their sides. Some writers have decided, from
this, that Gardner's work should be held in suspicion. But let's not forget
that he was working at a time when no standards for photojournalism had
yet been established.
138 **Morse referred to his output as "photographic paintings"**: Silverman, *Lightning Man*, chap. 9.
139 **"the dead they too vividly represented"**: Holmes, *Soundings*, 267.
140 **"How shall I speak?" says the war-hardened soldier:** Melville, *Battle-
Pieces*. The quotation comes from the poem "Lee in the Capitol," which,
like the others in this volume, was originally published in *Harper's*. It was
inspired by reports of Robert E. Lee's postwar testimony before the Reconstruction Committee of Congress. In the poem, Melville, adopting
Lee's voice in an act of poetic license, renounces "his cold reserve," as

Melville writes in a footnote to the poem, and removes the cloak to "feelings more or less poignant."

141 **"by the strange spell that dwells in dead men's eyes"**: "Brady's Photographs," *New York Times*, Oct. 20, 1862.

141 **"before they were relieved from their sufferings"**: "Battle of Antietam," 663.

141 **Patrons were charged twenty-five cents**: Harvey, *American* Art, 94–95.

142 **"shaddow"**: Lincoln, letter to Harvey G. Eastman, April 7, 1860, *CW*, 4:40. "While I was [in Chicago] I was taken to one of the places where they get up such things, and I suppose they got my shaddow, and can multiply copies indefinitely."

VIII. Preliminaries

145 **"without being hurt"**: Lincoln, telegram to McClellan, September 12, 1862, *CW*, 5:419.

145 **he had eighty thousand, while Lee had just thirty-seven thousand**: McPherson, *Tried*, chap. 5.

146 **countermarch to Washington**: This comes from an account by Nathaniel Paige, a war correspondent for the *New York Tribune*, as referenced in Nevins, *War*, 231.

146 **casualties . . . had reached 212,249**: Greer, "Counting Civil War Casualties."

146 **"When Lee came over the river"**: Holland, *Life*, 395. The meeting with Boutwell occurred in October, well after Antietam. Boutwell was pressing Lincoln on a published account that held that Lincoln had only moved to issue the Preliminary Proclamation because he was experiencing pressure from loyal state governors who were about to gather for a conference.

147 **God himself "had decided this question in favor of the slaves"**: Donald, *Chase Diaries*, 149–50; also Welles, *Diary*, 1:143, entry for September 22, 1862.

148 **"He liked to think he was the attorney of the people"**: Brooks, *Observed*, 216.

149 **"He looked like a glove-stretcher"**: Twain, "On Artemus Ward."

150 **Stanton was particularly offended at the president's**: Donald, *Chase Diaries*, 149.

150 **"His decision was fixed"**: Welles, "History of Emancipation," 847.

150 **"the disposal of the subject to a Higher Power"**: Welles, *Diary*, 1:143, entry for September 22, 1862.

151 **"perplexities" was the evocative word**: Nicolay and Hay, *History*, 6:154.

152   **he suspended the writ of habeas corpus:** Lincoln, letter to Winfield
      Scott, April 27, 1861, *CW*, 4:348.
152   **"I can touch a bell on my right hand":** Stahr, in *Seward*, has an interest-
      ing discussion of this. There, he says the story is probably best understood
      not as fact but as demonstrating Seward's enthusiasm for suspending the
      writ and how he was viewed by many, especially his critics, as arrogant and
      autocratic.
153   **As a young man, he freed his own slaves:** Simon, *Lincoln and Taney*,
      epilogue.
154   **about to serve with his tenth president:** The ten are Jackson, Martin
      Van Buren, William Henry Harrison, John Tyler, James Polk, Zachary
      Taylor, Millard Fillmore, Franklin Pierce, James Buchanan, and Lincoln.
      Taney swore seven of these into office. Harrison and Taylor died in office
      and so their vice presidents were sworn in by a circuit court judge without
      ceremony. Taney's predecessor, John Marshall, swore in Jackson.
154   **"throw the weight of the judiciary against":** *New York Times*, May 29,
      1861.
155   **supported on the arm of his grandson:** Brown, *Baltimore*, 89.
155   **The president had carried less than 3 percent:** Here is Maryland's
      vote breakdown for the 1860 election: Breckinridge (Southern Democrat)
      45.93%; John Bell (Constitutional Union), 45.14%; Stephen Douglas
      (Democrat) 6.45%; Abraham Lincoln (Republican) 2.48%.
155   **"Mr. Brown, I am an old man":** Brown, *Baltimore*, 90.
155   **"at the will and pleasure of the army officer":** Simon, *Lincoln and
      Taney*, 192.
156   **"with free institutions in each section":** Letter from Roger Taney to
      Franklin Pierce, June 12, 1861, in "Some Papers of Franklin Pierce," 368.
156   **"cast ourselves upon the judgment of the people":** Seward in letter to
      A. G. Andrews, in Seward, *Seward at Washington*, 608.
156   **"the very assembling of which might be prevented":** *CW*, 4:431. It is
      important to note that Lincoln's argument was not that the Constitution
      gave the executive the power to suspend the writ and not the Congress.
      He acknowledged the significance of its being in Article I. But as Amar
      notes in *America's Constitution*, Lincoln read this as meaning that "*ultimately*
      the decision was Congress's. The president could merely act temporar-
      ily, as Congress's faithful on-duty servant maintaining the pre-rebellion
      status quo precisely in order to preserve Congress's options." A proposal
      to approve Lincoln's suspension of the writ was debated in Congress's
      July 1861 session and again in the December session. The end result, the
      Habeas Corpus Suspension Act of 1863, was not an approval of the presi-
      dential suspension but the suspension of the writ by Congress itself.

157 **only one has since, Ulysses S. Grant:** On congressional authorization, Grant suspended the writ in 1871 to stem the progress of white-supremacist terrorist groups operating throughout the South. Proclamation, October 17, 1871, in Simon, *Grant Papers*, 176.

158 **"wherein a General *or a President* may make permanent rules":** Lincoln, letter to Orville Browning, September 22, 1861, *CW*, 4:533.

158 **had already been discussed individually with the cabinet members:** Welles, *Diary*, 1:144. entry for September 22, 1862.

160 **"did not care much about the phrases he had used":** Chase, *Diary*, 89.

161 **"despotic":** Welles, *Diary*, 1:145, entry for September 22, 1862. "There is in the Free States a very general impression that this measure will insure a speedy peace. I cannot say that I so view it. No one in those States dare advocate peace as a means of prolonging slavery, even if it is his honest opinion, and the pecuniary, industrial, and social sacrifice impending will intensify the struggle before us. While, however, these dark clouds are above and around us, I cannot see how the subject can be avoided. Perhaps it is not desirable it should be. It is, however, an arbitrary and despotic measure in the cause of freedom."

162 **"puff of wind over an accomplished fact":** Piatt, *Memories*, 150. The historian Walter Stahr believes that Piatt inflated his relationship with Seward and that this exchange is therefore questionable for its intimacy. But Stahr also believes that Seward had serious doubts about the proclamation as far back as the first reading in July. Stahr cites Stanton's notes from that cabinet meeting where the secretary of war writes, "The Attorney General and Stanton are for [the proclamation's] immediate promulgation. *Seward against it*; argues strongly in favor of cotton and foreign governments." The principal source for Seward's favoring the proclamation in the July meeting is the artist Carpenter. That Stanton's notes were written contemporaneous to the event and years afterward might suggest that Seward's supposed support for the proclamation was a story developed over time so as to make him appear to be on the right side of history. Stahr cites Browning, Brooks, and a letter that Seward wrote to Henry Adams as further evidence that Seward was dragging his feet on the subject. See Stahr, *Seward*, chap. 12.

163 **"Here it is. Mr. Lincoln's own hand.":** Stoddard, *Inside*, 168.

163 **"What I did," he told them, "I did":** Lincoln, "Reply to Serenade in Honor of Emancipation Proclamation," September 24, 1862, *CW*, 5:439.

163 **The crowd dispersed and made its way:** Chase, *Diary*, 94; Burlingame and Ettlinger, *Inside*, 41; Niven, *Chase*, chap. 23.

IX. Dissent

166   **"will be the last Hundred Days of Slavery"**: *National Republican*, September 23, 1862.

166   **"the beginning of the end of the rebellion"**: *New York Daily Tribune*, September 23, 1862.

166   **"shout for joy"**: "Emancipation Proclaimed," *Douglass' Monthly*, October 1862.

167   **"imaginary interest in persons not yet in existence"**: *National Republican*, August 11, 1862, 2.

167   **"nigger-freeing" mission or a "damned abolition war"**: Neely, *Fate*, chap. 3.

168   **"The Union is unnatural"**: Hawthorne, letter to Henry A. Bright, December 17, 1860, in Hawthorne, *Letters*, 232.

170   **consumed with this "nigger business"**: Klement, *Dissent*, 107.

170   **"To maintain the Constitution as it is"**: Ibid., 97.

171   **run from the stage at the Cincinnati Opera House**: *New York Times*, March 25, 1862.

171   ***"the niggers where they are"***: Klement, *Dissent*, 106.

171   **"fire in the rear"**: Sumner, Charles. Letter to Francis Lieber, January 17, 1863, as found in Pierce, *Memoir and Letters of Charles Sumner*. 4:114.

173   **"Where is it written in the Constitution"**: Remini, *Webster*, 128.

173   **It didn't, and Taney's unpublished opinion**: Anderson, *Draft*, 207–18; Amar, *Unwritten*, chap. 2.

174   **the Thirteenth Amendment, abolishing slavery**: During World War I, when the Selective Service Act of 1917 instituted a draft to fight the war in Europe, opposition to it focused on the argument that conscription violated the Thirteenth Amendment's ban on slavery. Only with the Selective Draft Law Cases of 1918 was the issue settled, at least as far as the Supreme Court was concerned. In a unanimous decision, the Court focused on Congress's Article I power "to raise and support armies" as determinative. The Court said that to challenge whether the government has the power to force its citizens to military duty would be to challenge "the existence of all power, for a governmental power which has no sanction to it and which therefore can only be exercised" upon consent "is in no substantial sense a power."

174   **though the accepted estimate is around fourteen thousand**: Neely, *Fate*, chap. 6.

175   **to say that three-quarters of those signing up**: Ibid., chap. 3.

175   **"hooting and noise"**: Ibid.

175   **The caesars in Rome, the Bourbons**: Mahony, *Prisoner*, 44.

176   **to France, referred to as a "military bastillle [*sic*]"**: Klement, *Dissent*, 163.

176 **"kind assurance of support":** No record exists of this telegram, only a reply from Burnside, who thanks Lincoln for his "kind assurance of support." *CW*, 6:216.

176 **Lincoln adjusted the sentence, banishing him:** The former congressman was then transported in secrecy down the Ohio River to Louisville, across Kentucky, and into Tennessee, where he was unceremoniously dumped behind enemy lines. There, Vallandigham approached a soldier and announced, "I am a citizen of Ohio, and of the United States. I am here within your lines by force and against my will. I therefore surrender myself to you as a prisoner of war."

The response to Lincoln's action on Vallandigham was harsh from both sides of the political spectrum. But when a group of New York Democrats organized a public response to the Vallandigham affair, declaring it an affront to the Constitution and all manner of civil liberties, Lincoln countered with a public letter in which he famously asked, "Must I shoot a simpleminded soldier boy who deserts while I must not touch a hair of a wily agitator who induces him to desert?" This appealing, homespun, accessible way of making his argument ignored a central tenet of free speech: American law punishes acts, not words. Lincoln insisted that Vallandigham's speech was indeed "action"; it was intended to disrupt the activities of the military. But this was simply not true: Vallandigham had been careful not to urge his audiences to evade the draft, and his plea was for them to remove Lincoln from office by the ballot box, not violence.

177 **a big, bulky figure who had been a law partner:** The historian David Donald wrote that Lamon had a "dog like devotion to Lincoln."

178 **"the old regiments are reduced to mere skeletons":** McClellan, telegram to Henry Halleck, September 26, 1862, 10 a.m., in Sears, *McClellan Papers*.

178 **"These people don't know what an army requires":** McClellan, letter to his wife, Mary Ellen McClellan, October 2, 1862, in McClellan, *Own Story*, 654.

178 **"hopelessly stupid" . . . "[he] would say one thing":** Ibid., 137.

178 **get off with nearly every caisson, tent, wagon:** Richardson, *Secret Service*, 289.

178 **"masterpiece of art":** McClellan, letter to Mary Ellen McClellan, September 18, 1862, in McClellan, *Own Story*, 612.

178 **"I will leave the service":** McClellan, letter to Mary Ellen McClellan, September 20, 1862, in Sears, *McClellan Papers*.

179 **"accursed doctrine":** McClellan, letter to Mary Ellen McClellan, September 25, 1862, ibid.

179 **"the action of the people at the polls":** McClellan, telegram to Abraham Lincoln, October 7, 1862, 11:35 p.m., ibid.

179 **"That is not the game":** *CW*, 5:443.

181   **"long legs doubled up so that his knees"**: Nevins, *Wainwright Journals*, 109.

182   **Lincoln turned to Lamon and asked him to sing a favorite song:** Lamon, *Recollections*, 145–47. Here are the second and third verses:

> Near by the spring, upon the elm you know I cut your name,
> Your sweetheart's just beneath it, Tom; and you did mine the same.
> Some heartless wretch has peeled the bark, twas dying sure but slow,
> Just as she died whose name you cut, some twenty years ago.

> My lids have long been dry, Tom, but tears came to my eyes;
> I thought of her I loved so well, those early broken ties:
> I visited the old churchyard, and took some flowers to strew
> Upon the graves of those we loved, some twenty years ago.

182   **"Picayune Butler"**: Ibid., 147. Fehrenbacher notes that Lamon often mixed the stories of others into what he presented as his own "recollections," making him a questionable source. But the story of the "ribald song" is credible in that opposition newspapers did indeed criticize Lincoln for the incident and Lincoln wrote a response to them. In 1864, Lamon confronted Lincoln about the abuse the president was receiving in the opposition press over this story and how Lamon intended to reply. Lincoln read Lamon's reply, found it too bitter, and then tried his own hand at it. This text, in Lincoln's handwriting but signed by Lamon, appears in Basler's *Collected Works*, 6:549. It notes, "Neither Gen. McClellan or any one else made any objection to the singing; the place was not on the battlefield, the time was sixteen days after the battle, no dead body was seen during the whole time the president was absent from Washington, nor even a grave that had not been rained on since it was made." Yet this, too, was never sent to the papers. "You know, Hill, that this is the truth," said Lincoln of the statement, "but I dislike to appear as an apologist for an act of my own which I know was right." Finally, a word about "Picayune Butler," which is a study in itself. Though no hard evidence proves it, it has long been accepted that a black New Orleans banjo player in the 1820s and 1830s went by that name. Several white minstrel players claimed to have learned songs from him, among them "Picayune Butler's Comin' to Town." The song became quite popular in the 1840s and 1850s and is probably the one that Lamon sang for Lincoln. As to its being "ribald," that reputation would seem to have derived solely from its being about a black banjoist, since the lyrics are simple and plaintive.

X. A Different War

186   **"It was eleven days"** Richardson, *Secret Service*, 324. Fehrenbacher finds this passage dubious because Richardson also has Lincoln saying that he ordered McClellan to "move on Richmond," which was never Lincoln's goal. He wanted McClellan to move on Lee, not Richmond. But as with so many of the quotes attributed to Lincoln, the specific words may be in doubt but the thrust of the idea—here, his frustration with McClellan for not pursuing Lee—seems on the mark.

186   **"inert mass":** Letter from Halleck to Hamilton R. Gamble, October 30, 1862, *OR*, series 3, 2:703–4.

186   **"with an auger too dull to take hold":** Letter of Francis P. Blair to Montgomery Blair, November 7, 1862, in Smith, *Blair Family*, 144.

187   **"not the slightest expression of feeling":** McClellan, *Own Story*, 660.

187   **"Come back to us, McClellan!":** "McClellan's Farewell," *Daily Alta California*, December 5, 1862.

187   **"Alas, for my poor country":** McClellan, *Own Story*, 660.

188   **"so as to be on hand . . . when treason wanted them":** Grant, *Memoirs*, 150.

188   **Two months after Lincoln arrived in Washington:** Here is Grant's summation of Floyd: "General Floyd, the commanding officer, who was a man of talent enough for any civil position was no soldier, and, possibly, did not possess the elements of one. He was further unfitted for command, for the reason that his conscience must have troubled him and made him afraid. As Secretary of War, he had taken a solemn oath to maintain the Constitution of the United States and uphold the same against all enemies. He had betrayed that trust. . . . Well may he have been afraid to fall into the hands of National troops. He would have no doubt been tried for misappropriating public property, if not for treason, had he been captured." Grant, *Memoirs*, 206.

188   **"I am prepared to vote to abolish the West Point Academy":** *Congressional Globe*, Senate, 37th Congress, 2nd sess., December 23, 1861, 164–65.

189   **"wild onions" and "musquetoes":** Lincoln, July 27, 1848, *CW*, 1:510. In his speech on the House floor, Lincoln referred to his own paltry military service as he ridiculed the Democratic presidential nominee, Senator Lewis Cass of Michigan. "By the way, Mr. Speaker, did you know I am a military hero? Yes sir; in the days of the Black Hawk war, I fought, bled, and came away. . . . If Gen. Cass went in advance of me in picking huckleberries, I guess I surpassed him in charges upon the wild onions. If he saw any live, fighting Indians, it was more than I did; but I had a good many bloody struggles with the musquetoes; and, although I never fainted from loss of blood, I can truly say I was often very hungry."

189   **"strategical works":** Nicolay and Hay, *Lincoln*, 5:155.
190   **Lincoln checked the book out of the Library of Congress:** Wilson, *What Lincoln Read*, 69. Carol Reardon in *Jomini* points out that Lincoln's son Robert checked out Jomini's *Operations Militaire* in March 1865, but of course by then the war had just about run its course.
190   **Halleck's work would have explained:** This has been a much-debated issue ever since General J. D. Hittle wrote, in 1947, "Many a Civil War general went into battle with a sword in one hand and Jomini's *Summary of the Art of War* in the other." T. Harry Williams followed the same tract in his *Lincoln and His Generals*. More recently, several historians have urged caution on such a judgment, arguing that it is unlikely that many officers thought of themselves as "Jominian" or the follower of any other philosopher, but that would only be the most obvious test of influence. All one needs to see is that McClellan thought and acted like a Jominian and that Grant and Sherman—and Lincoln, too—did not.
191   **representing a kind of "Military Enlightenment":** Lynn, *Battle*.
191   **"which are by their nature invariable":** The phrase, as John Shy points out in his essay in Paret, ed., *Makers of Modern Strategy*, 148, belongs to the Welshman Lloyd, whom Jomini credited as an influence. Lloyd, Jomini, and the others seemed to have had more success at articulating the *idea* of a science of war than they did in actually formulating one. As Shy, again, points out, Napoléon read Lloyd and showed his disdain in the scribbles that can be found across his copy: "Ignorance . . . Ignorance . . . Absurd . . . Absurd . . . Impossible . . . False . . . Bad . . . Very bad . . . How absurd . . . What absurdity!"
191   **"the impulsion and repulsion of physical masses":** Gat, *Military Thought*, 85.
191   **the "Palladio" of siege warfare:** Keegan, "Grand Illusions"; Lynn, *Battle*, 118.
192   **they continued to form the defense of France:** Fussell, *Great War*.
192   **Vauban is even credited with inventing:** Paret, *Makers*, 78; chap. 3: "Vauban: The Impact of Science on War" by Henry Guerlac.
193   **his was a "simple theory," not an "absolute" rulebook:** Reardon, *Jomini*, 3.
193   **"liberty of action":** Jomini, *Art of War*.
194   **"our people will harass and destroy his army":** Davis, speech in Macon, Georgia, September 24, 1864, in Davis, *Writings*.
195   **"to impose that order and discipline":** Rafuse, *McClellan's War*, 38.
196   **the one person Lincoln feared could be his assassin:** Lamon, *Recollections*, 269.
196   **"armies can be reckoned into blocks of stone":** *Deseret News*, July 30, 1862, in Reardon, *Jomini*, 68.

196 **"You can never destroy [the enemy] by building fortifications"**: *Congressional Globe*, Senate, 37th Congress, 3rd sess., January 15, 1863, 164–65.

196 **"The military situation is far from bright"**: Livermore, *My Story*, 556. Again, Fehrenbacher doubts the word-for-word nature of this story, but the gist of it probably does represent Lincoln's mood.

197 **"hard, tough fighting"**: *CW*, 5:485; also in Livermore, 242.

198 **"War is the continuation of politics by other means"**: Clausewitz, *On War*, 16.

198 **"senseless thing without an object"**: Ibid., 596.

199 **"'I have been studying the art of war'"**: Vidal, *Lincoln*, pt. 2, chap. 1. The author is clever in that he has Hay reading Clausewitz—not Lincoln—and serving as translator for Lincoln. As Bassford in *Clausewitz in English* tells us, Lincoln could have learned of Clausewitz from any of several German-born officers, particularly Carl Schurz, whose memoirs demonstrate knowledge of Jomini and Clausewitz. Bassford writes, "As for war and politics, the statement that 'war is a continuation of politics by other means' is important not because Clausewitz said it but because it reflects a fundamental reality. That reality would have been obvious to a professional politician in the throes of a political crisis that had led to war. What is surprising is not this insight but that Lincoln should have had the self-confidence and strength of will to pursue it over the resistance of men with what must have seemed far better credentials than his own."

199 **evidence suggests that a few of those around Lincoln *had* read Clausewitz**: In his 1839 two-volume *Manual of Political Ethics*, Lieber writes, "General Clausewitz, in his work *On War*, a work which bears the imprint of a powerful mind, says 'War is the act of compelling an opponent to submit to one's will.' Thus, force is the medium, and submission is the object, and the latter can only be obtained by the development of the former." Lieber, *Manual of Political Ethics*, 2:631.

199 **"that son of crime and sin"**: Freidel, *Lieber*, 9.

200 **"youthful ardor to assist the oppressed and struggling"**: Ibid., 30.

200 **into the personal library of Abraham Lincoln**: Ibid., 81. Freidel's sources include Robert Lincoln, who told Nicholas Murray Butler that an 1851 edition of the encyclopedia was among his father's possessions.

200 **"it is no injustice to have slaves"**: Keil, "Francis Lieber's Attitudes." Lieber also writes, "Where slavery exists, it is far better to own slaves than to hire them. They feel attached to the master, because they are entirely dependent upon him, and the master not only feels more interest in them but can also do something for them, habituate them to good manners, etc., whereas he has no influence over hired slaves."

200 **"Why, my dear doctor"**: Freidel, *Lieber*, 305.

201   **"yet to learn it in the phase":** Lieber, letter to Charles Sumner, March 23, 1862, ibid., 325.

201   **"Well, Mr. President, won't you give us a little fight?":** Lieber, letter to Henry Boynton Smith, ibid., 308.

201   **"Happiness Period":** *New York Times*, October 27, 1861.

202   **his pamphlet became the guide for officers:** Lieber, *Guerilla Parties*.

202   **"Domestic traitors, who seek the overthrow":** Halleck, letter to Major General Horatio G. Wright, November 18, 1862, *OR*, series 1, vol. 20, pt. 2, p. 67.

203   **in the Lieber Code (as it would come to be known):** For all references to the text of the Lieber Code, refer to General Orders, No. 100, *OR*, series 3, 3:148–64.

XI. Weakened

206   **sitting at once on "two stools":** James C. Welling, in Rice, *Reminiscences*, 531.

206   **"a civil necessity":** James C. Welling, ibid.

207   **"unstable as water":** Harris, *Chandler*, 61.

208   **"scenes as bloody and dark":** *Ottawa Free Trader*, October 25, 1862.

208   **"the ample powers conferred upon him by the Constitution":** Pratt, "Repudiation of Lincoln's War."

209   **"so dark with negroes":** "Negroes Pouring In," *Cairo Gazette*, August 19, 1862. "The levees yesterday were so dark with negroes that pedestrians found it difficult to peregrinate without lanterns. We never before saw just such a lot of darkies in our life. Uncle Toms, Aunt Chloes and Topsys were abundant. What this eternal raft of negroes will find to do here, is more than we can foretell. The government may find employment for a small per cent of them, but the greater portion must either starve or become government paupers. . . . We cannot dispel from our mind the fear that not only this new population will suffer, but that their presence will so affect the laboring class of white men that the pinch of want will become general. We sincerely hope that time will prove these fears to be groundless, but it is hoping almost against hope."

209   **a full quarter of the Army of the Potomac absent:** Lonn, *Desertion*, 145. See also *OR*, series 1, vol. 22, pt. 2, p. 78.

210   **his hair "grizzled, his gait more stooping":** Brooks, *Observed*, 13–14.

210   **"I suppose it is good for the body":** Brooks, "Personal Reminiscences," 673.

210   **Annual Message to Congress:** Lincoln, "Annual Message to Congress," December 1, 1862, *CW*, 5:519.

213 **leave the country, and all that at a cost:** The tally at the end of the last week in November 1862 (ending November 29) was 189,783 Confederate casualties and 230,196 Union for a total of 419,979. Darroch Greer's "Counting Civil War Casualties Week by Week for the Abraham Lincoln Presidential Library and Museum."

216 **"hallucination":** Pease and Randall, *Browning Diary*, 1:591.

218 **13,353 Union men . . . 4,567 for the Confederates:** Civil War Trust, Battle of Fredericksburg site, http://www.civilwar.org.

218 **"terrible sight":** Holmes, letter to Amelia Jackson Holmes, December 12, 1862, in Howe, *Fire*, 74.

218 **"certain and useless death":** Holmes, "In Our Youth Our Hearts Were Touched by Fire," Memorial Day address, May 30, 1884, in Holmes, *Selected Works*.

218 **The Fifty-First New York Volunteers were there:** Reynolds, *Whitman*.

219 **Burnside's incompetence at Fredericksburg:** Here is how Lee's biographer Douglas Southall Freeman describes it: "General Burnside most obligingly was preparing to waste in costly assault the great odds his country had given him. The Unionists did not even choose the weakest part of Marye's Heights for their assault. They made their advance against the steepest part of the heights and directly against the sunken road. They planted three standards defiantly, but in the very act received the full blast of the artillery almost in their faces. So intense was the fire and so perfectly laid that the ranks thinned at the very first round and soon were, melting back to the ditch in blue and blood."

219 **"the attempt was not an error":** Lincoln, "Congratulations to the Army of the Potomac," December 22, 1862, *CW*, 6:14.

220 **Lincoln wishing for a decisive battle:** Stoddard, *Inside*, 179. Regarding the following remarkable quote from this book, Fehrenbacher writes that one wishes it came from a more reliable source: "There is sense in the awful arithmetic propounded by Mr. Lincoln. He says that if the same battle were to be fought over again, every day, through a week of days, with the same relative results, the army under Lee would be wiped out to its last man, the Army of the Potomac would still be a mighty host, the war would be over, the Confederacy gone, and peace would be won at a smaller cost of life than it will be if the week of lost battles must be dragged out through yet another year of camps and marches, and of deaths in hospitals rather than upon the field."

221 **whether they should ask the president to shake up:** Pease and Randall, *Browning Diary*, 1:599.

221 **"He is Lincoln's evil genius":** Hollister, *Colfax*.

221 **"back stairs influence":** Fessenden, *Life*, 234.

221 **"cold courtesy":** Welles, *Diary*, 1:203, December 20, 1862.
222 **running to the president two or three times a day:** Ibid., 1:132, September 16, 1862.
222 **"bitter and malignant Democrats":** Donald, *Lincoln*, chap. 14.
222 **"largely pro-slavery men":** Fessenden, *Life*, 241.
223 **"but I am like the starling":** Seward, *Seward at Washington*, 147.
223 **"earnest and sad session":** Beale, *Bates Diary*, 269–70. The account of this scene comes largely from Bates.
223 **who was, at the moment, packing boxes:** Stahr, *Seward*, chap. 12.
224 **come there to be "arraigned":** Fessenden, *Life*, 244.
224 **"national ailment":** Welles, *Diary*, 1:133, September 16, 1862.
224 **"They wish to get rid of me":** Pease and Randall, *Browning Diary*, 1:600.

XII. A Birthing. January 1, 1863

227 **visited the president to urge him to stay the course:** The story is mostly taken from Tarbell, *Life*, 2:123–24. But other renditions of it have different detail and I have borrowed from these as well to form an amalgamation. For instance, in Emanuel Hertz's *Lincoln Talks: A Biography in Anecdote*, Robbins alone visits Lincoln, and so it is to Robbins that Lincoln says, "Peter denied his master." That account also has Lincoln meeting Robbins a few days after he had signed the proclamation and saying, "Well, friend Robbins, I beat Peter." If we are to choose, it makes more sense that Lincoln would have made the biblical reference to the preacher Sunderland, not Robbins, but who knows? That both men are reported as having recalled it tells us that it likely happened in some manner. Robbins was Lincoln's patent attorney. He filed the patent on Lincoln's device to lift boats, mentioned in chapter 3. An 1872 letter written by Sunderland was published in its entirety in the appendix of Barton's *Soul of Abraham Lincoln*. There, Sunderland tells more about what was presumably the same meeting as the one discussed here, though he mentions nothing of the anecdote I have related. Instead, he offers a long quote from Lincoln, which by its very length is dubious. But the content is consistent with other statements by Lincoln. Sunderland quotes the president as saying that he is "an instrument of Providence. . . . Nevertheless, I am no fatalist. I believe in the supremacy of the human conscience, and that men are responsible beings; that God has a right to hold them, and will hold them, to a strict personal account for the deeds done in the body."
230 **"tend but to make him more abominable":** In the Penguin edition of *Aesop's Fables*, the editor's note says that the original version of the fable was about an Indian, not an Ethiopian. Robert Bray, in his *Reading with*

Lincoln, tells us that the story only appeared in some of the editions of *Aesop's Fables*, and the one that Lincoln likely read was the Aitken *Aesop* published in 1777. Bray also says that *Pilgrim's Progress* and the poetry of Hood were favorites of Lincoln's. For Hood, Bray relies on Orville Browning, whose diary mentions a story in April 1862, when Browning visits Lincoln at the White House, and Lincoln, upon learning that Browning had not read some of Lincoln's favorite Hood poems, has an edition of Hood's works brought to them and reads the poems out loud to his guest. Pease and Randall, *Browning Diary*, 542.

231 **the final Emancipation Proclamation text and read it aloud:** Welles, *Diary*, 1:209, December 29, 1862.

232 **"wild and lawless":** Sumner, *Works*, 3:267.

233 **he rejected Blair's idea of making the slaves show:** Chase's rather thorough critique can be found in a letter to the president, dated December 31, 1862, in Schuckers, *Life*, 514–15.

234 **"he is of opinion he may thus best subdue the enemy?":** Curtis, *Executive Power*, 17.

235 **as to whether native-born, free "colored men" are citizens:** Schuckers, *Life*, 477.

236 **delivered his opinion to Chase on November 29:** Bates, *Opinion*. The attorney general's reasoning rested in part on refuting Taney's assertion that political rights are inextricably linked to political power. The authors of a 1997 article in *Civil War History*, "Circumventing the Dred Scott Decision: Edward Bates, Salmon P. Chase, and the Citizenship of African Americans," refer to Bates's letters to Francis Lieber in order to explain. There, Lieber argues, "To suppose that political right & political power are one and the same—that a person is not a citizen unless he have a portion of the power of Government . . . would exclude entire categories of the population, such as women and under-aged males, from citizenship."

237 **"secession against the Constitution":** *CW*, 6:28.

238 **his father stayed up this entire night:** "Emancipation Proclamation: Lincoln's Own Story."

238 **father's study, and eventually Lincoln would pick up the boy:** Donald, *Lincoln*, chap. 15.

240 **"transcendent executive power":** Curtis, *Executive Power*, 9.

240 **"moving in deep-cut channels forever and forever":** All quotes in this paragraph on Lincoln's personal philosophy from Hertz, *Hidden Lincoln*, 142.

241 **"I am a man under orders. I cannot do otherwise":** The story comes from two articles in the *Christian Science Monitor*, and both ran without byline. The first was called "New Light on Lincoln's Character" and appeared in the paper on February 12, 1935. Anticipating Lincoln's birthday,

the paper had run a tribute to Lincoln earlier in the week. In response, a
letter arrived from Mrs. Florence W. Stanley, who said that she had known
Robert Todd Lincoln since she was four years old (Robert Todd Lincoln
died in 1926), and he had once told her the story of New Year's Eve 1862.
The letter is reproduced in the *Monitor*, and its essential details are what
I have recounted here. The *Monitor* published a second story about the
same letter on September 22, 1937. Both are available through the *Monitor*
archives.

241 **"to save writing"**: This comes from a letter that Lincoln wrote on October 26, 1863, in *CW*, 6:540. The letter was written to the "ladies . . .
in charge of the North-Western fair" for the "Sanitary Commission" in
Chicago. They had requested the original draft of the final Emancipation
Proclamation to auction off at a fund-raiser. "I had some desire to retain
the paper," Lincoln told them, "but if it shall contribute to the relief or
comfort of the soldiers that will be better." The Chicago Historical Society purchased the manuscript from the Sanitary Commission, but it was
destroyed during the Chicago Fire of 1871.

241 **"whereof *I have hereunto set my hand"***: Eberstadt, *Emancipation*, 14–17.

241 **Lincoln went to the Blue Room to meet his guests:** Seward, *Seward at
Washington*, 151.

242 **men supporting the army from the loyal state of New York:** Brooks,
Washington, 42; Brooks, *Observed*, 14–15.

242 **"But, any way, it is going to be done":** Seward, *Seward at Washington*,
151.

243 **using a steel pen with a wood handle:** This detail about Lincoln's
gnarled pen ("a habit that he had when composing anything that required
thought") comes from Benjamin Perley Poore, a journalist who wrote for
Republican newspapers and was published in Rice, *Reminiscences*, 230. The
pen was later given to Charles Sumner to give to George Livermore, author of a book on slavery and the early republic.

243 **"he will yet send us all into eternity":** Carpenter, *Six Months*, 75. This
famous and colorful quote frequently attributed to Lincoln comes solely
from Carpenter, who asserts that he heard it from Edwin D. Morgan, who
heard it from Lincoln's lips. According to Carpenter, Morgan, who had
arrived at the White House "soon after the issue of the proclamation,"
was on official business as the governor of New York. The story suffers
some credibility in that Morgan was actually no longer governor on January 1, 1863. He would, however, soon be elected by the New York State
legislature as a US senator and serve from March 1863 to March 1869.
Carpenter may have had the timing wrong or cited the wrong reason for
Morgan's visit to the White House.

243 **"he had not shown himself a man of heroic measures"**: Douglass, *Life and Times*, 428.

246 **"of an inferior race"** . . . **"peaceful and contented laborers in their sphere"**: Davis, Message to the Confederate Congress on January 12, 1863, in Davis, *Essential Writings*.

246 **"length and breadth the land of liberty!"**: Du Bois, *Black Reconstruction*.

247 **"in the fight for the rights of my people"**: Albright's story can be found in Ward, *Slaves' War*, 108. The oral histories done for the Federal Writers' Project have come under some criticism; oral histories are always suspect. They rely on the memory, and memory cells can embroider and embellish the truth. But these histories have additional problems in that, by the 1930s, more than seventy years had passed since the Emancipation Proclamation, so those recalling slavery were recalling experiences deep into their pasts, likely from childhood or, like Albright's, from adolescence. What they saw and heard, therefore, was through a child's eyes and ears. Furthermore, the interviewers for the project were likely to have been white and Southern, which, as many scholars have suggested, could not have made it comfortable for their subjects.

247 **"would throw down his hoe or quit his plow"**: Wilson, *Black Phalanx*, 131.

247 **93,542 recruits came from the Confederate states alone**: Gladstone, *Colored Troops*, 120.

248 **"heard the thunder, and that was the big guns"**: Humez, *Tubman*, 135.

248 **"You say you will not fight to free negroes"**: Lincoln, letter to James C. Conklin, August 26, 1863, *CW*, 6:407.

249 **"Every slave withdrawn"**: Halleck, letter to Major General U.S. Grant, March 31, 1863, *OR*, series 1, vol. 24, pt. 3, pp. 156–57.

249 **North was acting contrary to the rules of "civilized nations"**: Confederate secretary of war James Seddon, letter to Robert Ould, June 24, 1863, *OR*, series 2, 6:241–47.

BIBLIOGRAPHY

Books

Adams, Henry. *The Collected Works of Henry Adams.* Houston: Halcyon Press, 2009. Kindle edition.

Adams, Michael C. C. *Fighting for Defeat: Union Military Failure in the East, 1861–1865.* Lincoln: University of Nebraska Press, 1992.

Agassiz, Elizabeth Cabot, ed. *Louis Agassiz: His Life and Correspondence.* Public domain book. Kindle edition.

Alexander, Archibald. *A History of Colonization on the Western Coast of Africa.* Philadelphia: William S. Martien, 1846.

Alexander, Ted. *The Battle of Antietam: The Bloodiest Day.* Charleston, SC: History Press, 2011.

Amar, Akhil Reed. *America's Constitution: A Biography.* New York: Random House, 2006.

———. *America's Unwritten Constitution: The Precedents and Principles We Live By.* New York: Basic Books, 2012.

———. *The Bill of Rights: Creation and Reconstruction.* New Haven, CT: Yale University Press, 1998.

Ambrose, Steve E. *Halleck: Lincoln's Chief of Staff.* Baton Rouge: Louisiana State University Press, 1996. Kindle edition.

Anderson, Martin, ed. *The Military Draft: Selected Readings on Conscription.* Stanford, CA: Hoover Institution Press, 1982.

Ayers, Edward L., ed. *America's War: Talking About the Civil War and Emancipation on Their 150th Anniversaries.* American Library Association, 2011. Kindle edition.

Bake, Jean H. *Mary Todd Lincoln: A Biography.* New York: W. W. Norton, 2008. Kindle edition.

Baker, George E. *The Works of Henry Seward.* Vol. 1. New York: Redfield, 1853.

Barrett, Joseph Hartwell. *Abraham Lincoln and His Presidency.* Vol. 2. Cincinnati: The Robert Clarke Company, 1904.

———. *Life, Speeches, and Public Services of Abraham Lincoln.* Cincinnati: Moore, Wilstach and Baldwin, 1865.

Barton, William Eleazar. *The Paternity of Abraham Lincoln: An Essay on the Chastity of Nancy Hanks.* New York: George H. Doran, 1920.

———. *The Soul of Abraham Lincoln.* New York: George H. Doran, 1920. Google Books.

Basler, Roy P., ed. *The Collected Works of Abraham Lincoln.* New Brunswick, NJ: Rutgers University Press, 1953.

Bassford, Christopher. *Clausewitz in English: The Reception of Clausewitz in Britain and America, 1815–1945.* New York: Oxford University Press, 1994.

Bates, David Home. *Lincoln in the Telegraph Office.* New York: Century, 1907.

Bates, Edward. *Opinion of Attorney General Bates on Citizenship.* 1863. Public domain book.

Beale, Howard K., ed. *The Diary of Edward Bates, 1859–1866.* Washington, DC: Government Printing Office, 1933.

Bennett, Lerone, Jr. *Forced into Glory: Abraham Lincoln's White Dream.* Chicago: Johnson Publishing, 2007.

Berlin, Ira. *The Making of African America: The Four Great Migrations.* New York: Penguin, 2009. Kindle edition.

Betros, Lance, ed. *West Point: Two Centuries and Beyond.* Abilene, TX: McWhiney Foundation Press, 2004.

Black, Charles L., Jr. *A New Birth of Freedom: Human Rights, Named and Unnamed.* New Haven, CT: Yale University Press, 1997.

Blair, William A., and Karen Fisher Younger, eds. *Lincoln's Proclamation.* Chapel Hill: University of North Carolina Press, 2009.

Bordewich, Fergus M. *America's Great Debate: Henry Clay, Stephen A. Douglas, and the Compromise That Preserved the Union.* New York: Simon and Schuster, 2012. Kindle edition.

Borritt, Gabor. *The Gettysburg Gospel: The Lincoln Speech That Nobody Knows.* New York: Simon and Schuster, 2006.

Bray, Robert. *Reading with Lincoln.* Carbondale: Southern Illinois University Press, 2010. Kindle edition.

Brooks, Noah. *Abraham Lincoln.* New York: Fred DeFau, 1894.

———. *Lincoln Observed: Civil War Dispatches of Noah Brooks.* Edited by Michael Burlingame. Baltimore: Johns Hopkins University Press, 2002.

———. *Washington in Lincoln's Time.* New York: Century, 1894.

Brown, George William. *Baltimore and the Nineteenth of April 1861: A Study of the War.* Vol. 3. Baltimore: Isaac Friedenwald, 1867.

Browne, Francis F. *The Every-day Life of Abraham Lincoln: A Narrative and Descriptive Biography with Pen-Pictures and Personal Recollections by Those Who Knew Him.* Originally published by Browne and Howell in 1913. Project Gutenberg ebook.

Bunting, Josiah, III. *Ulysses S. Grant.* The American Presidents Series. New York: Times Books, Henry Holt, 2004.

Burlingame, Michael. *Abraham Lincoln: A Life.* Baltimore: Johns Hopkins University Press, 2008.

Burlingame, Michael, and John R. Turner Ettlinger, eds. *Inside Lincoln's White House: The Complete Civil War Diary of John Hay.* Carbondale: Southern Illinois University Press, 1997.

Carman, General Ezra A. *Maryland Campaign of September 1862.* Volume 1, *South Mountain.* Eldorado Hills, CA: Savas Beatie, 2010. Kindle edition.

Carnahan, Burrus M. *Act of Justice: Lincoln's Emancipation Proclamation and the Law of War.* Lexington: University Press of Kentucky, 2007.

Carpenter, F. B. *Six Months at the White House with Abraham Lincoln: The Story of a Picture.* New York: Hurd and Houghton, 1866.

Carwardine, Richard. *Lincoln: A Life of Purpose and Power.* New York: Vintage, 2006.

Charnwood, Lord. *Abraham Lincoln.* Garden City, NY: Henry Holt, 1917.

Chase, Salmon P. *Diary and Correspondence of Salmon P. Chase.* Washington, DC: Government Printing Office, 1903.

———. *The Salmon P. Chase Papers: Correspondence, 1858–March, 1963.* Kent, OH: Kent State University Press, 1996.

Clausewitz, Karl von. *On War.* Translated from the original German by Matthijs Jolles. New York: Random House, 1943.

Cleveland, Henry, ed. *Alexander H. Stephens in Public and Private, with Letters and Speeches Before, During, and Since the War.* Philadelphia: National Publishing, 1866.

Clinton, Catherine. *Mrs. Lincoln: A Life.* New York: HarperCollins, 2009.

Cohen, Eliot A. *Supreme Command: Soldiers, Statesmen, and Leadership in Wartime.* New York: Anchor Books, 2002.

Colton, Calvin, ed. *The Works of Henry Clay: Comprising His Life, Correspondence and Speeches.* Vol. 3. New York: Henry Clay Publishing Company, 1897.

———. *The Works of Henry Clay: Comprising His Life, Correspondence, and Speeches.* 10 vols. New York: G. P. Putnam's Sons, 1904.

Curtis, Benjamin Robbins. *Executive Power.* Boston: Little, Brown, 1862.

Dattel, Gene. *Cotton and Race in the Making of America: The Human Costs of Economic Power.* Lanham, MD: Rowman and Littlefield Publishing Group, 2009.

Davis, David Brion. *Inhuman Bondage: The Rise and Fall of Slavery in the New World.* New York: Oxford University Press, 2006. Kindle edition.

Davis, Jefferson. *Jefferson Davis: The Essential Writings.* New York: Random House, 2004. Kindle edition.

———. *The Rise of the Confederate Government.* New York: Barnes and Noble, 2010.

Dawes, Rufus R. *Service with the Sixth Wisconsin Volunteers.* Marietta, OH: E. R. Alderman and Sons, 1890.

Delbanco, Andrew. *The Abolitionist Imagination.* Cambridge: Harvard University Press, 2012.

de Saxe, Maurice. *Reveries on the Art of War.* 1757. Reprint, New York: Dover 2011. Kindle edition.

Diggins, John Patrick. *On Hallowed Ground: Abraham Lincoln and the Foundations of American History.* New Haven, CT: Yale University Press, 2000.

———. *The Promise of Pragmatism: Modernism and the Crisis of Knowledge and Authority.* Chicago: University of Chicago Press, 1994.

Donald, David. *Lincoln's Herndon.* Read Books. Kindle edition. Originally published by Alfred A. Knopf in 1948.

———. *Charles Sumner and the Coming of the Civil War.* New York: Alfred A. Knopf, 1960.

———, ed. *Inside Lincoln's Cabinet: The Civil War Diaries of Salmon P. Chase.* New York: Longmans, Green, 1954.

———. *Lincoln.* New York: Simon and Schuster, 2011. Kindle edition.

———. *Lincoln Reconsidered: Essays on the Civil War Era.* New York: Vintage, 2001.

———. *We Are Lincoln Men: Abraham Lincoln and His Friends.* New York: Simon and Schuster, 2003. Kindle edition.

Douglass, Frederick. *Life and Times of Frederick Douglass.* Boston: De Wolfe and Fiske, 1892.

———. *The Most Complete Collection of Written Works and Speeches by Frederick Douglass.* Boston: De Wolfe and Fiske, 1892. Northpointe Classics. Kindle edition.

Du Bois, W. E. B. *Black Reconstruction in America: Toward a History of the Part Which Black Folk Played in the Attempt to Reconstruct Democracy in America, 1860–1880.* New Brunswick, NJ: Transaction Publishers, 2012. Kindle edition. Originally published by Harcourt and Brace, 1935.

Eberstadt, Charles. *Lincoln's Emancipation Proclamation.* New York: Duschnes Crawford, 1950.

Eisenhower, John D. *Agent of Destiny: The Life and Times of General Winfield Scott.* Norman: University of Oklahoma Press, 1997.

Emerson, Jason. *Giant in the Shadows: The Life of Robert T. Lincoln.* Carbondale and Edwardsville: Southern Illinois University Press, 2012.

———. *Lincoln, the Inventor.* Carbondale: Southern Illinois University Press, 2009.

Epstein, Daniel Mark. *Lincoln's Men: The President and His Private Secretaries.* New York: HarperCollins, 2009. HarperCollins ebook.

———. *The Lincolns: Portrait of a Marriage.* New York: Ballantine Books, 2008. Kindle edition.

Fabian, Ann. *The Skulls Collectors: Race, Science, and America's Unburied Dead.* Chicago: University of Chicago Press, 2010.

Falkenstein, George N. *Pennsylvania: The German Influence in Its Settlement and Development*. Part VIII: *The German Baptist Brethren or Dunkers*. Lancaster: Pennsylvania German Society, 1900.

Farber, Daniel. *Lincoln's Constitution*. Chicago: University of Chicago Press, 2003. Kindle edition.

Faust, Drew Gilpin. *This Republic of Suffering: Death and the American Civil War*. New York: Alfred A. Knopf, 2008.

Fehrenbacher, Don E. *Slavery, Law and Politics: The Dred Scott Case in Historical Perspective*. New York: Oxford University Press, 1981.

Fehrenbacher, Don E., and Virginia Fehrenbacher. *Recollected Words of Abraham Lincoln*. Stanford, CA: Stanford University Press, 1996. Kindle edition.

Fessenden, Francis. *Life and Public Services of William Pitt Fessenden*. Vol. 1. Boston: Houghton Mifflin, 1907.

Fischer, Leroy H. *Lincoln's Gadfly, Adam Gurowski*. Norman: University of Oklahoma Press, 1964.

Flower, Frank Abial. *Edwin McMasters Stanton: The Autocrat of Rebellion, Emancipation, and Reconstruction*. New York: Saalfield Publishing, 1905.

Foner, Eric. *The Fiery Trial: Abraham Lincoln and American Slavery*. New York: W. W. Norton, 2010.

———. *Forever Free: The Story of Emancipation and Reconstruction*. New York: Vintage, 2005.

———. *Nothing but Freedom: Emancipation and Its Legacy*. Baton Rouge: Louisiana State University Press, 1983.

———. *The Story of American Freedom*. New York: W. W. Norton, Company, 1998.

Franklin, John Hope, ed. *The Diary of James T. Ayers, Civil War Recruiter*. Baton Rouge: Louisiana State University Press, 1999.

———. *The Emancipation Proclamation*. Wheeling, IL: Harlan Davidson, 1995.

Fredrickson, George M. *Big Enough to Be Inconsistent: Abraham Lincoln Confronts Slavery and Race*. Cambridge: Harvard University Press, 2008.

———. *Racism: A Short History*. Princeton, NJ: Princeton University Press, 2002. Kindle edition.

———. *The Black Image in the White Mind*. New York: Harper & Row, 1971.

Freeman, Douglas Southall. *Lee* (abridged one-volume edition of the four-volume original). New York: Scribner, 1997.

Freidel, Frank. *Francis Lieber: Nineteenth Century Liberal*. Baton Rouge: Louisiana State University Press, 1947.

Fussell, Paul. *The Great War and Modern Memory*. New York: Oxford University Press, 1975.

Gallagher, Gary W., ed. *The Antietam Campaign*. Chapel Hill: University of North Carolina Press, 1999. Kindle edition.

———. *The Union War*. Cambridge: Harvard University Press, 2011.

Garrigus, John D. *Before Haiti: Race and Citizenship in French Saint-Domingue*. New York: Palgrave Macmillan, 2006.

Gat, Azar. *A History of Military Thought: From the Enlightenment to the Cold War.* New York: Oxford University Press, 2001.

Gilmore, Paul. *Aesthetic Materialism: Electricity and American Romanticism.* Stanford, CA: Stanford University Press, 2009.

Gladstone, William. *United States Colored Troops, 1863–1867.* Thomas, 1996.

Goethe, Johann Wolfgang von. *Theory of Colors.* London: John Murray, 1840.

Goodwin, Doris Kearns. *Team of Rivals: The Political Genius of Abraham Lincoln.* New York: Simon and Schuster, 2005.

Gould, Stephen Jay. *The Mismeasure of Man.* New York: W. W. Norton, 2006.

Grant, Ulysses S. *Memoirs and Selected Letters.* New York: Library of America, 1990.

Graves, Joseph L. *The Emperor's New Clothes: Biological Theories of Race at the Millennium.* New Brunswick, NJ: Rutgers University Press, 2001.

Greeley, Horace. *The American Conflict: A History of the Great Rebellion.* 2 vols. Hartford, CT: O. D. Case, 1866.

Greiner, James M., Janet L. Coryell, and James R. Smithers. *A Surgeon's Civil War: The Letters and Diary of Daniel M. Holt, M.D.* Kent, OH: Kent State University Press, 1994.

Guelzo, Allan C. *Abraham Lincoln: Redeemer President.* Grand Rapids, MI: William B. Eerdsman Publishing, 1999. Kindle edition.

———. *Fateful Lightning: A New History of the Civil War and Reconstruction.* New York: Oxford University Press, 2012. Kindle edition.

———. *Lincoln's Emancipation Proclamation: The End of Slavery in America.* New York: Simon and Schuster, 2004. Kindle edition.

Gurowski, Adam. *Diary from March 4, 1861 to November 12, 1862.* Boston: Lee and Shephard, 1862.

Halleck, Henry Wager. *Elements of Military Art and Science: or, Course of Instruction in Strategy, Fortification, Tactics of Battles.* New York: D. Appleton, 1846.

Hanson, Victor David. *The Father of Us All: War and History.* New York: Bloomsbury Press, 2010.

Harlow, Ralph Volney. *Gerrit Smith: Philanthropist and Reformer.* New York: Henry Holt, 1939.

Harris, Wilmer C. *Public Life of Zachariah Chandler, 1851–1875.* Lansing: Michigan Historical Commission, 1917.

Hartigan, Richard Shelly. *Lieber's Code and the Law of War.* Chicago: Precedent Publishing, 1983.

Harvey, Eleanor Jones. *The Civil War and American Art* (exhibition catalog of the Smithsonian American Art Museum). New Haven, CT: Yale University Press, 2012.

Hattaway, Herman, and Archer Jones. *How the North Won: A Military History of the Civil War.* Champaign: University of Illinois Press, 1991.

Hawthorne, Nathaniel. *Selected Letters of Nathaniel Hawthorne.* Columbus: Ohio State University Press, 2002.

Heidler, Daniel S., and Jeanne T. Heidler. *Henry Clay: The Essential American.* New York: Random House, 2011.

Herbert, Walter H. *Fighting Joe Hooker.* Indianapolis: Bobbs Merrill, 1944.

Herndon, William H., and Jesse W. Weik. *Herndon's Lincoln.* Urbana: Knox College Lincoln Studies Center and the University of Illinois Press, 2006.

Hertz, Emanuel. *Lincoln Talks: A Biography in Anecdote.* New York: Viking Press, 1939.

———. *The Hidden Lincoln: From the Letters and Papers of William H. Herndon.* New York: Blue Ribbon Books, 1940.

Hofstadter, Richard. *The American Political Tradition and the Men Who Made It.* New York: Vintage, 1989.

Holland, Josiah Gilbert. *The Life of Abraham Lincoln.* Springfield, MA: Gurdon Bill, 1866.

Hollister, O. J. *Life of Schuyler Colfax.* New York: Funk and Wagnalls, 1886.

Holmes, Oliver Wendell, Jr. *Selected Works.* Public domain book. Kindle edition.

Holmes, Oliver Wendell, Sr. *Soundings from the Atlantic.* Boston: Ticknor and Fields, 1864.

Holt, Dean W. *American Military Cemeteries.* Jefferson, NC: McFarland, 2010.

Holzer, Harold. *Emancipating Lincoln: The Proclamation in Text, Context, and Memory.* Cambridge: Harvard University Press, 2012.

Howe, Mark DeWolfe. *Justice Oliver Wendell Holmes: The Shaping Years, 1841–1870.* Cambridge: Belknap Press of Harvard University Press, 1957.

———, ed. *Touched with Fire: Civil War Letters of Oliver Wendell Holmes, Jr.* New York: Fordham University Press, 2000.

Hubbard, Mark, ed. *Illinois's War: The Civil War in Documents.* Athens: Ohio University Press, 2013.

Humez, Jean M. *Harriet Tubman: The Life and the Life Stories.* Madison: University of Wisconsin Press, 2003.

Janken, Kenneth Robert. *Walter White: Mr. NAACP.* Chapel Hill: University of North Carolina Press, 2006.

Jomini, Antoine-Henri. *The Art of War.* Public domain book. Kindle edition.

Jones, Archer. *Civil War Command and Strategy: The Process of Victory and Defeat.* New York: Free Press, 1992. Kindle edition.

Keckley, Elizabeth. *Behind the Scenes, or, Thirty Years a Slave, and Four Years in the White House.* Chapel Hill: University of North Carolina Press, 2011. (Originally published in 1868.)

Keegan, John. *The American Civil War.* New York: Vintage, 2010.

———. *The Face of Battle.* New York: Penguin, 1976.

Kendrick, Paul, and Stephen Kendrick. *Douglass and Lincoln: How a Revolutionary Black Leader and a Reluctant Liberator Struggled to End Slavery and Save the Union.* New York: Walker Publishing, 2008.

Klement, Frank L. *The Limits of Dissent: Clement Vallandigham and the Civil War.* New York: Fordham University Press, 1998.

Kurland, Philip B., and Ralph Lerner, eds. *The Founders' Constitution.* Web edition, University of Chicago Press. http://press-pubs.uchicago.edu/founders/.

Lamon, Ward Hill. *Recollections of Abraham Lincoln.* Chicago: A. C. McClurg, 1895.

Lande, Nathaniel. *Dispatches from the Front: A History of the American War Correspondent.* New York: Oxford University Press, 1996.

Laski, Harold J. *The American Presidency: An Interpretation.* New York: Harper and Brothers, 1940.

Lester, Charles Edwards. *Life and Public Services of Charles Sumner.* New York: John F. Trow and Sons, 1874.

Levin, Bruce. *Confederate Emancipation: Southern Plans to Free and Arm Slaves During the Civil War.* New York: Oxford University Press, 2006.

Lewis, David Levering. *W. E. B. Du Bois: The Fight for Equality and the American Century, 1919–1963.* New York: Henry Holt, 2000.

Lieber, Francis. *Guerilla Parties Considered with Reference to the Laws and Usages of War.* New York: D. Van Nostrand, 1862.

Lieber, Franz. *A Manual of Political Ethics.* 2 vols. Boston: Charles C. Little and James Brown, 1839.

Lincoln, Abraham. *Abraham Lincoln on the Coming of the Caterpillar Tractor.* Peoria, IL: E. A. Jacob, 1929.

Lind, Michael. *What Lincoln Believed: The Values and Convictions of America's Greatest President.* New York: Anchor Books, 2004.

Livermore, Mary A. *My Story of the War.* Hartford, CT: A. D. Worthington, 1896.

Lonn, Ella. *Desertion During the Civil War.* Lincoln: University of Nebraska Press, 1998.

Lynn, John A. *Battle: A History of Culture and Combat from Ancient Greece to Modern America.* Cambridge, MA: Westview Press, 2003.

Mabee, Carleton. *The American Leonardo: The Life of Samuel F. B. Morse.* Fleischmanns, NY: Purple Mountain Press, 2000.

Mahony, D. A. *Prisoner of State.* New York: Carleton, 1863.

Maltby, Charles. *The Life and Public Services of Abraham Lincoln.* Stockton, CA: Daily Independent Steam Power Printing, 1894.

Marcou, Jules. *Life, Letters, and Works of Louis Agassiz.* Vol. 1. New York: Macmillan, 1895.

Marszalek, John F. *Commander of All Lincoln's Armies: A Life of General Henry W. Halleck.* Cambridge: Harvard University Press, 2004.

McClellan, George B. *The Armies of Europe: Comprising Descriptions in Detail of the Military Systems of England, France, Russia, Prussia, Austria, and Sardinia.* Philadelphia: J. B. Lippincott, 1861.

———. *McClellan's Own Story.* New York: Charles L. Webster, 1887.

McCullough, David. *The Greater Journey: Americans in Paris.* New York: Simon and Schuster, 2011.

McDonald, William, ed. *Select Statutes and Other Documents Illustrative of the History of the United States, 1861–1898.* New York: Macmillan, 1903.

McFeely, William S. *Grant: A Biography.* New York: W. W. Norton, 1981.

McPherson, James M. *Abraham Lincoln.* New York: Oxford University Press, 2009.

————. *Abraham Lincoln and the Second American Revolution.* New York: Oxford University Press, 1991.

————. *Crossroads of Freedom: Antietam.* New York: Oxford University Press, 2002.

————. *The Negro's Civil War: How American Blacks Felt and Acted During the War for the Union.* New York: Vintage, 2003.

————. *Tried by War: Abraham Lincoln as Commander in Chief.* New York: Penguin, 2008.

Melville, Herman. *Battle-Pieces and Aspects of the War.* New York: Harper and Bros., 1866.

Menand, Louis. *The Metaphysical Club: A Story of Ideas in America.* New York: Farrar, Straus and Giroux, 2002.

Meron, Theodore. *War Crimes Law Comes of Age.* New York: Oxford University Press, 1998.

Miller, William Lee. *Lincoln's Virtues: An Ethical Biography.* New York: Alfred A. Knopf, 2007.

————. *President Lincoln: The Duty of a Statesman.* New York: Alfred A. Knopf, 2008.

Mitchell, James. *Report on Colonization and Emigration Made to the Secretary of the Interior by the Agent of Emigration.* Washington, DC: Government Printing Office, 1862.

Monaghan, Jay. *Lincoln Bibliography: Collections of the Illinois State Historical Library.* Springfield: Illinois State Historical Library, 1943.

Morris, Errol. *Believing Is Seeing: Observations on the Mysteries of Photography.* New York: Penguin, 2011.

Murfin, James V. *The Gleam of Bayonets: The Battle of Antietam and Robert E. Lee's Maryland Campaign.* Baton Rouge: Louisiana State University Press, 2010.

Neely, Mark E., Jr. *The Fate of Liberty: Abraham Lincoln and Civil Liberties.* New York: Oxford University Press, 1991.

Nevins, Allan, ed. *A Diary of Battle: The Personal Journals of Colonel Charles S. Wainwright.* New York: Da Capo Press, 1998.

————. *The War for the Union.* Vol. II: *War Becomes Revolution, 1862–1863.* New York: Charles Scribner's Sons, 1960.

Nicolay, John George, and John Hay. *Abraham Lincoln: A History, in Ten Volumes.* New York: Century, 1890.

Niven, John. *Gideon Welles: Lincoln's Secretary of the Navy.* New York: Oxford University Press, 1973.

————. *Salmon P. Chase: A Biography.* New York: Oxford University Press, 1995.

Noll, Mark A. *A History of Christianity in the United States and Canada.* Grand Rapids, MI: William B. Eerdmans Publishing, 1992.

Nott, J. C., and George R. Gliddon. *Types of Mankind or Ethnological Researches, Based upon the Ancient Monuments, Paintings, Sculptures, and Crania of Races, and upon Their Natural, Geographical, Philological, and Biblical History.* Philadelphia: Lippincott, Grambo, 1854.

Paludan, Phillip Shaw. *The Presidency of Abraham Lincoln.* Lawrence: University Press of Kansas, 1994.

Panzer, Mary. *Mathew Brady and the Image of History.* Washington, DC: Smithsonian Books, 1997.

Paret, Peter, ed. *Makers of Modern Strategy from Machiavelli to the Nuclear Age.* Princeton, NJ: Princeton University Press, 2010. Kindle edition.

Parish, Peter J. *The American Civil War.* New York: Holmes and Meir, 1975.

Pease, Theodore Calvin, and James G. Randall. *The Diary of Orville Hickman Browning.* Volume I, *1850–1864.* 2 vols. Springfield: Illinois State Historical Library, 1925.

Peterson, Merrill D. *Lincoln in American Memory.* New York: Oxford University Press, 1994.

———. *The Great Triumvirate: Webster, Clay, and Calhoun.* New York: Oxford University Press, 1987.

Piatt, Don. *Memories of the Men Who Saved the Union.* New York: Belford, Clarke, 1887.

Pierce, Edward Lillie. *Memoir and Letters of Charles Sumner.* Volume 4. London: Sampson Low, Marsten and Company, 1893.

Pratt, Harry E. *The Personal Finances of Abraham Lincoln.* Springfield, IL: Abraham Lincoln Association, 1943.

Putnam, Harriet. *The Life of Abraham Lincoln for Young People: Told in Words of One Syllable.* New York: McLoughlin Brothers, 1905.

Quarles, Benjamin. *The Negro in the Civil War.* New York: Da Capo Press, 1989. Originally published by Little, Brown in 1953.

Rafuse, Ethan S. *McClellan's War: The Failure of Moderation in the Struggle for the Union.* Bloomington: Indiana University Press, 2005.

Randall, James G. *Constitutional Problems Under Lincoln.* Urbana: University of Illinois Press, 1951.

Reardon, Carol. *With a Sword in One Hand and Jomini in the Other: The Problem of Military Thought in the Civil War North.* Chapel Hill: University of North Carolina Press, 2012.

Rehnquist, William H. *All the Laws but One: Civil Liberties in Wartime.* New York: Vintage, 1998.

Reilly, Philip R. *Abraham Lincoln's DNA and Other Adventures in Genetics.* Cold Spring Harbor, NY: Cold Spring Harbor Laboratory Press, 2000.

Remini, Robert V. *At the Edge of the Precipice: Henry Clay and the Compromise That Saved the Union.* New York: Basic Books, 2010.

———. *Daniel Webster: The Man and His Time.* New York: W. W. Norton, 1997.

Reynolds, David S. *Walt Whitman's America: A Cultural Biography.* New York: Vintage, 1996.

Rice, Allen Thorndike. *Reminiscences of Abraham Lincoln by Distinguished Men of His Time.* New York: North American Publishing, 1886.

Richardson, Albert Deane. *The Secret Service: The Field, the Dungeon, and the Escape.* Hartford, CT: American Publishing, 1866.

Richardson, James D., ed. *A Compilation of the Messages and Papers of the Presidents: Lincoln.* Project Gutenberg. Ebook edition.

Schantz, Mark S. *Awaiting the Heavenly Country: The Civil War and America's Culture of Death.* Ithaca, NY: Cornell University Press, 2008.

Schlesinger, Arthur M., Jr. *War and the American Presidency.* New York: W. W. Norton, 2004.

Schuckers, J. W. *The Life and Public Services of Salmon Portland Chase.* New York: D. Appleton, 1874.

Scott, Robert Garth. *Fallen Leaves: The Civil War Letters of Major Henry Livermore Abbott.* Kent, OH: Kent State University Press, 1991.

Scripps, John Locke. *Life of Abraham Lincoln.* Peoria, IL: Edward J. Jacob.

Sears, Stephen W., ed. *The Civil War: The Second Year Told by Those Who Lived It.* New York: Library of America, 2012.

———, ed. *The Civil War Papers of George B. McClellan.* New York: Ticknor and Fields, 1989. Kindle edition.

———. *George B. McClellan: The Young Napoleon.* New York: Ticknor and Fields, 1988; New York: Da Capo Press, 1999.

———. *To the Gates of Richmond: The Peninsula Campaign.* New York: Houghton Mifflin, 1992.

Seward, Frederick W. *Seward at Washington as Senator and Secretary of State: A Memoir of His Life, with Selections from His Letters.* 2 vols. New York: Derby and Miller, 1894.

Silverman, Kenneth. *Lightning Man: The Accursed Life of Samuel B. Morse.* New York: Alfred A. Knopf, 2003. Kindle edition.

Simon, James E. *Lincoln and Chief Justice Taney: Slavery, Secession, and the President's War Powers.* New York: Simon and Schuster, 2006.

Simon, John Y., ed. *The Papers of Ulysses S. Grant.* Vol. 22. Carbondale: Southern Illinois University Press, 1998.

Smith, Jean Edward. *Grant.* New York: Simon and Schuster, 2001.

Smith, William Ernest. *The Francis Preston Blair Family in Politics.* Vol. 2. New York: Macmillan, 1933.

Sotos, John G. *The Physical Lincoln.* Mt. Vernon Book Systems, 2008.

Spiller, Roger. *An Instinct for War.* Cambridge: Harvard University Press, 2005.

Stahr, Walter. *Seward: Lincoln's Indispensable Man.* New York: Simon and Schuster, 2012.

Stampp, Kenneth M. *The Imperiled Union: Essays on the Background of the Civil War.* New York: Oxford University Press, 1980.

Stanton, William Ragan. *The Leopard's Spots: Scientific Attitudes Towards Race in America, 1815–1859.* Chicago: University of Chicago Press, 1960.

Staudenraus, P. J. *The African Colonization Movement, 1816–1865.* New York: Columbia University Press, 1961.

Stauffer, John. *Giants: The Parallel Lives of Frederick Douglass and Abraham Lincoln.* New York: Twelve, 2008.

Stoddard, William O. *Inside the White House in War Times: Memoirs and Reports of Lincoln's Secretary.* Lincoln: University of Nebraska Press, 2000.

Stone, Geoffrey R. *Perilous Times: Free Speech in Wartime.* New York: W. W. Norton, 2004.

Stout, Harry S. *Upon the Altar of the Nation: A Moral History of the Civil War.* New York: Penguin, 2006.

Sumner, Charles. *Charles Sumner: His Complete Works.* Vol. 7. Boston: Lee and Shepard, 1900.

Symonds, Craig K. *A Battlefield Atlas of the Civil War.* Baltimore: Nautical and Aviation Publishing Company of America, 1983.

Tarbell, Ida Minerva. *The Life of Abraham Lincoln.* New York: Doubleday & McClure, 1900.

Thomas, Emory M. *The Confederacy as a Revolutionary Experience.* Englewood Cliffs, NJ: Prentice Hall, 1971.

Trachtenberg, Alan. *Reading American Photographs: Images as History, Mathew Brady to Walker Evans.* New York: Hill and Wang, 1989.

United States Department of War. *The War of the Rebellion: A Compilation of the Official Records of the Union and Confederate Armies.* Washington, DC: Government Printing Office. Searchable at http://ebooks.library.cornell.edu.

Van Deusen, Glyndon G. *William Henry Seward.* New York: Oxford University Press, 1967.

Vidal, Gore. *Lincoln.* New York: Vintage, 2000.

Vorenberg, Michael. *The Emancipation Proclamation: A Brief History with Documents.* Boston: Bedford/St. Martin's, 2010.

Ward, Andrew. *The Slaves' War: The Civil War in the Words of Former Slaves.* New York: Houghton Mifflin Harcourt, 2008.

Warren, Robert Penn. *The Legacy of the Civil War.* Lincoln: University of Nebraska Press, 1961.

Waugh, John C. *The Class of 1846. From West Point to Appomattox: Stonewall Jackson, George McClellan, and Their Brothers.* New York: Warner Books, 1994.

———. *Lincoln and McClellan: The Troubled Partnership Between a President and His General.* New York: Palgrave Macmillan, 2010.

Weigley, Russell F. *A Great Civil War: A Military and Political History, 1861–1865.* Bloomington: Indiana University Press, 2000.

Welles, Gideon. *Diary of Gideon Welles.* 3 vols. Boston: Houghton Mifflin, 1911.

———. *Lincoln and Seward.* New York: Sheldon and Company, 1874.

Wheeler, Tom. *Mr. Lincoln's T-mails: How Abraham Lincoln Used the Telegraph to Win the Civil War.* New York: Collins, 2006.

White, G. Edward. *Oliver Wendell Holmes, Jr.* New York: Oxford University Press, 2006.

White, Ronald C., Jr. *A. Lincoln: A Biography.* New York: Random House, 2010.

———. *Lincoln's Greatest Speech: The Second Inaugural.* New York: Simon and Schuster, 2002.

Wilentz, Sean, ed. *The Best American History Essays on Lincoln.* New York: Palgrave Macmillan, 2009.

Wiley, Bell I. *The Life of Johnny Reb and the Life of Billy Yank.* New York: Book-of-the-Month Club, 1994. Originally published by Bobbs-Merrill in 1943 (*Johnny Reb*) and 1951 (*Billy Yank*).

Williams, T. Harry. *Lincoln and His Generals.* New York: Vintage, 2011. Kindle Edition. Originally published in 1952.

Wilson, Douglas L. *Lincoln's Sword: The Presidency and the Power of Words.* New York: Alfred A. Knopf, 2006. Kindle edition.

Wilson, Douglas L., and Rodney O. Davis. *Herndon's Informants: Letters, Interviews, and Statements about Abraham Lincoln.* Urbana: University of Illinois Press, 1998. http://Lincoln.lib.niu.edu/Herndon.

Wilson, Edmund. *Patriotic Gore: Studies in the Literature of the American Civil War.* New York: W. W. Norton, 1994.

Wilson, Joseph Thomas. *The Black Phalanx: A History of the Negro Soldiers of the United States in the Wars of 1775–1812, 1861–65.* Hartford, CT: American Publishing, 1890.

Wilson, Rufus Rockwell. *What Lincoln Read.* Washington, DC: Pioneer Publishing, 1932.

Witt, John Fabian. *Lincoln's Code: The Laws of War in American History.* New York: Free Press, 2012.

Zall, P. M., ed. *Abe Lincoln Laughing: Humorous Anecdotes from Original Sources by and About Abraham Lincoln.* Knoxville: University of Tennessee Press, 1995.

Articles and Reports Cited

With Byline

Brooks, Noah. "Personal Reminiscences of Lincoln." *Scribner's Monthly* 15, no. 5 (February–March 1878): 561–69, 673–81.

————. "Recollections of Abraham Lincoln." *Harper's New Monthly Magazine* 31 (July 1865).

de Roulhac Hamilton, J. G. "The Many-Sired Lincoln." *American Mercury* 5, no. 18 (June 1925).

Douglass, Frederick. "Emancipation Proclaimed." *Douglass' Monthly*, October 1862.

Du Bois, W. E. B. "Opinion of W. E. B. Du Bois." *Crisis* 24, no. 3 (July 1922): 103.

Keegan, John. "Grand Illusions." *New York Review of Books*, July 17, 1986.

Keil, Hartmut. "Francis Lieber's Attitudes on Race, Slavery, and Abolition." *Journal of American Ethnic History* 28, no. 1 (Fall 2008).

McClure, James P., Leigh Johnsen, et al. "Circumventing the Dred Scott Decision: Edward Bates, Salmon P. Chase, and the Citizenship of African Americans." *Civil War History* 43, no. 4 (1997).

Morse, Samuel F. B. *An Argument on the Ethical Position of Slavery in the Social System, and Its Relation to the Politics of the Day.* New York: Society for the Diffusion of Political Knowledge, 1863.

Moser, Benjamin. "Pioneers." Review of *On Africa's Shore: A History of Maryland in Liberia, 1834–1837,* by Richard L. Hall. *New York Review of Books*, April 6, 2006.

Pratt, Harry E. "The Repudiation of Lincoln's War Policy in 1862: Stuart-Swett Congressional Campaign." *Journal of the Illinois State Historical Society* 24, no. 1 (April 1931): 129–40.

Sherwood, Henry Noble. "The Formation of the American Colonization Society." *Journal of Negro History* 2, no. 3 (July 1917).

Shieps, Paul J. "Lincoln and the Chiriqui Colonization Project." *Journal of Negro History* 37, no. 4 (October 1952): 418–53.

Strother, David Hunter. "Recollections of the War." *Harper's New Monthly Magazine* 36 (February 1868).

Thayer, William Roscoe. "Lincoln and Some Union Generals." *Harper's Monthly Magazine* 130 (December 1914–May 1915): 93.

Twain, Mark. "Mark Twain on Artemus Ward." *Brooklyn Daily Eagle*, November 22, 1871.

Welles, Gideon. "The History of Emancipation." *Galaxy*, December 1872, 838–51.

Wiley, Bell Irvin. "Billy Yank and Abraham Lincoln." *Abraham Lincoln Quarterly* 6, no. 2 (June 1950).

Without Byline

"The Battle of Antietam." *Harper's Weekly*, October 18, 1862, 663.

"Brady's Photographs: Pictures of the Dead at Antietam." *New York Times*, October 20, 1862.

"Early History of the American Colonization Society." *African Repository and Colonial Journal* 12 (February 1836).

"Emancipation Proclamation: Lincoln's Own Story Retold." *Christian Science Monitor*, September 22, 1937.

"McClellan's Farewell." *Daily Alta California* 14, no. 4670 (December 5, 1862).

"New Light on Lincoln's Character." *Christian Science Monitor*, February 12, 1935.

"Some Papers of Franklin Pierce." *American Historical Review* 10, no. 1 (October 1904).

INDEX

emancipation issue and, 58–59, 72
Garrison and, 45
habeas corpus and, 152–58, 239, 306*n*
Lincoln's proposed amendments to, 212–13, 225
secession issue and, 61, 237
Seventeenth Amendment to, 207
slavery issue and, 17–18, 30, 35, 41–44, 74, 79, 98, 153, 159, 174
slave trade and, 290–91*n*
Thirteenth Amendment to, 174, 236, 308*n*
Cook, John F., Jr., 100
Cooper Union address (1860) (Lincoln), 15, 16, 65
Copperheads (Peace Democrats), 170
Cornerstone address (1861), 78–79
Costin, John T., 100–101
cotton, 34, 84
cotton gin, 34
Cowper, William, 120
Crimean War (1853–56), 137, 303–4*n*
Crisis, 1
Cromwell, Oliver, 208
Curtis, Benjamin, 234, 240

daguerrotypes, 138
Daily National Intelligencer, 106
Davis, David, 122
Davis, Jefferson, 194, 246
Crimean War and, 304*n*
West Point and, 189
Dawes, Rufus, 133
D-Day (June 6, 1944), 130
Dead at Antietam, The (Gardner), 141
Declaration of Independence (1776), 161, 245
secession issue and, 60
slavery issue and, 40–41, 42–44, 78–79, 98, 160
Delaware, 59
Democratic Party, 19
Copperhead faction of, 170
election of 1862 and, 207–9, 217
election of 1864 and, 182–83
McClellan and, 23
Preliminary Emancipation Proclamation and, 169, 170
slavery issue and, 15, 23

Department of Ohio, 176
Department of the South, 83
Deseret News, 196
Dialectic Society of West Point, 194–95
Dickson, William M., 67
diseases, 12–13, 130, 220
District of Columbia, *see* Washington, DC
Dixon, Archibald, 274
Douglas, Stephen A., 15–16, 53
death of, 216
election of 1860 and, 306*n*
Illinois State House speech of (1857), 80
Kansas-Nebraska Act and, 36–37
Lincoln's 1858 debates with, 15–16, 38–47, 122, 290*n*, 296*n*
McClernand and, 177
popular sovereignty and, 36, 39, 46
racial views of, 80
Douglass, Frederick, 31, 45
African colonization issue and, 104–5
Emancipation Proclamation's signing and, 243
escape from slavery by, 102
incompatibility of races issue and, 104
Lincoln and, 102–5, 166, 243
McClellan and, 103
Preliminary Emancipation Proclamation and, 166
Douglass' Monthly, 103
draft (conscription), 172–77, 308*n*
Dred Scott v. Sanford (1857), 18, 38, 74, 76, 83, 153, 235–36, 287*n*
Du Bois, W. E. B., Lincoln and, 1–4, 6, 7–9
Dubuque Herald, 175
Dunkers, 134
dysentery, 12, 130

Eckert, Thomas, 55, 57–58, 292–93*n*
"Egmont Overture" (Beethoven), 244
Eisenschiml, Otto, 293*n*
elections:
of 1824, 93
of 1832, 93
of 1844, 93
of 1848, 121–22

ABOUT THE AUTHOR

Todd Brewster is a journalist and historian who is co-author, with the late Peter Jennings, of the #1 *New York Times* bestseller *The Century.* He has served as both a writer and editor at Time-Life, a senior producer at ABC News, a Knight Fellow at Yale Law School, and the Don E. Ackerman Director of Oral History at West Point. Brewster has written for *Vanity Fair, Time, Life,* and the *New York Times.* A graduate of Indiana University, he lives with his wife and two sons in Ridgefield, Connecticut.